A SPECTACLE OF DUST

A Spectacle of Dust

THE AUTOBIOGRAPHY

Pete Postlethwaite

Weidenfeld & Nicolson

LONDON

First published in Great Britain in 2011
by Weidenfeld & Nicolson

3 5 7 9 10 8 6 4 2

The author and publisher are grateful to the *Shropshire Star* for
permission to reproduce photographs unless otherwise credited.

A CIP catalogue record for this book
is available from the British Library.

ISBN-13   978 0 297 86493 6
TPB 978 0 297 86653 4

Printed in Great Britain by CPI Mackays, Chatham ME5 8TD

Weidenfeld & Nicolson

The Orion Publishing Group Ltd
Orion House
5 Upper Saint Martin's Lane
London, WC2H 9EA

An Hachette Livre UK Company
www.orionbooks.co.uk

The Orion Publishing Group's policy is to use papers that are natural,
renewable and recyclable products and made from wood grown in sustainable
forests. The logging and manufacturing processes are expected to conform
to the environmental regulations of the country of origin.

Thanks:

Jax, Will, Lily
Andy Richardson, Pippa Markham, Alan Samson,
Alex Irwin, Sue Johnston, Olivia Stewart, Gerry Conlon,
Dick Penny, Nigel Cooke, George Costigan,
Kevin Spacey, Beau Gordon, Sean Bean, Bill Nighy,
Bryan Singer, Chris McQuarrie, Alison Steadman,
Gabriella Martinelli, Timothy Spall, Anton Monsted,
Baz Luhrmann, John Shea, Greg Hersov, Philip Jackson,
Stephen Tompkinson, Maryanne Macdonald, Otto Bathurst,
Tracey Seaward, Lucinda McNeile, Celia Hayley, Nick Hamm,
Mark Herman, Sandy Johnson, Daniel Day-Lewis,
Ralph Fiennes, Tamsyn Manson, Carl Jones, Sarah-Jane Smith,
Stuart, Ann, Wendy, Judy and Jane and a cast of thousands.

Pete wanted this book to be written. As his health deteriorated he recognised that he would need help to complete
his story. The writer Andy Richardson came to his aid, and
through conversations with Pete and others he achieved
this. Had Pete lived long enough to write all of this himself
it might have been a different book; but then had Pete lived
longer it would also have been a different story.

ONE

Climbing the Eiger

∾

If the dots of the matrix line up, what else can you do but join them together? We're here today and gone tomorrow, we have to live every moment as though it were the last. Letting fear get the better of you, or finding a reason not to do the thing you love the most, is as pointless as refusing to dream.

The dots of the matrix aligned for me when Liverpool was named the European Capital of Culture for 2008. 'Great,' I thought, when I heard the announcement, the cogs in my brain already whirring into action. 'That'll be great for the city, for its people.' Little did I know that I would be asked to play a major part in the event.

Before we go any further, I should explain this much: Liverpool is central to my story and throughout my childhood I felt the city's gravitational pull. As children, Liverpool, rather than Manchester, drew us in. It was an exotic, otherworldly, mesmerising place, and trips into town were as welcome as presents on Christmas morning. I re-member once as a kid in Warrington hearing a story: 'You go to Liverpool, and when you get onto the staircases in the shops, they move, they actually move, you don't even have to walk up, they take you right to the top.' It was an interesting description of an escalator.

My home town of Warrington was like a minor planet, orbiting Liverpool's great sun. The city had stunning shops, great places to hang out, fashionable clothes and an amazing arts scene. My dad was from Bootle, so we had always supported Liverpool FC anyway, not Everton ... and, of course, we were Catholics. We'd go for days out at New Brighton, which was a massive trip for us; we'd come in on the steam train from Warrington and then catch the ferry across the Mersey before going to the tea shop and the beach.

I was born soon after the end of World War II and as a teenager, at the start of the 1960s, I watched the first three professional plays of my life at the Everyman, on Liverpool's Hope Street. I saw *Waiting for Godot*, *Look Back in Anger*, John Osborne's iconic kitchen-sink drama about real people in modern Britain; and *Murder in the Cathedral*, a sublime verse/poem. They were all by the same company, with the same actors playing different roles.

I went to see those plays with my friend from sixth form, Davie Broadbent, and we'd sit in the stalls, feeling the magic of the performance. We were captivated by the excitement of the drama; we relished every nuance, every twist and turn. For two hours, Davie and I would be transported from the humdrum of our normal existence to a different reality in which anything could happen. 'This is realer than real life,' Dave would say.

One evening, as we were making our way home on the bus, I remember turning to him and confiding in him. 'Dave,' I said, 'I don't know what it is they do up there ... but I have to do that. I'm going to do that some day. I want to be an actor.' Some forty-odd years later, during the run of *Lear* in the same theatre, he reminded me of this conversation!

The Everyman hadn't done with me, however, and more intimate engagements lay in store. During the early part of the 1970s, at the start of my acting career, Liverpool's magnetism pulled me back again. At that time, the city was still the most creative, vibrant, exciting, dangerous and magical place on earth. It was a carnival of delights, a smorgasbord of thrilling excitements. We'd been through the swinging sixties, a decade in which the Beatles and Merseybeat had dominated the world, and the region remained at the cutting edge of contemporary culture. Quite simply, there was nowhere else like it. Forget California's counter culture or London's vibrant clubs, forget New York's art houses too; Liverpool was where it was at. The city's painters and musicians, actors and writers were mavericks, re-imagining the world for a population that was eager to escape the harshness of their daily lives. The economic troubles of the times were grist to the mill, they fuelled our creative fires.

By then, I'd been through drama school at Bristol and was on my way to becoming an established actor. In that small, tatty, derelict little theatre in Hope Street, I learned my craft with Bill Nighy, Jonathan Pryce, Julie Walters, George Costigan, Matthew Kelly, Antony Sher ... the list goes on and on. If you looked at that roll call of names now you'd say they would never be in the same room, building, county or country together, let alone in one small creative space: it was an absolute pantheon of stars.

Those years were a magical mystery tour. They were some of the most illogical, demanding and potent of my life. They taught me why I wanted to be an actor and showed me that acting wasn't just a silly game, that it had meaning and could change people's lives for the better. I'm forever grateful to the Everyman because it changed my perception of life and taught me that drama was substantial. In my eyes, there was never any doubt at all; the Everyman was unique.

Defining those times is a joy because they were limitless and enchanting. Each time we stepped through the heavy front doors off Hope Street there was a feeling that something special was in the air. My digs in those days were nearby, in Canning Street, where I had a small flat, and I remember standing on the opposite side of the road from the Philharmonic, just thinking: 'This is it, this is what I want to do, there's no going back.'

It was an exceptional time in the Everyman's history; to be honest, that golden era still ranks alongside the greatest of times that any theatre in the world has experienced. We were part of the city and the business of doing plays made absolute sense in terms of the community. It didn't matter whether we were doing Shakespeare or Brecht, if it didn't relate directly to Liverpool and the surrounding community then it was out the window. 'Acting's a worthwhile career,' I thought. 'There's a reason to pursue this.' Everything had to be done very much on a budget and we had to find a way in which the local community could identify with the work. One of our theories was that 'we may be cheap but we are not shoddy'.

There was less division between the theatre and the real world than in other, more formal theatres. The cast of the Everyman felt as though it belonged to the city, as though we were the people's players. 'Ar ay, lar,' someone would say to us, after we'd finished a play that we'd adapted to more accurately reflect the lives of our constituents. 'I really got that, you know. That really said something to me about my life.' Such moments reaffirmed my love for the stage.

There were times when as actors we had no money, not a shilling, but we were forever being helped out, either as individuals, or as a company. On one occasion, Trevor Eve and

I couldn't afford to make ends meet and hadn't got enough money for food, but a local grocer came to the rescue. 'He'yar, lads,' he said, handing over ripe green avocados. 'Eat these, they'll be good for you.' And we did, we subsisted on a diet of donated avocados. I'll tell you something else, they were delicious.

Liverpool felt like a spiritual home and I returned to it at other times. In 1981, we did a TV play called *The Muscle Market*, with Alan Bleasdale. I played a character called Danny Duggan, who was an out-of-his-depth building contractor. In one scene, I had to escape retribution from a gang of thugs by hanging on to the back of a bus as it sped through the city streets. The director, Alan Dossor, who was directing for TV for the first time, filled the vehicle full of extras and I had to cling on to the outside of it as it swung wildly down the road to a particular tune. I remember it even now: it was 'Yesterday', by the Beatles. A police car watched us for a little while, and then gave chase, imagining that I was a ne'er-do-well who was up to no good. As the cop car came level with the driver, the policeman shouted 'Eh, mate, there's a fella hanging off the outside of yer bus.' The driver, a Scouser, fired back: 'Well, there's no room inside, where d'ya expect him to go?'

It wasn't that things like that don't happen anywhere else, it was the sheer amount of them and the way people revelled in a bit of repartee. Liverpool seemed to thrive on its ribald humour, an ability to see the good in bad and to laugh at things that outsiders might not have found funny. It's a phrase stated so often that it is practically a truism; but Liverpool is genuinely unlike anywhere else. So when it was named the European Capital of Culture, I knew that I had to be involved. Macca, Ringo, Sir Simon Rattle and countless others were on board. Another Everyman alumnus was also planning his own performance: the actor and presenter Matthew Kelly was due to play alongside his son, Matthew Rixon, in Samuel Beckett's classic *Endgame*. I didn't want to let the event pass without making my own, meaningful contribution. My friend, the theatrical director Rupert Goold, conceived of an idea. Throughout my career, I'd always coveted one theatrical role above all others: King Lear. So when Rupert telephoned me and suggested that we take a production to the city, it seemed like the perfect plan.

I'd appeared in various performances of *King Lear* at different times, from a formative production during my early days at teacher training college through to a stirring RSC run in Stratford-upon-Avon in 1982. The Stratford performances were particularly notable: I appeared alongside a then-fortysomething Michael Gambon, who gave a stupendous performance as the doomed King. My Everyman friend Antony Sher played a brilliant red-nosed Fool who sat on his master's knee like a ventriloquist's doll. I played Cornwall, opposite Jenny Agutter, who was sublime. I also understudied Michael's Lear. I adored the role, it seemed the most complete characterisation in all of Shakespeare. No, scratch that, it wasn't just the most complete part that Shakespeare created, it was the most accomplished, four-dimensional role in all of theatre.

I'd always viewed Lear as a role that an actor 'had to' play, rather than one that an actor might consciously choose. It was in my blood. I longed to test myself against Shakespeare's moving and complex text. The play was a great gift from the Bard; in my mind, there seemed to be no greater examination of an actor's skill than the fragile, tormented, doomed king. If I'm really honest, Lear had always been in the back of my mind from the start of my career, even though it may seem like an obvious choice. Above all else, the reason I wanted to play Lear was because I thought I understood it.

I'd worked with Rupert Goold before, during a successful one-man play called *Scaramouche Jones* that we took to Australia, New Zealand and Canada. We spoke to Gemma Bodinetz, the artistic director of the Everyman/Playhouse, and she loved the idea instantly. 'That would be a real coup,' she said, brimming with enthusiasm at the prospect. 'Pete, you playing King Lear at the Everyman during the Capital of Culture Year would be the right play in the right place at the right time.' There was nothing more to discuss. And so began my ascent of theatre's most challenging and perilous climb. I was interviewed by the local paper, the *Echo*, about my forthcoming performance. 'It's the acting equivalent of tackling the North Face of the Eiger,' I told them, and that was precisely how it felt. 'Doing Lear is a big, big privilege – terrifying and exciting at the same time. If we can do something special on that stage, then we will have fulfilled our dreams.'

It's impossible to underestimate the excitement that we felt about that production. Once Gemma had agreed to our idea I started to immerse myself in the project; it was a chance in a lifetime to deal with something like that. There was, of course, an equal measure of pressure that went hand-in-hand with the anticipation. It was as though somebody had said to me: 'Here's your chance to paint the Sistine Chapel, you can do the ceiling of the Sistine Chapel.' And I thought: 'What, have I got the guts to do that?'

I returned to my home in Shropshire to plunge myself into the work and, just as importantly, to grow an enormous beard. I wanted my Lear to be hirsute, so I stopped shaving. The beard came with the territory; my portrayal would be of a wizened old man ranting and stumbling around on a ferocious heath. I couldn't imagine Lear would have been paying too much attention to personal hygiene; he had other things on his plate. I could have stuck a beard on, but that would have looked phoney. No, if Lear was going to have a beard, it was going to be a proper one. It was nine months in the growing and I hated it. 'It's a bit sackcloth and ashes,' I thought to myself. 'But it's the price for the privilege of saying some of the finest lines ever written; I have to live up to them.' The regulars in my rural local gave me some stick. 'What's that stuck to your chin?' they'd ask, as I sat in a quiet corner, buried beneath a hat and huge scarf, supping my pint of Guinness, and filling in my *Guardian* crossword at a quiet table. 'Can't you afford a razor?'

One afternoon, I took a walk along our local high street and popped into a charity shop. I'd been studying the text and I'd misread a line, in which I thought it had said Lear has a 'dress of flowers'. I went to pick up some laundry and in the hospice shop, hanging up on the rail, was a dress covered in flowers. I went in and said to the lady on the counter: 'How much is that dress?'

'Two pounds fifty,' she said, looking at me curiously.

'I'll have it.'

A flash of delight darted through her eyes: 'Oh, you'll look very nice in that, dear,' she said.

'I hope so, I think it'll be a perfect fit.'

She gave me an old-fashioned look. I left the shop thinking: 'Great, now it's going to be all round town that Pete Postlethwaite dresses up in women's clothes.'

I was familiar with *King Lear*'s script but I re-read it at home as though it was the first time I'd ever seen it. The words ran through me as though they were electric. Every line, all eight hundred of them, was slowly confined to memory, and I started to understand the structure and form of Shakespeare's narrative. The play is a profoundly dark and notoriously unforgiving work. The character is the most troubled of Shakespearian souls, written to capture the extremes of the human condition. All of the double-crossing, manipulation, evil scheming and madness started to make sense and I vowed that my Lear would be the real deal. He would be tortured and borderline insane. No stone would be left unturned.

We got through rehearsals, working hard and making sure we made good progress. Being in the city during the Capital of Culture Year was a great experience because every day there was something new and unusual, something unexpected. At one point, a giant fifty-foot spider was attached to an office block to launch a five-day festival of street theatre. It was made from steel and wood and operated by twelve people who were strapped to it. There were lots of other things going on, it was just like being back in the melting pot that was the seventies. Our production was described as being a 'hot ticket', a phrase which made me laugh. I imagined myself picking up the stub for my seat, and getting burned fingers. We tried to take such flattery with a pinch of salt. We were simply part of Rupert Goold's team in *King Lear*. Besides, nothing we could do could top the giant spider.

Walking through the city was an eye-opening experience and the people I met on my way into Hope Street were tremendously hospitable. It was energising to be back. On one particular day, two different ladies came up to me in the street, one was aged about forty-five and the other was about seventeen; they both stopped me, just out of the blue, on Hope Street. The elder lady came up and said, 'Can I give you a hug?' and I said 'Why?' 'I'm for peace and love,' she told me, as she wrapped her arms around me in a warm, comforting embrace. She had no idea who I was. The other wanted to kiss me and I asked why she wanted to do that. She paused for a moment, looked into my eyes, and declared: 'Because you're you.' I felt very humbled and glad to be so warmly welcomed, the response was unbelievable.

The people of Liverpool seemed to be so kind to me because of my long-held affection for, and association with, the city. It seemed as though the work we did back in the 1970s was still remembered, people seemed to recall who we were, what we were and how we behaved. The connection was very special. Although I'd long since departed, I didn't feel like an outsider coming in and doing something before jetting back out, I felt like somebody who belonged.

There were ideas knocking around to create a huge new theatre in Liverpool and inevitably we were asked to offer our opinions. The plan was to knock down the Everyman and rebuild it as part of a £41 million project to revitalise theatre in Liverpool. Its sister theatre, the Playhouse, was also told it would be given a complete refit amid warnings that both venues faced a long lingering death if the money wasn't found. The Everyman had apparently been declared 'unfit for purpose'. I disliked the idea of a supertheatre, big enough to accommodate popular shows on a regular basis. Liverpool already had terrific theatres. Big wasn't always beautiful. I've never believed that hugely expensive productions mean that the quality is any better, although it's nice not to have to share a dressing room with a goat, which happened to us during one early Everyman production.

The Everyman itself had changed by now and the stage was close to the people. I loved that because it meant there would be a strong connection with the audience. When I first started in the 1970s, things were completely different. There was a cross-arch stage and there was also a gallery. At one point the stalls were covered over and it became an arena; there'd been continual development over time. But the latest incarnation was my favourite of all. I loved being inches away from the people in the front row, to be among the audience and not be divided by a fourth wall was brilliant, it was an exciting prospect.

As we got closer to the opening night, our work intensified and a round of media interviews began. The critics began to hover for interviews and they drew parallels with roles that I'd played before. One of the themes that kept recurring was that I was well suited to the role of the flawed patriarch. Writers and broadcasters reasoned that some of my better-known roles had been difficult, proud men who had made misjudgements or been forced to explore their own personalities in extremis. Characters like Giuseppe Conlon, in *In the Name of the Father*; the bandleader Danny, in *Brassed Off*, and the violent, abusive, alcoholic dad in *Distant Voices, Still Lives* were all corralled into a one-size-fits-all theory. Parallels were also drawn with Max, from Harold Pinter's *The Homecoming*, whom I'd played a few years earlier. He'd also been a flawed father with three kids, just like Lear.

The theories were neat, but I didn't buy them. You see, if you look a little more closely at those characters, you realise how different they all are. The father in *Distant Voices, Still Lives* was a drunken aggressive wife-beater, Giuseppe Conlon in *In the Name of the Father* was one of those Northern Irish, Catholic working-class men who was full of integrity. Giuseppe was basically a saint-like figure who went through the world and the events that affected him and his son in an extremely honest and stoical way. Danny in *Brassed Off* was actually a fascist fanatic in terms of the music, even though he had a big change of heart towards the end. So they were three very different characters. Of all of the patriarchal figures that I'd been involved with, however, Lear was the one most riven with complexity and malfeasance, he was the ne plus ultra. His problems were of his own making, they were his responsibility. He'd brought them all on himself and caused his own chaos. What sort of man makes his daughters compete for their inheritance by asking them to make public declarations of filial love? It didn't help his cause that he was a king, of course, because kingship is a malady; as the script said: 'To say aye, or no, to everything I said.' Power corrupts, just look at some of our recent prime ministers.

My Lear was going to be bad, mad and sad. In my eyes, he was misogynistic and fixated on femininity, hence my decision to wear 'the dress of flowers' from the charity shop. His description of the vagina, for instance, was quite remarkable: 'There's hell, there's darkness, there is the sulphurous pit, burning, scalding, stench, consumption …' Lear couldn't bear the feminine side of himself for some reason and I wondered if his madness partly came from his lack of self-knowledge. Certainly, his two scheming daughters, Goneril and Regan, were on to him: he has 'ever slenderly but known himself', one of them said. So that's where I was coming from. I corresponded with a professor of English at Oxford, who also had his own theories; he basically agreed with a number of my observations. He had very elaborate ideas, really highfalutin stuff, and his observations became part of my research. Like the rest of the company, I wanted to make sure that our interpretation of *Lear* would take the audience on a journey, that it would resonate with something deep within everybody who came to see it.

Our rehearsals for *King Lear* were a huge challenge. We tried to inject our own blend of humour, which was very dark and wild, and that aspect was crucially important to me. Though I no longer had my Catholicism, my faith had left an indelible imprint on me, and I wanted to find some redemption in the story, but it proved to be a tough play to find any in. I took comfort from the fact that we were doing it on Hope Street, instead.

But gradually, comfort started to feel in short supply. As a company we found ourselves divided over the way we were approaching the production. The kitchen sink was being thrown at our performance, with props, songs, overt politics and more besides. We were due to transfer *King Lear* to London for two months following our month-long run at the Everyman and at one point I got the distinct impression that all of our work was focused on getting it right for the capital city. During a discussion with Rupert, I told him I felt we'd got parts of our production wrong, that we were not being true to Shakespeare and that we were short-selling Liverpool. There was a lot wrong with our *Lear*, there was too much gimmickry and I told Rupert as much. He explained the reasoning behind the production and suggested it would improve as we went along. He seemed to have a view that by the time we got to London, for a two-month run at the Young Vic, we'd be flying. The critics would return and garland us with praise. But that infuriated me because the whole point of doing *Lear* was that it was back in Liverpool at the theatre that had helped to shape my creative life. To my mind, we had to get it right for the Everyman, not London, it shouldn't have been a work in progress, it should have been right from the very start. Liverpool shouldn't have been used as a 'try out' place.

As we moved closer to opening night, the fear inside me built. The performance was so important to me, I was working with a great group of people and we all wanted to get it right. On the night before our preview performance I'd stayed with friends to relax and prepare myself for curtain up. But suddenly my tongue started to swell. The swelling became worse and worse until my tongue was double its normal size and I literally couldn't speak. 'Pete, we're going to have to take you to A&E,' said my friends, as they ushered me into their car and rushed me to the Royal Liverpool University Hospital. The doctors told me I'd suffered some kind of allergic reaction. 'Jesus,' I thought. 'This wasn't in the script.' I was given steroids and an adrenaline injection, which reduced the swelling. 'Great, I can talk again,' I thought. 'Lear has a voice.'

But for all of the relief at being able to go ahead with the opening performance, the tortuous feeling of unease remained. My stomach was a knot of worry and stress. It felt as though a surgeon had performed some nefarious operation while I was asleep; replaced everything inside with steel cables that had been twisted out of shape.

I disagreed with the doctor's textbook diagnosis that I'd suffered an allergic reaction, that seemed too simple an explanation. I'd done nothing any different to any other day of the week, so it had to be something else. This is how I see it. My return to the Everyman created tremendous expectation among the media, people in Liverpool and the audience. I'd become a big story with interviews on TV, for radio and in the national and local press. The preparation to our opening night, however, had been far from perfect. We'd thrown everything at the production but there were a lot of aspects that I wasn't happy with – and there was no time to change them. I had to put a brave face on things, try to downplay the hype while simultaneously being outwardly confident. It was a tough balancing act. 'How does it feel to have men in pubs talking about your performance as King Lear?' asked an interviewer from Radio Merseyside. I dealt with the question, but the expectation was almost overwhelming.

We were all so keen to get it right that we created a cauldron of pressure and there were continual disagreements over the production of the play, with changes being made up to the opening night and then throughout the first week. Being King Lear became difficult, really hard. You can't have someone playing Lear who doesn't endorse every single bit of that production. Psychologically, I was between a rock and a hard place. I couldn't speak, I literally couldn't speak. My tongue swelling seemed to me like a physical manifestation of the things that had been going on in my head and in my heart. Here I was, playing a great, doomed king, and the power to make my voice heard seemed to have been taken away from me.

The confusion that we faced over our work was mirrored by a private disorder, the magnitude of which I had yet to comprehend. A tumour had started to grow inside me, on my kidney; I had cancer. In many ways, the external discord over the play was matched by the internal tumult of my health. My weight had dropped from eleven stone to nine and a half stone and I was exhausted, both physically and emotionally. As a team, we'd worked relentlessly to make the play as good as it could be, even though we had failed to unite on one vision. Outside, turmoil was being created, but inside, there was turmoil too. The production of *King Lear* seemed to be falling apart, as was my body. I knew about one, but not yet about the other.

On the night before we launched, I stayed in hospital overnight for observation and managed a little sleep, but by the morning, I just needed to get out and get back to the theatre; I couldn't let myself down, or the theatre: I was responsible to the cast. 'Are you okay, Pete? Is everything going to be all right?' The people at the Everyman were understandably worried that the opening performance would be cancelled, but I couldn't let that happen. 'I'm fine,' I lied, though the truth was, I was despairing. We had to get off to a flying start. On the first night there seemed to be almost as many critics in the stalls as there were members of the audience. Somehow, we got through it, but when I opened the papers the next morning, my dreams of a triumphant homecoming crumbled to dust. 'Terrible,' was the almost unanimous view of critics. They hated the fact that we'd opened with a clip of Margaret Thatcher quoting from St Francis of Assisi:

'Where there is discord, may we bring harmony.' In truth, they weren't alone on that, I wasn't the only member of the cast who'd thought that an odd way to start. They didn't like the fact that the Fool performed 'Singing in the Rain' in the middle of one of Shakespeare's darkest tragedies. Reading their reviews, it was clear that they didn't bloody well like anything. The production was assassinated while the performances didn't fare much better. 'Self-indulgent' and 'clumsy' were among the kinder phrases employed. The director came in for particularly heavy criticism. 'Goold's bright ideas often seem self-indulgent and reductive, drawing flashy attention to the director's role of theatrical razzle-dazzle without serving the text,' wrote Charles Spencer in the *Daily Telegraph*. 'It lacks dignity to a degree and is flawed by numerous misjudgments,' noted Christopher Hart in *The Times*. I sat stupefied as I read those words. They'd been similar to the thoughts that I'd tried to convey to Rupert. The reviews made for uneasy reading in the dressing room on Hope Street. Digesting phrases like 'For anyone who knows and loves the play, some scenes are truly painful to behold' increased the pressure tenfold. Even my own paper, the *Guardian*, didn't like it. Its reviewer, Michael Billington, was particularly acidic, saying something like: 'Postlethwaite's Lear falls from a very low height.' To be honest, it was difficult not to agree with many of the reviewers. We'd talked over and over about our differences, but we seemed to have been lumbered with a production that we didn't really want and didn't really believe in. Going into a show like that, it was no surprise that we came in for such excoriating criticism. In some ways, I'd almost been ready for the kicking.

After that terrible first night, we got one good review, which was from my local newspaper in Shropshire. I read it with immense relief. The writer had seemed to understand what it was we were trying to convey. He had ignored the needless tinsel of the production and connected with the performances of the players. He noted the 'heart-rending terror of madness' that I'd tried to convey and admired some of the interplay between members of the cast. He seemed to join us on our journey into Lear's dark heart. I cut out his review and pinned it on my dressing-room wall, to keep me going. I needed a chink of light to keep my spirits up. During that first week in Liverpool the pressure was all-consuming. Fear is good, in small doses, but the level of fear I felt was unhealthy. I was thinking, 'I'll fall down any set of stairs I can find. I'll get out of this one way or another.' I did not want to go on. I have never felt so despairing. It was nadir time; horrendous, really horrendous. Going to the wall to portray a character like Lear is a big ask of any actor, but to walk that line when you don't believe in what you're doing is insidious. The doubt and self-recrimination creep up on you like terrors in a dream.

The first week of *Lear* was a blur. What I needed most was my own sense of rightness and my own ability to concentrate. But I didn't have that. I didn't quite know … I just knew I had to get through it. We were old enough and wise enough to get up to speed with the critics. For instance, it was easy to see why using the Thatcher clip, for instance, was a mistake. The first thing you want to hear in a Shakespeare play normally, I would have thought, would be Shakespeare. You don't come in with something other than those first lines. It was symptomatic of the way in which we'd misjudged a number of elements. So, during the first week, we changed things around. We ditched the Thatcher clip, got rid of some of the ephemera and took the play back to the Bard's original vision. The politics – left, right or indifferent – were abandoned and we accepted that they had no place in the play. We stripped out everything that distracted us or seemed in any way unhelpful. We honed in on the themes of the play, on a purer interpretation of Shakespeare's words, and the response from the audiences was great. We went from being an unhappy, despairing band of actors to a very happy bunch of bunnies bounding onto the stage every night, being enraptured by one of theatre's great stories.

A little while later, once we'd accepted our shortcomings and improved the quality of the production, I went onto Radio 4's *Front Row* to talk about our version of *Lear*. 'We were overwhelmed, I think, by the ideas,' I told them. A number of elements had been jettisoned since the play opened. The most expensive props that we'd bought had been ditched. We'd spent money on what looked like three large tables, on wheels, they were similar to the ones that architects use to create models of towns and villages. They went; the play was better without them. Anything that we found unhelpful, distracting, not true to the story, was washed away. It was like a bonfire of vanities. Publicly, I accepted that the critics were right and that the production had lost its way in adapting Shakespeare's great tragedy. Rupert was also bold enough to say, 'Right, that didn't work,' as we pared back on some of the grander ideas that had no real relevance to Shakespeare or Liverpool. There was no temptation on our part to beat ourselves up for the sake of it. As a group, as far as we were concerned, it wasn't all bad, there was a lot of really good stuff going on, bubbling underneath, that just needed releasing. I don't suppose I won any popularity competitions by speaking out publicly, but it was something that needed to be done. We needed to let the people know that we acknowledged our shortcomings and had addressed them.

When the run ended, just before Christmas, I returned home to my family and enjoyed a well-earned rest. 'Cheers, Pete,' said the guys in my local. 'Welcome back.' There was time to spend a delightful Christmas at home. It was heavenly to be back among my family and friends. I gained a sense of perspective on my portrayal of King Lear: it had been a redemptive experience, the light had followed the darkness. As the New Year began, it was time to get back to it as the production shifted to London, to the Young Vic. The crew reunited to rehearse in the Jerwood Arts Space before we opened. It was as though we'd only just started, as though those days in Liverpool were a nightmare. I was exhilarated, elated; I knew *Lear* was within our grasp: I knew that we wouldn't experience the traumas of Liverpool. My only thought was, 'Bring on London, bring on the Young Vic, mate.'

When the show opened, the response was incredible. Having come through the experience of an unsuccessful opening, the success was actually sweeter. Had it been handed to us on a plate … I don't know. I'd shuffle into the theatre each day, with my carrier bag of sandwiches, wrapped up against the cold in a huge, warm scarf. As we waited for the performance to start, we'd be rapt with nervous anticipation.

During one of the early performances, I also learned a very important lesson: Playing a good Lear involves more than intensity, poise and terror – it also requires a good pair of shoes. At the beginning of the run, I decided to play Lear barefoot. It seemed like the sort of thing the character would have done. Lear was a madman, consumed by insanity, he wouldn't have been getting up each morning looking for his hand-stitched loafers. He'd have pulled on whatever clothes he could find before stumbling into the wilderness. In one scene, I had to carry Amanda Hale, who was playing Cordelia, across the stage. 'Shit,' I thought, as I slipped in a puddle that had formed on one of the stage's steps with Amanda still in my arms. There were gasps of horror as the

audience realised a very modern tragedy was about to unfold. We'd been using stage rain to evoke a wild, untamed
environment. The elemental conditions, however, almost did
for me. As I descended the watery steps – badum, badum,
badum – I just about recovered my footing and stopped short
of falling. I mean, I couldn't have done, could I? However
mad Lear was, he was a king and kings have dignity. They
don't fall over, especially not when they're carrying their
most beloved daughter in their arms. The experience taught
me a valuable lesson: I made sure Lear had a pair of shoes
to wear for every remaining show.

The negative opening in Liverpool was quickly forgotten.
The production got better and better and better and by the
end of the two-month run we felt as though we were invincible. 'Pete, we've had offers to extend the run and move it
to a bigger theatre in the West End,' one of the producers
told me one morning. We were thrilled by the interest but
turned them down. 'Tell them thanks, but no thanks,' we
said. Four of the cast had got other work in different productions and though we could have replacements, there was
no way any of us would continue without them. We'd come
so far together that the idea of bringing on board people
who hadn't completed the first part of the journey with us
made no sense at all. It didn't matter to us that the offers
were very good, that they involved bigger stages further into
the West End and more money for the cast and crew. What
mattered was how we felt. If we'd accepted, it would have
seemed as though we were going backward, almost as though
we were betraying ourselves. We were like musketeers,
all for one and one for all.

Throughout the production of *Lear*, I hadn't thought
about anything else. I remember one interviewer asking me:
'What's next – post *Lear*?' I didn't have an answer, it had
been difficult to look beyond *Lear*. I just wanted to do that

and then see what happened. There was no goal other than the performances at the Everyman and the Young Vic. The interviewer looked at me, expecting more. 'Truthfully,' I said, 'there is no other goal.' From the outset, we knew that *Lear* was going to be a hell of a climb and we had to commit one hundred per cent to that. Beyond *Lear*, I thought about my daughter's birthday and whether or not my dog was in good health, but in terms of work, well, I didn't have any further plans. When the final curtain call came on 28 March, I was exhilarated but exhausted. Lear had always been my biggest ambition. I'd overcome my fear and reached the highest peak.

TWO

A Lover for the Rest of My Life

❧

'Get your bucket and spade,' said Mum, standing in the doorway of the prettily painted railway carriage that was our home for the week at Browns Holiday Camp in picturesque North Wales. I was playing in the sandy grass outside, feeling the heat of the midday sun radiate against my uncovered pink skin. 'We're going to the beach. Come on, Pete.' It was the second day of our family holiday, in Gronant, a glorious, perfectly formed village in Flintshire.

Every year, Mum and Dad packed our cases and loaded the family car so we could make our annual pilgrimage from Warrington. It wasn't a long trip and we travelled in high spirits, sitting quietly in the back for most of the way. 'Are we nearly there yet?' we'd pipe up as our journey neared its end, when we could contain our enthusiasm no longer. My father, William, shook his head sagely; he knew we'd been looking forward to our holiday for months.

Browns was our destination of choice most years and it never failed to please. The days seemed to go on forever and it was heavenly. Every moment was filled with sunshine and laughter. Buckets and spades, ice-cream cones, deck chairs and sun burn; our holidays were a cornucopia of quintessentially British thrills. They were bliss. Gronant sat on the tip of the North Wales coastline and the dunes were wonderful, their golden sands rising and falling like a mini mountain range, all the way to Prestatyn. We'd run up and down them, happy and carefree, exhausting ourselves by playing until our lungs almost burst. Nearby, there were beautiful marshes and a gorgeous beach of shingle and sand. It was wild and untamed splendour.

Home for the week was an outrageously romantic former railway carriage that had been taken off the railways some years before, its wooden frame lovingly restored, and kitted out with berths and beds, a cooker and cupboards. The carriage was a relic of a bygone era, when craftsmen took great pride in their work and such things were built to last.

In other years, we'd stay in similar resorts further along the coast, in towns like Towyn or Prestatyn, and the days seemed to go on forever. Our holidays were punctuated each year, however, by a peculiar order from Mum and Dad. They would corral us into the car so that we could make an annual sojourn to a particular address in Prestatyn. 'We're just going to meet a man,' was all they'd say, mysteriously, and we'd troop dutifully behind them, filing into the car for the short trip. We never really knew why they went to see the same man at the same address each year, at least, not until much later when we realised that they'd been paying the year's rent for our home, at 101 Norris Street, Warrington.

It must have been hard work for them, saving a year's worth of rent. We weren't rich and we pretty much lived from hand to mouth. Back home, Dad went out to work each morning and Mum, Mary, was the matriarch. She ran the family with great diligence and pride, making sure everything was shipshape and Bristol fashion. We daren't step out of line for fear of invoking her not inconsiderable wrath.

Though Mum ran a tight ship, she placed great importance on our happiness. There were six of us in our terraced house in Warrington, mother and father, my two elder sisters, Anne and Pat, my elder brother Mike and me. We were brought up to be deeply religious and very devout. Our Catholicism was all-pervasive. Religion was an integral part of our lives from the year dot. I can't remember a time when we didn't go to church. We'd attend Mass every Sunday and there were religious icons and images in the home. I sometimes wonder whether serving Mass as an altar boy may have turned me towards acting. I was up there on the altar-stroke-stage, ringing the bell. I was offering the priest the bowl to wash his fingers, swinging the thurible, incense burning, audience right there.

Dad worked in a bike shop, then was a cooper, a job that's now gone – it's all kegs now – then a batman for a US padre and then the caretaker of a local Catholic primary school, where he was so well loved that when he retired they made him a governor. Everybody loved him. He was more for a quiet life but he would completely condone whatever Mary thought. The two of them were complete opposites; Mother was a whirlwind of energy, unstoppable. The idea of going behind Mum's back and trying to get Dad to gang up against her, so that we could have our own way, didn't enter our minds. Her word was law and Dad seemed to be entirely happy with that. 'Whatever Mum thinks will probably be right in the long run, so I might as well agree,' was the way he seemed to think. That may appear harsh, as though Father were a wimp, but he wasn't, far from it. Dad was very much his own man. He was staunch in his love for us and cared deeply for us all. He knew what he wanted and what he liked and put great faith in his family. In some respects, Dad was a very simple man; his passions and pleasures were straightforward, he was uncomplicated and didn't want very much.

The most important thing to him was Mother's happiness, it meant everything to him. She was his lifelong love. As long as he had his pipe and my mother, that's all he cared about. He once told me that he'd never had a dream in his life. Mother and Father were inseparable for almost their entire lives. They were together from the age of five. They met at junior school and went through life together. They went into secondary school and got married not long after leaving. They'd just celebrated fifty years of marriage, their golden wedding, when my father died.

Mother and Father brought us up in a terraced house, two up and two down, right next door to the Co-Operative Society shop. On Friday nights Mum would say: 'Go and get sixpence worth of broken biscuits,' and we'd smile as she handed us the money, excited by our impending treat. We loved that Friday-night routine, it was really good, a highlight of the week. Our living accommodation was reasonably cramped. We kids shared a bedroom, me and Mike and Anne and Pat, and Mum and Dad had their own. There was a loo at the end of the yard but no bathroom. We didn't get a bathroom for years and, when we did, it was built downstairs, beyond the kitchen.

If any of us wanted a bath, we'd have to move everything out of the way in the kitchen and then put a board up against the back door so that nobody came in to catch us in our birthday suits. We'd lock the kitchen door and fill the bath with water, it was a right palaver. There was an art to bathing in our house. You'd try and get the bath on a night when nobody else was using it, so that you could make the most of the hot water. Before that, when we were nippers, we had a tin bath in front of the fire and we'd bathe on a Saturday night. Being the youngest, I was normally the last in, so it wasn't quite as hot for me as it was for everyone else.

Growing up was a happy process and our family had plenty of friends. As we grew older, mother got a job, cleaning for the Yanks, in Burtonwood. There were lots of Americans there, working at a US Air Base. Mum became close with a couple called Sue and Robbie, who also had two children, of about our ages. Mum became great friends with them.

It was a tearful occasion when they boarded their flight back to America, but they gave us a permanent reminder of our friendship: Queenie, a marmalade-and-white cocker spaniel. She stayed with us when they left and we adored her, she had big floppy ears and we loved her with real gusto while Mum gave Sue and Robbie regular reports on her progress. Queenie's eventual death, from water on the belly, was very distressing. Mike and I found it particularly difficult to comprehend because we'd never experienced death at such close quarters. 'What are we going to do without her?' said our Mike. 'We've never known anything die before.' Mum had the answer and she took us out for a treat, she bought us roller skates to ease our grief. I'd have been nine or ten at the time and while long afternoons roller-skating outside our home didn't make the pain any less acute, it did give us something else to think about. Mum always knew what to do.

Life may have been simple, but it was filled with joy. We waited for nights like Christmas and 5 November with great anticipation. As soon as autumn came, we'd start to look forward to Bonfire Night, it was a great occasion. In the streets, the other kids would talk about their plans and describe the extraordinary figurines of Guy Fawkes that they planned to create. It was a magical, fantastic time; utterly beguiling for us children. Come Bonfire Night, the skies were lit up with wonder as the compounds created a rainbow of explosive light. The sulphurous smell of fireworks would linger in the air as house after house sent rockets skittling into the sky with loud, long, explosive 'weeeeeezzzzzzzzz-pop' sounds. The kaleidoscopic pyrotechnics were visible for miles around.

Every street would have its own bonfire, with wood piled up and old sofas and armchairs all around. Sometimes there'd be a fire on an allotment and the air would be filled with the harsh, crackling noise of dry wood being burned. People would bake apples and a toffee that was so hard we'd almost crack our teeth biting into it. We'd stand around gazing heavenwards, our eyes filled with wonder, as the fireworks exploded. And we knew that better was to come: 'Great,' we'd say to ourselves. 'Christmas is not long now. Fifty days to go. We'll count 'em down, one by one.'

Soon enough, we'd arrive at the best day of the year and when we opened our eyes and the light peered through our curtains on Christmas morning, we were enraptured by the sorcery and magic. We'd hardly have slept on Christmas Eve, concentrating as hard as we could to stay awake, forcing our eyelids to stay open in case we saw Him. Of course, as the clock advanced, our stamina would fade and we'd drift into happy slumber. Then, when Mum and Dad looked in on us the next morning, we'd greet them: 'Has he been yet? Has he been?' We didn't know Father Christmas was my dad, but that wouldn't have spoiled our enjoyment. When we opened our presents, we'd find a stocking with a few little Dinky toys and a Mars bar and tangerine. Some years, we might even get a few nuts. It was brilliant.

There was always one big present, a big box, and it was always a surprise. We'd tear into the wrapping paper and rip through it like hungry jackals, desperate to find out what was inside. One year, there was compendium of games and another year a toy. The best present we ever had was a Scalextric, which was a joint gift for Mike and me to share.

It was out of this world. We unpacked it straight away, put the track together and raced our cars all day long. The box was a bit scuffed and I'm sure it was second hand, but it didn't matter.

My happiness at home was replicated at school. I went to an ordinary Catholic junior school, St Benedict's RC, which was attached to our local church. It was at St Benedict's Church that I had my first taste of theatre, when I played Jesus in the nativity play. 'Great,' I thought: 'I'm the star of the show.' My formative acting experience at the age of nine or ten brought with it an unexpected privilege. The girl playing Mary, who could only have been eleven, was a very well-developed girl for her age and I remember taking advantage of my elevated position, sidling up to her, amorously, offering my Holy blessing.

An acting experience that was even more influential came in a play called *The Upper Room*, which we performed at school when I was ten. The plot was dark and mysterious and I was captivated by the play's power. The story centred on a youngster who had been a serving boy, bringing food and drink to Christ and the Apostles, when they'd eaten together for the Last Supper. The action started the following morning and the boy – played by yours truly – was looking at a window at the back of the stage, as row upon row of spears went by. The spears were held by other members of the class who walked past the window and then scurried round to rejoin it. The audience couldn't see that, of course; to them, there was the illusion of a never-ending processing of spear-carriers. We were creating the scene at Calvary where Jesus was carrying the Cross. It worked a treat.

When the Cross went by, I distinctly remember being enthralled by two things. My sense of wonderment at the spectacle was almost overwhelming and yet, at the same time, I also knew that it was fake. The illusion, however, didn't trouble me. I was in Jerusalem. I was there in *The Upper Room*. In a sense, I hadn't suspended my disbelief because I knew there were other people marching round and round in a virtual loop. But I was still amazed by the fact that I was in two planes. I felt as though I'd been transported, as though I'd opened the door to a level of consciousness that I'd never previously experienced. I distinctly remember the moment when the curtains opened, for instance. When the play began, I had my back to the audience. Before we started, I remember thinking, 'Should I say my first line?' because I didn't know whether I should or not. My dad later told me that I actually turned around, very distinctly, and had a look, to make sure the curtains were open, so that I could get on with it. Then I delivered the first line of the play. The plain fact is that I fell into the warm and comforting embrace of the lover who was going to be a lover for the rest of my life: the audience. It was a perfect moment. The audience welcomed me and warmed to me. I, in turn, was enveloped by its delicate and sublime affection.

Even now, I can still recall the group of anticipative faces looking towards me. There were 200 or 250 people all crushed together on tiny primary school benches, craning their necks forward, alert to every movement and every breath. There was something profound about that sensation. I felt utterly calm, transported from reality. I was completely aware that I was at the centre of the storm; I felt as though everything in the world – everything in that elevated world of artistic performance – revolved around me. Then we started the play and I can't remember anything about it whatsoever, other than the fact that I know it was a huge success. The eager faces of the audience stayed with me, however. Every single person was there for a reason and I remember imagining their thoughts. 'What's going to happen next?' 'Is he supposed to turn round and look at us like that?' They didn't know. They didn't know. They were waiting. Only I knew what was about to unfold. 'Is he supposed to speak straight away?' 'Why put him facing away from us, if he's supposed to speak?' That was the first time that I encountered the sheer magic that theatre could give to an audience. The spirit of performance infected me so completely, so profoundly, that it's remained with me ever since. It has my adoration and forever will.

After primary school I went to the seminary. I'd been to a retreat, called Blythe Hall, in Ormskirk, for the Passionist Fathers. It ignited a passion deep within me. The seminary gave me a chance to breathe. For the first time I was away from the confining conditions of our small home and able to express myself. My faith ran through me like letters through a stick of rock, so entering the seminary seemed like a natural step. It was an opportunity to spread my wings. I was due to go to grammar school following my years at St Benedict's and, I suppose, pursue a formal education before getting a respectable job. That was the path that had been mapped out for me. But I wasn't going to do that, not on your nelly. I decided I'd rather take a place at Blythe Hall and train to be a priest. The idea of living away, in a boarding school, really appealed. As the youngest of four children, I'd naturally been in the shadow of my siblings. I had an innate desire to push myself and make my mark. It was also important to me to win the approval of others, especially my parents. There was a degree of rebellion, too. The decision was one that I made myself; my parents certainly didn't push me, even though, in my mother's heart of hearts, I knew she would rejoice. For her, to have a priest in the family would have been the be all and end all. It would have been unbelievable.

To their credit, and particularly to Mum's credit, both my parents tried to persuade me to go to grammar school. They wanted me to do my O-levels and then, when I was sixteen, if I was still determined to be a priest, I would have plenty of time to train for the Church. Their attitude, and apparent sacrifice, was remarkable, particularly considering how important their faith was to each of them. Both counselled patience and insisted the better course was to spend five years at grammar school, but I was adamant and I got my own way. Even as an eleven-year-old, I could be resolute.

The seminary was a huge influence. It suited me in all sorts of ways. I didn't have much time for the classical elements of the education; neither Greek nor Latin gave me a thrill. To be honest, I didn't have much time for maths or history, either. My penchant was for English literature and drama, which I adored. Both subjects were inspiring and transporting, taking me to new and distant worlds. French was good fun too, though our teacher was a frightful show off. He once took a holiday in France and, rather than describe himself as English, he somewhat pompously spoke French all the time, creating the illusion that he was a literate bohemian from Paris. He must have been convincing because as he was coming home, a Frenchman asked him: '*Quelle partie de Paris vous fait est venu de?*' – meaning, Which part of Paris do you come from? That pricked his ego and Father Basil had to admit that he wasn't actually from France but was a secondary school teacher from the north west. He was a big-headed bastard, even though he was a nice enough chap, and he got caught out that time.

There were times when I got really homesick when I was at seminary, and there were occasions when my family used to hide behind the bushes outside the gates to stare at their out-of-reach son. Home visits were infrequent. But for the most part, my new life was liberating. My new 'family' was a collection of immaculately dressed young boys, all neatly attired in freshly pressed uniforms and presided over by teachers who were often austere. The part that I loved, however, was acting. Throughout my time at seminary, drama was tickling me like a trout in water. As soon as we got towards Christmas and started planning the pantomime or play, my excitement level became almost uncontrollable. Whenever a performance ended, I yearned for my next fix. I didn't have to wait too long. I developed a good relationship with a teacher called Father Aidan, a magnificent man who gave us a love of English and also produced seasonal performances each Christmas. I remember them all, particularly the production of *Jack and the Beanstalk*, in which I played Jack. My friend Bill Johnson played my mother. When we talk now, I remind him about it. 'Yeah, but I was so bad that the next time we did a play they just had me building the set. They wouldn't let me act.' Bill was a brilliant footballer, mind, and a very good pupil, as well as being very handsome. He was typical head boy material. As for me, when I took to the stage, decked out in a verdant tunic, I was bewitched. I still have a photograph of me playing Jack. I'm in position, on a chair, wearing a fur hat and holding a sword, looking out to camera. It's been an interesting journey, from *Jack and the Beanstalk* to *King Lear*. It's been a massive arc.

The following year we did a very funny play, or rather, a very odd play, called *The Uninvited Guest*. The action was set at a séance and the lead character had paid a friend to appear, unannounced and at a certain time. The idea was to create the impression of interaction with spirits from the other world. The guy organising the séance went off script. I followed him and we were both busking for a while, though thankfully we got away with that.

I enjoyed the first three years at the seminary but my determined streak surfaced as the third year came to a close. I developed an urge to leave and join the grammar school system that I had previously rejected. My parents were again cautious, advising me to stay put. They wanted me to finish off at seminary and at least get my O-levels. 'We don't mind if you don't want to become a priest,' said my mum. 'We'll support you, whatever decision you make. You can continue your education at the seminary and then move on after your exams.'

But I was sure: 'No, no, I want to leave.' And that was it. West Park Grammar School, in St Helens, which had given me a place three years earlier, accepted me right away and I joined them for the fourth form. Cheerio, seminary.

My new surroundings were fertile ground for me to be led astray. At seminary, there had been Christian Brothers keeping me on the rails; we'd had breakfast, done games and studied. Everything was very regimented, we'd boarded in dormitories and, though there were great walks in the grounds, there was little else to do. We couldn't misbehave because there was no outlet for our frustration. We were all very obedient. There were no rebels at all.

To be honest, I used to hate the walks at seminary. We'd go round and round in a big circle, but I didn't see the point of it. There were elements of seminary life that were fun; I enjoyed the river running through the grounds and taking it in turns to risk the various jumps that went across it. Football was okay too. Moving to grammar school was a big shock. I went from a conservative, restrictive environment to one where there seemed to be hardly any rules. Inevitably, I went wild. I was kicking over the traces. Nobody was standing over me telling me what to do. I had tranches of time – entire evenings in my bedroom at home – that had previously been taken up with other activities. I seemed to have limitless freedom. 'Shall I do my homework or not?' I'd ask myself each evening. The answer, often as not, was no. There were no consequences; nothing too serious, anyway. If I didn't do as I was supposed to, nobody seemed to mind.

At St Helens, I didn't work the way I should have, I lacked commitment. It was no surprise when I passed only three O-levels. I'd let myself down and I knew it, because I was capable of much, much more. Brother Augustine, who was the headmaster there, called me into his office. 'Peter,' he said, his voice measured and calm, 'you can leave now and get a job, if that is what you want to do. I won't stand in your way.' He paused, to watch my reaction: 'But there is an alternative.' He looked at me seriously and lowered his tone, as though about to impart some state secret. 'Now, I don't say this to everybody, but in your case, I think you would benefit from another year in the fifth form.' I looked at him quizzically, digesting his words. 'Peter, I'm saying you can take your fifth year again, work harder, and redo your O-levels.' It was a tough choice. My friends were going into the lower sixth form and I was facing the prospect of being re-streamed with the previous year's fourth formers. Signing up to do resits meant I would have to acknowledge the mistakes I'd made. It was a no-brainer. I swallowed my pride. 'Yes, Brother Augustine. Thank you for giving me the opportunity,' and I signed on the dotted line.

Before I started, I sat down with Brother Augustine again. I'd drawn up a list of demands. I said: 'Well, I'll drop this subject and drop that.' In his wisdom, he'd asked me why I wanted to drop anything at all, so I told him it would allow me to free up time for other studies. 'No,' he said. 'You'll waste that time. Why don't you keep those subjects going. The more you do, the easier it becomes. You wouldn't use the spare time productively, you'd waste it.'

In retrospect, redoing my fifth year was the best decision I could have made. I made really good mates with all of the fourth form, and a few became lifelong friends. To this day,

I'm still in touch with some of them. David Broadbent was a great friend and shared my enthusiasm for drama. He was a very good student and we both kicked on and enjoyed our work. History, geography, English; it didn't matter what the subject was, we both had a real determination to give of our best. I kept up chemistry and physics too, and eventually ended up with seven or eight O-levels, which was much more respectable than it might have been. Then I went into the sixth form and felt very grown up. We used to sit around discussing theatre and literature, people like James Joyce, thinking we were seriously intellectual. For my A-levels, I focused on the arts side. I dropped maths and chemistry and physics and did English, history, geography and French. We made the most of those years and emerged with good results. Our interest in theatre flourished too, in part because the Everyman Theatre was just down the road. It had been opened by a scruffy bunch of bastards: Terry Hands, Peter James and Martin Jenkins. They were doing the most extraordinary stuff. David and I were captivated and, by the time we'd passed our exams and moved into the lower sixth, we were Everyman regulars.

We were also able to stage our own productions. At one point I was given the part of Lane in *The Importance of Being Earnest*. 'Cucumber sandwich, son ...?' I can still remember my lines today. David and I were in *A Man for All Seasons* together, produced by Brother Dominic. I think it was then that I first thought the acting profession was great, that it could allow me to be creative while giving me the opportunity to say things about life in general. From then on, everything revolved around theatre. It was my abiding passion.

I'd go to see films, as well, like Alan Sillitoe's *The Loneliness of the Long Distance Runner* and *Saturday Night and Sunday Morning*. I was transfixed by both of them; by

Tom Courtenay and Michael Redgrave in *Long Distance* ... and by Albert Finney and Shirley Anne Field in *Saturday Night*. I realised, watching them, that you didn't have to be poncey to be an actor. But I still had this cloud above me, this feeling that if you came from where I did, acting wasn't a proper job. Working-class boys from Warrington weren't encouraged to emote, particularly Catholic boys who, like me, had been set on becoming priests. Even so, I loved the fact that there were writers like Osborne and Pinter and actors like Finney and Courtenay who were producing stuff that meant something to people. I thought, 'Hang on, this is about real life.' That was vital for someone like me, a boy from a Northern town who was looking for role models. I'd think, 'Yes, I can do that.' There were other role models, of course. I used to spend hours in front of the mirror, perfecting my Tony Curtis quiff. I think that's why I'm bald now.

Within the letter of the law there was an extraordinary freedom, providing you were doing your work. Our behaviour was pretty good, though we weren't above letting off steam in the local pubs and clubs. In those days, West Park was opposite Pilkington's, in Prescott Road, or we would all pop into the Bird in th' Hand for a little liquid refreshment after our A-levels. We'd also be on the fags; I'd started smoking at the age of ten. The father of another friend of mine was the landlord of The Sefton and that used to be another of our drinking spots. All of us developed a taste for the drink, and my appetite for it never really diminished.

At home, I was pretty well behaved. I was respectful of my parents and didn't rebel. I didn't get into much trouble; I'd kid Mother and Father that I'd done my homework when I hadn't, but as nonconformity goes, I was a novice. I maintained my religion and still went to church on Sundays, never missing my confessions. I remained very Catholic, the idea of not going to church simply didn't occur; religion was an important component of my identity and I was comfortable with it.

My brother, Mike, was more outwardly rebellious. He was a natural-born outlaw. He'd gone to a grammar school, Xaverian, in Manchester, which had a good reputation, but he spent more time at the cinema than he did in the classroom. Mike liked a wild life and rebelled very strongly. He was out there living it large, doing whatever the hell he pleased.

Mike stopped going to lessons altogether when he was in his mid-teens, at the age of about fourteen or fifteen. The day that my parents found out was awful. They'd been deceived by him and a pall of disappointment and sorrow hung over the house. Mike had been leaving for school every morning, satchel on his back, creating the impression of being the perfect student. 'Have a good day, Mike,' said Mum each morning, cheerfully, as he closed the front door. She did not realise he'd long since stopped going to school.

Then, one day, he came whistling down the yard late in the afternoon, pretending he'd been hard at it. 'Come in here, son,' said Dad, ushering him into the front room. The atmosphere was as thick and heavy as Northern smog. Dad spoke again: 'Sit down,' and Mike sat. My dad took a letter from the table and handed it to him. He nodded at Mike to read it. Mike's eyes whizzed across the text, absorbing the gravity of the situation. The school had written to say it was sorry about his poliomyelitis and considered it unfortunate that the condition had prevented him from attending lessons for the past three months. Mike's eyes glazed over, but he was quick to think on his feet. 'What's it all about?' asked Mum. 'Oh, it's a joke,' he bluffed. 'It's one of my mates, winding me up.' But it wasn't, it was the school. Worse was to come and Mike was expelled, eventually. He was the big black sheep of our family, our Mike.

Later on, at dancehalls, Mike would get into fights. He'd be carousing, drinking and smoking. I thought of him as being the arch villain, he was an absolute terror. To him, I was a proper goodie goodie, always on the right side of the law. He must have thought I was a right prissy bloody sockhole, and I probably was. I was going to church, but Mike was out there kicking ass, riding round on the back of motorbikes and breaking into Butlins holiday camps, looking for girls. He was a villain, through and through.

Later on in life, Mike saw the light and changed. Quite when his Road to Damascus moment happened, I don't know, but I know that it did. He reinvented himself. He stopped being an aggressive, selfish, angry and rebellious thorn in everybody's side to become one of the most thoughtful, compassionate, gentle human beings you could ever hope to meet. There was an extraordinary about-face. We started getting together more when I was down in Bristol, at drama school. He used to come and visit and see shows and we started to get to know each other really well. Our relationship blossomed. He became fascinated by theatre and made very perceptive observations about some of the plays that I was in.

On one occasion, when I performed *The Bofors Gun*, at Liverpool, we met up afterwards. 'What did you think?' I asked him, shortly after the curtain had come down. But before he'd had a chance to answer, I was off: 'You know, I think it's a shame that the theatre hasn't got enough money for props, so we couldn't afford a gun,' I said. 'In the last scene, when the lead character stabbed himself to death on a bayonet, we should have used a gun. It's a shame we didn't have one.'

Mike listened to me answering my own question then, when I'd run out of steam, he spoke. 'I enjoyed the play.' He was very measured: 'You know, I disagree with you, Pete. I don't think using props would have made it any better than what I saw. You should be pleased with the way you played it. You were the Bofors Gun, weren't you? The gun was you, O'Rourke, your character; he was the obsolete gun. He was the one that had to go. So he didn't really need the gun on stage. He didn't need any props.' Mike was a perceptive man.

When I finished my A-levels, at the age of nineteen, the tried-and-trusted path for a reasonably bright Catholic boy from West Park Grammar School was straightforward. I was expected to go to university and then apply for teacher training college. I wasn't under pressure from my parents, as such: social convention and peer pressure at school were the factors guiding me. Teacher training college promised a job at the end of it and one of the colleges that loomed into view was St Mary's, at Twickenham, which was an all-male institution. I was fairly athletic and St Mary's had a phenomenal PE department, so it seemed like a natural fit. Besides, after the decisions I'd made to go to the seminary, then to leave it, I was eager to stay on the right rails.

Sport was a big part of my life during those years and I was quick and lithe. I played rugby for the school and I was a reasonable player: not a star by any means, but I could hold my own. So my bags were packed and I was on my way to the adult world, intent on becoming a PE teacher. It was 1965. When I arrived at St Mary's, I was asked to choose two subjects to study. PE was a natural choice and I chose drama as my second subject. I felt very grown up. Moving to London was a big step. But I'd lived away from home before so I felt undaunted. It was exciting to be on the fringes of London, everything seemed to be within our reach. During the first year, we were in halls of residence and we were looked after. It was like a home from home. There were differences to the seminary, because we lived in shared houses, rather than dorms, but there was still an element of community about the college we called SIMs. The college was pukka and my parents approved. Happy days.

I blossomed during those years, unbelievably so. I was away from the subversive influence of Mike, cut free from my mother's apron strings and no longer the baby of the family. The freedom was extraordinary. And I was still motivated to do well. I'd thrived in the sixth form and the drive that had helped me through my A-levels was still with me. I wanted to concentrate on my work and do well, study and enjoy it.

My plans soon unravelled, however, because my head and heart were pulling in different directions. Within a short time of my arrival, I realised that drama was my real passion, not PE. I was the only student combining PE and drama, and the drama group and the PE group were like chalk and cheese. The PE department was filled with butch, testosterone-pumped, volleyball-playing, rugby-mauling, javelin-throwing swimmers. They were all wearing fashionable clothes: designer tracksuits, plenty of blue-coloured gear and white trainers. Man, those boys were pumped. They were really up for it. The drama department, in contrast, was filled with bohemian, beatnik, oddball, kaftan-wearing, reefer-smoking whackos. There's no other way to describe them.

The two departments never met, their paths never crossed, well, not until our second year, when they fused beautifully. I began spending more and more time in the drama department, skipping my PE lectures. The fact I didn't turn up for PE was indicative of my attitude, rather than a reflection on the department itself, which was great. The course included sports, anatomy, physiology, the history of sport and also looked at different activities around the world. It also looked at the sociology of sport, which was fascinating. It was a very, very thorough course.

One of the teachers was Joe Jagger, Mick Jagger's dad, and he used to take us for volleyball. We made the most of the Rolling Stones connection and used to go to Eel Pie Island every once in a while, to watch the band play. Back then, the 'Stones were second or third on the bill, supporting people like Long John Baldry. I wasn't impressed with them, they were a bunch of dead scruffy yahoos, as were the Beatles, whom I'd encountered back in Liverpool at the Cavern Club, when I still lived in Warrington. I used to promote nights at a social club in Warrington and I asked them to play. The gig was at the Bell Hall, where I'd done *The Upper Room*. That was where we held our weekly, Friday-night youth club. They were paid about £10 but they didn't deserve it, they were terrible. We used to put on Friday-night socials for the young guns and on that particular night we had Gerry and the Pacemakers, the Beatles and the Undertakers on the bill. The Undertakers did them all. They were the best, they were brilliant. Their speakers were shaped like coffins, they wore stovepipe hats and they had saxophones as well as guitars. Gerry and the Pacemakers were quite good, but they were all 'la la lar, la la lar'. But the Beatles were a dirty, foul-mouthed, leather-jacketed bunch of insurrectionary yobs. You could just sense that they really could have done without being in Warrington in our club, that's the attitude they had. So much for Beatlemania.

PE started to drift at SIMs, it just didn't work. I was into drama and that was that. I spent my time poring over new plays that were popular in the mid-1960s. We were in the era of John Osborne, Samuel Beckett, Harold Pinter's *The Homecoming* and plenty of American and European play-wrights. There were influences from around the world like the Theatre of Cruelty, the Theatre of the Absurd, Ionesco;

and over in the States there was Eugene O'Neill and Arthur Miller. They were extraordinary times. I began to see the world in a completely different light. No longer did it seem like the cosy little community that I'd once believed in. The veneer was shattered. The world seemed very fractured. The Theatre of the Absurd was a particularly strong influence. It made me feel as though the world was mad, the way we looked at it was complete nonsense. It made me wonder why people behaved the way they did.

In every way, the drama course sustained the transformative feeling that I'd experienced all those years earlier while playing in *The Upper Room*. For instance, in Franz Kafka's *Metamorphosis*, there was a scene when a character turned into a monstrous insect. I was completely carried away by it, to the extent that I'd think: 'Yes, that's real. It is an insect.' In drama, I seemed to view everything with widescreen, panoramic, hyper-sensory vision. The SIMs environment changed everything about me; the way I thought, the way I interacted with people and even my views on the Church. My Catholic faith started to ebb away very quickly and I railed against organised religion to the point where I disliked it. My unshakeable faith mutated and I developed a strong agnosticism. Because of their Catholicism, my parents were raging Tories, but I rebelled against their beliefs when I went to teacher training college, and we used to have fierce arguments. My childhood was all cigars at Christmas and chicken on Sundays. But the thing that felt safe and comforting could also be inhibiting. My father had always been my hero, he'd always told me he didn't have dreams. But studying drama at college opened up a whole new world for me, and I began to question the foundations of my life. I started to dream.

On one occasion, Roy Groves, Joe Jagger's second-in-command in the PE department came into the drama department, looking for me. I was hanging upside down from a scaffold in the theatre, fixing a lamp. I must have looked like a bat. 'Look, Pete,' he said as I viewed him from on high. 'You've not been to a lecture this year yet.' He spoke to me in a reasoned tone, there was no condescension or frustration in his voice. I descended from the scaffold so that we could talk. 'You know, if you don't turn up for the course, we're going to have to fail you. Just turn up and it'll be okay. We know you're into your drama, we know that's where you're heading. But just turn up.' I stood there, nodding, thinking Roy was right, I ought to go to lectures. But I knew my heart wasn't in it.

Roy's chat persuaded me to continue with the PE course and I struggled through. But as the months passed, drama became my religion. It took over and became all-consuming. To a young man, moving from childhood to adulthood, drama had elements of everything that mattered. It had politics, sex, sexual politics, power and much more besides. We were doing incredible plays, like Jean-Paul Sartre's *No Exit*, with its famous line 'Hell is other people'. We were discussing sexuality, looking at what was male and what was female. Nothing was taboo. My beliefs in religion and theatre weren't necessarily incompatible, it was just that one took over. By osmosis, I was more committed and devoted and in awe of theatre than I was of religion. That's the long and short of it. The intellectual dimension of theatre thrilled me. Yes, drama was artifice, yes it was construction, but, when it was put together well, when it was performed with the right commitment, there was a reality that was more real than our day-to-day lives. Drama had greater resonance, greater depth than anything that we considered to be 'real life'.

In real life, there was so much that wasn't true. We didn't live in an equal nation, we lived in one where one person had this, the other had that and the other had nothing at all. Nothing that we were supposed to believe in was true. But in theatre, we were learning about spirit and soul, about humanity. The texts of our plays became my bible. They became my hymns. They became the priests and nuns of my existence.

None of us were stunning actors, by any means, but we were all so passionate about it that we'd commit to the nth degree. We did a production of *King Lear*, in which I played Gloucester, rather than Lear. My instincts for the best parts were honed, even then, and I was miffed not to get Lear. We had a guy who was older than me who had a big beard and was really mature. He was absolutely right to play Lear and did a good job. And Lear or not, I thoroughly enjoyed it. There was a unity among the drama people, we all helped each other and just pulled through.

The PE department had started to connect with the drama department by that point. The big, gruff PE lads who were used to pumping iron and chasing girls were getting into our esoteric work in our theatre. They came one night to see a production of Pinter's *Homecoming* and they couldn't believe their eyes. From then on, they were theatre-goers. Instantly, they'd been converted. It was a peculiar marriage between the butch world of the football players and the bohemian world of the drama group.

At the time, I was seeing a girl called Sheila Aspen, from Blackburn. But she grew weary of my commitment to drama. One night, she snapped and screamed at me to be less absorbed. I'd been playing a character called Faro in a play and I remember her yelling: 'It's you I want, not Faro.' She wanted me to stop talking about theatre and Faro, and start being Pete, Pete Postlethwaite. But I couldn't. That was how wrapped up in it I'd become, and eventually we went our separate ways.

I found myself at SIMs. When I went back to Warrington, for a break, I'd find it difficult to reassimilate. I'd go and get work in the Post Office at Christmas, to make a few bob, which I'd save for when I was back in London. When I reached my early twenties, I was a long-haired, wild-eyed, loon-pant-wearing, beer-swilling radical; completely in tune with the beatnik generation. But my seemingly unrestrained lifestyle was, in fact, curtailed by social convention. When I got to the end of my teaching course, I qualified and had the option of applying for drama school. I decided not to. One member of our group went for it, but it wasn't for me. Perhaps it was my working-class upbringing, perhaps I felt a sense of responsibility to enter a steady profession. Perhaps, perhaps, perhaps. In spite of Tom Courtenay, Albert Finney, et al, working-class men didn't become actors.

So I turned against it and became a teacher. 'Learn the lessons from the seminary and your wasted year in the fifth form,' I told myself. 'Go and teach for a couple of years. If you still want to act at the end of that, then go back.' I followed the advice that I'd ignored all those years before and taught.

My first year was in an approved school, St George's, at Formby, in Southport. It wasn't really teaching, it was social work. A lot of the kids who attended had led troubled lives and part of my job was to try to lead them back onto the straight and narrow. It was a tough place to work because a lot of the boys were obviously jail fodder. As teachers we had our hearts in the right places and we tried to do what was right for the boys there. It didn't always work, of course. There were plenty of times when I'd be asked to go to court to speak for someone's good character. On one occasion, I went to see the magistrate and told them that a particular boy had been working hard to get himself back on track and deserved another chance. Then, about a week later there was a phone call from the police. 'Mr Postlethwaite,' said the constable on the other end of the line, as serious as can be, 'someone has knocked over the court house.' Apparently, the kid had used his day in court to case the joint.

I enjoyed the work and did my best to make life better for the boys, until an incident happened there that made me leave. I came back to the class and found one of the staff having a fight with a boy. The boy had been a bully and a thug, but I'd been encouraging him to change. I'd made him head of house and he'd started to improve. But when I came back to the class, he was fighting.

Later, I sat down with the teacher. 'You didn't see that, did you?' he said.

I looked him in the eye. 'But I did.'

'No, no, no. You don't understand. You didn't see any-thing, did you?' His tone was hard and the implication hung heavy in the air. He wanted me to lie for him, to pretend I'd seen nothing, to betray the boy that I'd nurtured.

The headmaster called us in and asked me what had happened. I told him the truth, that there had been a fight and that I'd been asked to cover up for another member of staff.

'There was a fight,' I said. 'I'm sorry, but there was. And here's my resignation.' I handed him the letter. 'I can't work in an environment like this.' And so I left. It wasn't an unhappy job but it was a corrupt system. And then I went from one extreme to the other. I took a post at Loreto, a well-heeled Catholic grammar school for girls whose parents were very wealthy. The world I was entering couldn't have been more different to the world I was leaving behind. It was set in the midst of what was then a fairly run-down area of Manchester, Moss Side; though the school itself was well-heeled. There was a huge number of staff, led by a determined lady called Mother Victorine. She was made from steel.

I found from the beginning, almost without trying, that fortune was favouring the brave. Or the foolish. The lately retired and much-loved head of music, Michael Murphy, had left the school a unique legacy. The lower sixth had learned and knew by heart every aria, chorus and four-part harmony of *The Pirates of Penzance*, Gilbert and Sullivan's witty operetta, and we spent many fruitful hours in class, and after school, simply building a production around their extraordinary voices. One grey, rainy Thursday afternoon, another member of staff happened to watch our efforts and enthusiastically urged us, rather compellingly, to mount the whole thing on stage in the school hall and make a production of it. With ingenuity, tired voices and invaluable help from countless others, we did just that. It was brilliant.

We packed the school hall to its gunnels for four consecutive nights with audiences enraptured by the rollicking gay abandon and bittersweet melancholy of Gilbert and Sullivan's subtly subversive magic. Even Mother Victorine, who had expressed various doubts earlier on, was bound into silence by the sheer energy and joy of it all and, of course, the considerable box-office takings.

Was it the subversiveness of it that had worried her? I didn't know. I do know she took exception to the sight of me during the frenetic and chaotic dress rehearsal, gluing and sticking false moustaches and whiskers onto the chins of semi-clad schoolgirls, a detail that had escaped me completely: the semi-clad thing, not the whiskers. I was oblivious to it. She did ask me shortly afterwards to 'avoid wearing floral ties' as a small measure of her dominion over me – so I took to wearing floral socks instead, a fashion statement about which she could do very little. Hey ho.

The unexpected success of *Pirates* and kudos that went with it gave me the chutzpah to create a drama department of which, of course, de facto, I would be head. So I sailed away from the English department, with their blessing, and plunged into teaching drama exclusively and full-time. Happiness.

The upper sixth, on the other hand, were not content. Not to be outdone by the lower sixth, they had been clamouring for me to do something 'deep and serious' with them. Had Mother Victorine's ears got wind of that ambivalent exchange, the Lord only knows in what direction her labyrinthine mind would have raced!

What to do with the upper sixth? I remembered vividly the cauterising effect that playing the Common Man in *A Man for All Seasons* had had on me in my own sixth form days. But it faced me with a tricky dramatic dilemma. My school had been all male; Loreto, all female. Only two of Bolt's characters were women, the rest were men. But what a challenge! What an acting challenge for the girls!

'You're insane.' 'We're doomed.' 'What a fantastic play.' 'We'll be laughed off the stage.' 'It's radical.' 'We're all mad.' These were the excited babblings of the girls after a hushed reading of the play, and their continued enthusiasm and courage were to prove electric and infectious. They almost cast the play themselves, so everyone was happy in their role, everyone was on board and 'the caravan was on its way'.

The stumbling block from Mother Victorine came right out of left field, almost as soon as the casting was made public. She buttonholed me in the corridor the next day during the lunch break. 'Mr Postlethwaite, you cannot have Juliet playing the role of St Thomas More.'

'Really, Mother? Why ever not?'

'For the very good reason, Mr Postlethwaite, that she is a self-confessed atheist.'

I have absolutely no idea, even now, where my next sentence came from. 'I am aware of that, Mother, and I understand your concern. But, you see, to me, that is the whole point. Thomas goes through an excruciating crisis of conscience in the play, even, at one of his lowest ebbs, questioning his very relationship with God himself. Juliet has that exact problem herself at present and it makes her ideal casting. But, also, the experience of going "right through that" might just swing her round to the point of view that you profess and hold dear, who knows?'

Utter silence.

'Proceed as you think fit, Mr Postlethwaite. Proceed as you think fit.'

A flurry of black gabardine, a gleam of wimple and she was gone. *A Man for All Seasons* followed *Pirates* into the burgeoning annals of the young drama department at Loreto, even securing good reviews in the *Manchester Evening News* and the local press; high praise indeed. The work we were doing was worthwhile, the satisfaction immense and the prospects golden and unlimited. The girls were willing to attempt any project with brio, while their commitment, passion and work rate never needed prodding. As a young (or old) drama teacher, I doubt you could wish for a more rewarding position.

Then the letter arrived.

There was something in the way that Mother Victorine handed it to me, peering down at me over the top of her polished horn-rimmed glasses. She had asked me to take a seat, so she towered above me, even from behind her headmistress's colonial desk. Funny ole thing – power. It was 1969, only three years since England had nicked the World Cup from Germany in 1966, and at twenty-three years of age I was by far the youngest member of the vast teaching staff.

'Well, Mr Postlethwaite,' she said, in her clipped Cork brogue. 'What do you make of that?' She turned away as if distracted to gaze out of the stained-glass window of her office. I read the letter in a vacuum of silence, totally unaware then that it was about to change my life, radically and forever.

By this time, I had begun to really enjoy teaching at Loreto: thoughts of a career as an actor had long faded into the past. It was the beginning of the summer term and during the recent Easter holiday I had spent some time down in London, catching up with old friends and seeing a couple of shows. I had also met up with Roger Lane, head of the drama department at St Mary's. Roger and I enthused for hours about my time at SIMs, Roger mooted the idea that I come down to London in a few weeks' time to adjudicate the third year's final pieces and to speak with them specifically about life in secondary education. It would mean a Friday afternoon away from school. It sounded worthwhile and I suggested he write to Mother Victorine, outlining his plan and making his request. It was Roger's letter I was reading in her office, still naïvely oblivious to the inner workings of her Machiavellian mind.

'Well, Mother,' I offered. 'If it wouldn't disrupt the timetable too much, it would seem to be a worthwhile thing to do. I'm somewhat flattered that Roger has seen fit to ask me to put something back into the old Alma Mater, as it were, and if it did prove to be feasible, I'd be happy to oblige. I mean ...' Something in her stare stopped me in mid-sentence. 'What, Mother? What do you make of it?' I still couldn't see it coming.

'It is not on college notepaper.'

'Beg pardon, Mother?'

'It is not, Mr Postlethwaite, written on college notepaper.'

Oh! My! God! She believed the letter to be a complete fabrication, an elaborate excuse allowing me to cut loose early on a Friday afternoon and enjoy an extended weekend away in London. She may even have doubted the very existence of Roger Lane himself. She certainly believed there was a gross deception afoot and that I was central to it. Scales fell from my eyes.

Taking a couple of long, deep breaths, I rose from my seat and handed her back the letter.

'Mother Victorine, I am due to take the fourth form for a double period this afternoon but you may wish to make alternative arrangements for I shan't be there. I'm going home now for the weekend to consider carefully the implications of what you have just said and I shall return on Monday morning to let you know exactly what I make of it. Good afternoon, Mother, and go well, go with God.'

I turned on my heels and left the office, the school, Manchester and the teaching profession. That weekend, I applied to the Bristol Old Vic Theatre School, down in the West Country, asking to join the two-year course they offered there, with a clear and crystal ambition to become a professional actor. I suspect I should be grateful to Mother Victorine; had she not been her, I may never have been me. Maybe she was the catalyst for which I had been subliminally waiting. Peace, Mother Vic. RIP. Hey fiddly-dee; an actor's life for me.

THREE

Face Like a Fucking Stone Archway

∾

Suitcase packed, I contemplated the times to come in Bristol. I could barely conceive that I was embarking upon a life on the stage. Me, a working-class, Catholic boy from Warrington: I was supposed to be a 'normal' teacher, priest or office worker; not have the temerity to act. But what did I care for normal? 'Ha,' I thought. 'Bring it on.' 'This is all I ever wanted,' I thought, 'it's perfect.'

By abandoning teaching for acting, I was leaving a safe and secure profession for one that was anything but. The decision to pursue acting had been the most momentous of my life. Until then, convention had been my guide and I'd followed it like the North Star; though in my heart I'd wanted more. All the while I'd been dutifully pursuing teaching, my passion for theatre had gnawed like a buzz saw at wood. Looking back, it's plain to see that everything had been leading me to this day: performance had captivated me throughout my life, I'd even invented a drama department at Loreto to satisfy my passions. Now I'd cut the ties with my former, 'normal' life and there was no going back. I wouldn't be

Ernold Same, with three kids, a wife, an office job and a Ford Cortina; I was going to act. The steady, dependable future mapped out by the lords of assembly had been ditched. My future was no longer about instilling discipline in future generations or offering life lessons to disaffected teens. The classroom was out; the green room was in.

But how would I pay for it? I'd got no savings and had already spent my grant on teacher training; the local council wouldn't fund me again. My mother and father believed acting was a phase, they assumed it would soon pass and I'd eventually find my way back to the classroom. There'd never been any acting in our family, my dad liked to sing and make speeches but nothing else, so my ambition had always seemed peculiar to my parents. But their apparent lassitude didn't ever spill over into disapproval. In fact, I always felt that I had my father's tacit support. I remember as a teenager participating in a public speaking contest. Everyone in the room seemed to think I'd done a great job and had it in the bag. The chairman then stood up to proclaim the results. I'd been downgraded because I'd exceeded the time limit and my father was enraged. 'Come on, son,' he said, standing up and turning to go. 'Get your bloody coat. You were better than the rest of them, we'll not wait any more.'

But whatever my parents thought, an irreversible journey had begun. All roads led to Bristol's Old Vic Theatre School, I just had to find a way of footing the bill. My place was deferred so that I could save enough money to pay my fees and I found a job in London as a sheet-metal worker. For the best part of a year I made beer kegs, spending a little on rent, booze and fags, and saving every remaining penny. The irony of my position wasn't lost on me; a generation earlier, my father had worked as a cooper, never once complaining about his difficult toil. To him, work was a means to an end, a way of putting food on the table and a roof over our heads. All that he really wanted was to come home to his beloved Mary and us children. I, meanwhile, hated the modern-day equivalent of that job, I detested every moment. Working night shifts, pressing and welding beer kegs, was the worst year of my life; it was dirty, nasty, smelly work. Its only redeeming feature was that it gave me the money to pay my way through drama school. I laboured manfully and finally, at the age of twenty-four, the bright lights of Bristol beckoned.

∾

'Mwah, mwah', the well-heeled pretty-young-things at the enrolment desk were air kissing their hellos when I arrived at the Old Vic. I stood out like a clown at a funeral among those children of Aphrodite. I didn't feel self-conscious though, why the hell should I? Besides, I was used to being the oldest member of the group; it had been that way since my final years at school, after deciding to resit my exams. I vowed to make the most of this fantastic opportunity that was opening for me. My course at the Old Vic Theatre School was to last for two years. The college was attached to the theatre for the training of actors and our tutorials involved speech training, movement, modern dance, ballet, fencing, theatre workshop and parts in a dozen plays, both modern and classical. I found myself jumping through emotional and spiritual hoops like a collie at Crufts. The course was a revelation. Every day was a new beginning, an opportunity to push myself further. My tutors made encouraging noises, both about my level of commitment and the potential I showed. As the end of term neared, however, I found myself stony broke, despite my efforts at the beer-keg factory. The Old Vic needed a few hundred pounds down, but I had no way of raising it. 'How am I going to complete the course?' Fear filled my stomach with lead. The head of the school took me aside: 'Listen,' he said, 'I have a hunch you're going to do all right in this business, so I'm going to put down the outstanding amount as a debt and then, in a few years' time, I'll write it off as a bad debt.' Wow. It was landing ten score draws on the pools: delight rushed through my veins. My tutor had neutralised my financial worries and, more importantly, I took his words to indicate a degree of confidence in my acting abilities. Almost instantaneously, however, that illusion was shattered.

'Of course, when you've got a face like a fucking stone archway, you can't go wrong.'

'Umm, thanks, I'll take that as a compliment as well, shall I?'

Come to think about it, I still haven't paid back the drama school those fees. I'd better go and find my cheque book.

I never worried about the pretty boys because acting was no longer the middle-class bastion it had been. My whole strength was my weakness – when you look hard at supposedly villainous-looking people, like me, there is invariably vulnerability. An audience never expects that, that is the strength. One teacher gave me a copy of *Zen in the Art of Archery*, which was apparently nothing to do with the art of acting but in fact applied exactly the same principle. This guy goes to learn archery and for two years the master won't let him pick up a bow. He had to learn that the target came to the arrow, and when everything was correct, when everything else was in place, it would just happen. I had no desire to get arty-farty and transcendental about the art of acting, but he was right; all the best work seems effortless. If someone really enjoys being a barman, there's freedom, grace and beauty to it. The same with acting.

After my first year, I received the *Bristol Evening Post*'s Theatre Merit award, made annually to the best student at the Old Vic School. I was thrilled: it vindicated my decision to move from teaching to acting, and reflected my hunger for my new profession. Besides, I needed the money. The award was made in advance, to enable me to continue my studies, and I was the guest of honour at a dinner at the *Evening Post* offices. 'Great,' I thought. 'At least I don't have to worry about how I'll pay for that meal.'

Kept afloat by the *Evening Post* scholarship, I lived happily as I learned more and more each day. The cash was a life-saver and I lived on it for six months. It paid for me to take a part in *Who's Afraid of Virginia Woolf?* at the Little Theatre, a small company with links to the Old Vic. I'd walked a long road to get to the professional stage, though I kept a sense of perspective. In essence, the performance was no different to those back in college or school, except, of course, that I was being paid to do the thing I loved most.

The media swooped and I tasted my first local newspaper headlines when a story appeared recognising my achievement. My parents, correctly noted as being from Delery Drive, Padgate, were succinctly described by the reporter as 'thrilled' and Mother cut out the article. It became the first page in a career-long collection of scrapbooks that she compiled. Whether she thought acting was a phase or not, I was still one of her children and the interest she took in my career underscored her unconditional love and support.

The second year was simultaneously challenging and rewarding and as it drew to a close I began my search for work in repertory. My task wasn't easy: after all, there were around a thousand trained applicants across the UK and only three hundred jobs. Failure wasn't an option. Without my Equity card I'd have been out. I'd have been swallowed whole by the life I'd escaped; two-up, two-down domesticity and unfulfilling jobs.

'Pete, can I have a word?' I was once again taken into

the head's office. I braced myself for more 'face-like-a-stone-archway' schtick, or to be offered platitudes along with my P45. 'We'd like you to stay.'

'What?' The heavens seemed to open.

'The company can only take on two new members each year, and we'd like you to be one.'

It was a marvellous and beautiful moment, beyond my expectations.

'Thank you,' I said. 'I would love to stay in Bristol.' And that was that.

With joy in my heart, I contemplated the forty weeks of professional work, after which I'd become a full member of Equity. The Equity card was like gold, the equivalent of a pilot being given his licence or a doctor being told he could practise. I started to count down the weeks like days on an extended Advent calendar: 39, 38, 37 ... 10, 9, 8 ... 3, 2, 1 ... When my term ended I'd be able to work for whoever had the balls to employ me: I'd also be able to write the word 'Actor' on my passport. It was the stuff of dreams.

The work in Bristol was a revelation. Our first piece, *The Bristol Road Show*, was thrilling. At that time, there'd been a furore in the city over the state of the roads, so we devised an agit-prop show that shone the spotlight on the mandarins at the town hall. It was an innovative piece with film, stage games from vaudeville, group music and farcical by-play. It was wonderful to be part of that modern, exploratory studio theatre. We spent a long time researching it and I played alongside Marcia King, Ian Marter, Lewis Michael and Paul Moriarty. The comedy was intended to tear at the heart of the planners' intransigence, to illuminate the human cost of their 'progress'. The homes of people in Totterdown were being bulldozed, communities were being divided forever by concentric lines of tarmac. We felt our job as actors was to hone in on those issues, to initiate public debate, to offer catharsis to those affected.

I studied under Rudi Shelley at the Old Vic and he was a real legend. Rudi was more of a guru than a teacher. The other people he nurtured included actors such as Jeremy Irons, Daniel Day-Lewis, Peter O'Toole and Anthony Hopkins. He wouldn't let us settle into a comfort zone, he was constantly pushing for more. One afternoon, while rehearsing *Othello*, he stopped me dead in my tracks. 'What are you doing, Pete?' he said, in his heavy Eastern European accent.

'I'm rehearsing, Rudi,' I replied.

'I can see that, but what is it?'

'*Othello.*'

'Yes, but what is it?'

'It's a play,' I pleaded, growing ever more insecure.

'Well, fucking play it then,' Rudi said. I understood what he meant, he was telling me that by the doing of it, I would learn. 'You can analyse till the cows come home, but until you put yourself in that situation, who knows what it will pump up in you?'

The Old Vic Theatre School was a fantastic place to start. It also helped me to take theatre seriously. Though I'd always loved drama, I'd never really believed I'd be able to make a living from it. Bristol showed me that I could and I considered myself very lucky. The living wasn't great, of course. My wage was £18 a week, about half the national average: it was a pittance, but I'd have done it for nothing.

Equity card safely in hand, I ventured into rep; to Liverpool, London and Teesside. Brother Dominic, who all those years before had directed me in *A Man for All Seasons*, read about my progress in a Catholic newspaper and wrote to my parents:

Dear Mr and Mrs Postlethwaite,
This may come as a surprise! Hope you won't mind my
taking the liberty of writing to you. I read of Peter's
successful treading of the boards in a recent copy of
the Catholic Pic *and I felt I must write to offer my*
congratulations. It is indeed gratifying to know that I
played a small part in fostering this talent.

He kept in touch and later sent Christmas cards, telling me that all the world was a stage and wishing me luck on whichever boards I was treading.

The work came thick and fast and I started to gain experience in other theatres. Bristol Old Vic Theatre School had a fortnight's residency at the Theatre Royal and we played George Farquhar's *The Recruiting Officer*, a restoration comedy, and James Saunders' *The Borage Pigeon Affair*, which was another eccentric exercise about local government buffoonery. *The Workhouse Donkey* explored collective civil cant. I loved those agit-prop works, exploring the mad murky rituals of small-town politics. On another occasion, we did an American play at the Little Theatre, *Arsenic and Old Lace*. The basic formula was farce but it was handled in such a loony and sophisticated way that it took a while to realise that the old in-one-door-out-the-other routine was going on.

I was asked to perform at the Forum, in Billingham, where Timothy West had formed a new company for a season of plays. One was *We Bombed in New Haven*, a coruscating post-war drama by Joseph Heller that illustrated our collective helplessness in the face of high authority. I played Corporal Bailey, an aggressively avid conformist in the running for promotion, alongside Julian Glover, whose Captain Starkey organised orders to bomb. Before our opening night, Julian sent me a telegram from Billingham Town Centre:

'Don't worry, you'll get your promotion all right, after the mission and when you need the furlough. With confidence in your success. I mean that, corporal, with admiration.' Chocks away, Julian, chocks away.

Billingham was better known for its chemical industries than a nascent love of classical drama, but we played to full houses. When we did Congreve's *The Double-Dealer* for the workers at the chemical plant, Prunella Scales sent me a telegram saying I was the best Restoration truck driver she'd ever worked with. 'I'm the only Restoration truck driver you've ever worked with,' I laughed.

And then I was asked to return to the font of my creative ambition: the Everyman, in Liverpool. It was a moment of great fulfilment, the realisation of my dreams. I went to appear in *The Bofors Gun* and stayed for three or four years. It was the early 1970s, and I was in my mid-twenties. Life seemed full of opportunity.

The Everyman was brilliantly run by Alan Dossor, a remarkable man who brought gritty realism to the stage and offered real democracy to his actors. He brought together an extraordinary company who really believed that we'd change things for the better. He was the springboard for lots of actors – and also discovered great writers like Willy Russell. It was remarkable to be in that funky, miraculous converted chapel with people who were so talented. But at the time, I didn't contemplate that. We were all up-and-at-it, working together in harmony, wanting to extract the best from one another, to push the envelope. They were halcyon times.

The Bofors Gun, my first performance there, gave me an inkling of the Everyman atmosphere. At the Everyman, we were proud of our roots, we mucked in and got our hands dirty, running the bar, helping with the props, making the scenery or adding to the graffiti that had been daubed on the walls by the Liverpool Poets. Alan had hired a delightful man called Mike Mould to play all the heavies. With all respect to Mike – heavy he wasn't. I think he was relieved to be replaced by a chisel-faced dude from Warrington with an unpronounceable name. The lead, the weedy, ambitious Lance-Corporal Evans, was played by George Costigan, who was to become a lifelong friend. Tony Sher was there, playing Flynn, the Ulsterman. I played a Southern Irish madman, O'Rourke.

We worked out how to play one particular scene, in which I got into a tussle with Tony Sher. During rehearsals, I had to grab Tony's lapels. When I did, Tony knocked my hand away. I raised an eyebrow. 'I think my character could handle yours,' explained Tony.

A week later, we were rehearsing the same scene but the director wasn't on top of things and I was increasingly frustrated. I'd been spending time with my mother, who was unwell, and had a lot on my mind. I arrived at the theatre at 11 a.m. but wasn't used until 3 p.m. The rumours that I'd been in the theatre bar were true. Eventually, I was called upon to run through the scene. I grabbed Tony's lapel and he saw the fire in my eyes; sensibly, he decided not to knock my hand away. I was steaming drunk and the others eyed me with suspicion, as though I was an unexploded bomb. The next page of the script called for me to crash down on the bed and for my mate, George Costigan, to shake me and order me out. He came over, nervously, and said half his line; I exploded like a ball of human fury, grabbing him by his coat and lifting him horizontally into the air. I sent him crashing down onto the bed ... except, at the last possible moment, I took the weight of his momentum and cushioned his fall, lowering him as gently as possible. Nobody spoke. But that was the Everyman – a combustible atmosphere with free-flowing rehearsals where anything went. That spirit never left me.

Before the opening night, we decided to get into character and the entire cast descended on the local barber's so
that we could brush up. I went in sporting long hair and a
candy-striped shirt with kipper collars, feeling pretty good,
like some cool seventies hipster. When I emerged from
the salon of Francis Boyle-Ryan, I was a different man. I
looked like a squaddie: Francis had given me a short-back-
and-sides of military severity; he'd transformed me into a
skinhead.

We played *Bofors* to an appreciative audience and I tried
to give O'Rourke a hard, jumpy, all-but-maniacal power.
The reviews were good: another clipping for Mother's scrap-
book: pretty soon she'd start believing that I might be able
to make a career from this acting lark.

The next show was *The Good Woman of Setzuan*. I was
the baker or something tiny, and, bored, I covered myself in
a completely idiotic amount of make-up and indulged my
clown – giving myself a good deal more pleasure than either
the audience or, I imagine, Brecht. George called me out
on that: 'The inspiration for your character, it's not Dick
Emery, is it?' Hmmmm.

We also did a roadshow called Van Load, a raucous, devil-
may-care offshoot that went out into the pubs all round
Liverpool. Van Load was a real baptism of fire because
everybody in Liverpool was – is – a far better comedian than
any of us could ever be. But it was fertile, vibrant, dangerous
and exciting. When we toured Alan Bleasdale's *Scully*,
there was a night in Chester where a heckler was making
a nuisance of himself. I mooned him at some speed and
then demanded, 'Where were your lips, then?' That shut the
fucker up.

At times, we felt like a band of cultural revolutionaries,
waging war on the elitist strictures of other theatres. The less
conventional the venue, the more we loved it. There wasn't

anywhere we wouldn't perform: clubs, prisons, schools, borstals – you name it. We weren't afraid to take risks and if that earned the attention of the local police, well, then so be it. When the vice squad came calling following a tip-off about our industrial language, we didn't hold back. They waited for the verbals, and got a full blast. We didn't tone it down for the boys in blue. The common man was our audience; the sort of person who would previously have been too intimidated to step into a theatre. The city grew proud of what we stood for and embraced us, offering us free admission to clubs and making us its own. 'Here, they're from the Everyman, let them in, guv'nor,' became a regular refrain. We made the most of that generosity.

Our aim was to spread a bit of culture and earn some extra money. We were hard-working, hard-drinking, hard-living and hardly able to pay the rent. Not that we cared about that. We smoked, we drank, we partied, we enjoyed heady, illicit times and through a fug of marijuana smoke and Guinness portrayed the lives of people just like us. We survived on love and determination – as well as the occasional, donated box of avocados.

I hooked up with Julie Walters during those years and we got a Jack Russell terrier which we took into the theatre. It would root around in the dark recesses of the Everyman, occasionally returning with a dead rat clamped firmly between its jaws. Wagging its tail, it would look into my eyes, as though to say: 'Aren't I clever, look what I found for you.' Those days were incredible, looking back. We didn't even know whether we'd get a part in the next play. We played everyone from sacked Kirkby factory workers to Shakespearian kings. We had no fear and no safety net.

We'd take shows like Brecht's *Coriolanus* and make them seem as though they'd been written specifically for the people of Liverpool. It was courageous, cutting-edge, highly politicised theatre, especially in the dark days of 1975. We pushed it beyond the limit. *Coriolanus*, for instance, was flipped on its head and he was no longer the central figure in the tragedy, he became a pawn in a duel between patricians and plebs. I'd also rehearsed martial arts for the piece; it was like being in a kung fu flick rather than Shakespeare. I made him Churchillian, a scarred war-dog who was unacceptable to the bland multitudes in times of peace. Jules played Virgilia, alongside Jane Wood, as Valeria, and our costumes were meticulously fashioned in fustian, rope, hessian and linen. The theme that ran through it was that it would always be the little man who waged the wars engineered by the nobles – a motif that was apposite for inner-city Liverpool. During one performance, two girls in the audience giggled. I was onto them with the ruthlessness of a sniper, making them part of the performance, directing my spleen at them as though they were extras. They sat there, transmogrified. As a company, we tried to dazzle in everything that we did.

The Everyman grew more radical over the years, culminating in the visionary, rebellious style of Johnny Roche. Johnny carried on the tradition, finding invigorating and challenging new techniques and methods. 'I don't want you to be really good at acting angry,' he would say, while we were in rehearsal. 'If your character is angry, you've got to be angry.' Johnny craved authenticity. He wanted the audience to smell the emotion, to see the hostility in our eyes. He was an innovator too and found creative ways for us convey emotion. ''Ere,' he said, tossing colourful make-up sticks to members of the cast one afternoon. We put the sticks in our pockets. 'When you're angry, take the make-up sticks from your pocket and paint lines on your faces, angry lines, that make your faces look contorted and grotesque. I want green lines, red lines drawn across your face. Then say your words. I want anger, that's what I want to hear.'

At the same time, Ralph Steadman our extraordinary set designer would ask us most extraordinary questions. Take our production of *Widowers' Houses* by George Bernard Shaw, the classic play dealing with middle-class hypocrisy and economic exploitation. Our approach to this classic typified the Everyman way. Ralph spoke at length about the debilitating effects of Rachmanism, while he was designing, and he would constantly ask us questions. For instance, one afternoon we were working on a scene in which the characters were halfway up a Bavarian Alp. There was a line of dialogue: 'Here's a pencil.' And Ralph would say ... 'Here's a pencil, where's the pencil from? I don't understand it.' He had a forensic attention to detail. 'How can they have a pencil if they are halfway up a Bavarian Alp? Where has the pencil come from?'

'Yeah, right,' we'd say, thinking it was another of his flights of fancy. But Ralph wouldn't be moved. 'I need to sort this out because I'm designing that scene and I don't know where the pencil is from.' Ralph would have us racking our brains over such minutiae and then, triumphantly, he'd return. 'I've solved it, I've solved it,' he'd exclaim, satisfied smile writ large across his face. 'It's great, it really works well.'

We'd ask him what he'd discovered and he'd say: 'Look, they're halfway up this Bavarian mountain in a guest house. They have to sign this contract, which is why they need a pencil. Now, because they're halfway up the mountain they can't make it to the shops to buy provisions so they have to make their own supplies of milk and butter and so on. Cows are no good, because the hill is too steep, so they have to have a goat.' Ralph was extrapolating wildly. 'At this stage of the proceedings, the goat is being given a daily walk by a waiter. And waiters always have pencils behind their ears. So the waiter has got the pencil, that's where the pencil comes from.' He folded his arms. 'It makes perfect sense.' Thanks, Ralph.

So, on that occasion, we hired a bloody goat for the play. We brought it in from Southport every night, so that it could be taken for a walk by a waiter with a pencil behind his ear. It shared a dressing room with us; a dirty, smelly goat, and it walked across the stage. Johnny Roche loved it. He said the character who embodied the mean-spirited principles of Rachmanism was the devil and the goat's cloven hooves were symbolic. That vignette, in essence, summed up the Everyman. Everything had a reason. Nothing was haphazard or random, everything had logic, however peculiar it might have seemed.

Later, in rehearsals, Ralph was perturbed again. He said: 'Right, it's Act Two and the script says they're back in England. But how did that happen, how did they get back to England? They were in Bavaria in Act One.'

We reasoned: 'Ralph, does it matter, what's all this about?' But, as with the pencil, he ruminated on this new significant detail. Two or three days later, he returned and said: 'I've solved that problem.' And he had. Ralph asked our pianist, Roger, to play music that denoted a nautical mood – it happened to be '(There'll be Bluebirds Over) The White Cliffs of Dover'. Ralph got the crew to make a cardboard prop of a Stena Line ferry, with handles fixed to its back. Then he asked us, the cast, to stand behind it, start singing 'White Cliffs of Dover' and motion across the stage. 'That's how they got back,' said Ralph. That mise en scène, between Act One and Two, legitimised the action taking place back in England. We examined the verses of the song and found they were all about the poor in England, about the disastrous situation they found themselves in. Again, everything made sense. It was Everyman Gold.

Ralph's questions could verge on the surreal. We performed a piece in which one of the props on stage was a fireplace. During rehearsals, he would ask questions like: 'When can an actor walk behind the fireplace?'

'What are you on about? When can an actor walk behind the fireplace?'

Johnny Roche answered Ralph's question: 'Actors can only walk behind the fireplace when George Bernard Shaw's head is completely surrounding the Everyman Theatre, in Hope Street.' There was a logic to it. Even though we lived a reasonably lawless, wild rock'n'roll existence, we were utterly serious about our work.

On the first night of *Widowers' Houses*, none of us had any predetermined directions on stage. People knew the lines and how the drama would play out but, if they felt the action would be improved by the introduction of different movement, they were free to go for it. When the curtain went up, the only thing that we knew was what our characters wanted and what our characters needed. Our objective, as actors, was to try to get what we wanted from the other actors. We were deliberately rebuffing each other, making life hard, so we could get what we needed from the others. All we knew was that the other players would be there to do their lines, we didn't know how they would do them or what else they might do. Every night was different, every night was completely authentic. The cast couldn't 'phone it in'. We had to be on our toes, it was like walking the high wire every night. After a week or two, a little blasé-ness may have crept in. But that didn't replace the feeling of danger. During one performance, Nick Woodeson jumped on my back, completely unexpectedly. We were midway through a scene when he jumped up and clung to me like a limpet.

I couldn't carry on and had to go off stage to get him off. I think Nick was the one who went round the fireplace. He knew when George Bernard Shaw's head had completely enveloped the Everyman.

After we'd performed the first night, we had a letter from the chairman of the board, Alan Durban. Alan had been chairman for some time. 'I have never been so embarrassed,' he wrote. 'I found the performance absolutely disgraceful.' Poor man, he hadn't known what we were doing with George Bernard Shaw.

He wasn't the only one who was moved to write. We had letters of concern from school teachers, telling us we shouldn't change George Bernard Shaw's work like that. When Alan returned, for the final night, we got an equal and opposite letter. 'I would like to congratulate you on your incredible performance,' he wrote. 'It was innovative, fantastic, inspired. It was the most stunning production that I have ever seen.'

The curtain calls for *Widowers' Houses* were phenomenal. But, again, they'd been hard-earned. Johnny had spoken at length about curtain calls during rehearsal.

'It pisses me off,' he spat. 'In theatre, the audience can sit through an indifferent show but it still applauds politely and the actors accept that praise. The actors bow as though they've just performed the best thing. Well, they shouldn't. They should earn the applause.' Johnny would challenge us. 'Were you at your best? Because, if you weren't, you shouldn't come out for a bow.'

We took his words on board and the way we took the curtain call for *Widowers' Houses* was electrifying. By the end of the show, our faces had been daubed with the angry sticks of make-up that Johnny had given us; they were filled with angry lines and looked incredibly surreal, almost Dalí-esque. And we walked towards the front of the stage, smearing the greasepaint across our faces, singing a bitter refrain from John Lennon's 'Crippled Inside', looking more and more angry and monstrous. I remember looking into the whites of the audience's eyes, you could see them thinking: 'This is frightening, I hope they don't come off the stage.' But I'll bet George Bernard Shaw would have been galvanised by our interpretation. We viewed our work as being sacrosanct and the great man would have been thrilled to high heaven to see something so radical and honestly done. We ripped up the rule book and revolted against the norm. Our play tried to say something. We were showing the audience what capitalism was doing to people. We were showing them that it was destroying people's souls, making them cripples. And so that's how we ended up, as cripples.

∾

As summer ventured, there was magic in the air and our assembled ranks from the Everyman decided to head way out west for a season in Aberystwyth. Our soundtrack to the summer was not the anodyne strains of 'Summer Holiday'. Instead, we were plugged into the trippy psychedelia of our own 'Magical Mystery Tour', eagerly anticipating a sun-kissed season on the Welsh coast. The lyrics to that particular Beatles song were germane. The Everyman was looking forward to a creatively productive, alcohol-fuelled, ingeniously anarchic summer by the seaside. We wouldn't be needing buckets and spades, we'd got our stash of dope.

The Everyman closed each summer but members of the company willingly exploited the opportunity to carry on working. Not for us long, lazy holidays holding down dead-end jobs or doing nowt. We wanted to extend ourselves and perfect our art. Johnny Roche led us in our Aberystwyth summer season. The Everyman had already built a formidable reputation as a serious group who took a scalpel to poverty's deleterious effects. We were into the most radical, progressive and uncompromising work. We were devotees of Ken Kesey's *One Flew Over the Cuckoo's Nest* and Tom Wolfe's *Electric Kool-Aid Acid Test* and more besides. We were pioneering new creative frontiers, experimenting with drugs, gaining new perspectives on life and shattering preconceptions of contemporary drama. Anything that smacked of middle-class liberal convention was out of the window. That was not where we were at. We didn't set out to be overtly political, but we certainly wouldn't do the sort of bland theatre that went on at the nearby Playhouse. We wouldn't do *Anyone for Tennis?* for instance, or anything by Alan Ayckborn. If we'd been asked to perform those, there'd have been a significant caveat; we'd only have done them with a huge, leftfield slant.

Johnny had contacts with the university and had been told that we could take over for two shows during the summer season. Summer seasons, by their nature, were usually held at the end of piers and the plays would traditionally be potboilers. There'd be Brian Rix farces, typically, or similar light stuff. That type of froth, however, wasn't for us. We were the Everyman. We were at the vanguard of a new wave of British theatre. We weren't going to dumb ourselves down to please the good burghers of Aberystwyth. We were into blowing people's minds. So, summer season or not, there was no chance of a quintessential end-of-pier piece.

Johnny came up with a compromise. He said we'd play Arnold Ridley's *Ghost Train*, which was the sort of summer season fare people might have expected, but the price he'd extracted for that was a production of *One Flew Over the Cuckoo's Nest* by Ken Kesey. 'We'll put on *Ghost Train* for them, *Cuckoo's Nest* for us,' was the way Johnny and the rest of us saw it. *Ghost Train* wasn't a complete capitulation

on our part – far from it. In terms of that genre, it is unbelievably well written and well structured. It is exquisitely
composed. The people at Aberystwyth agreed and Johnny
set the season up. Our contract was wonderfully detailed
and even included a rider for regular supplies of hashish and
grass. We thought that was essential because we didn't want
people nipping off to London to score. The last thing we
needed was an actor going AWOL because he was looking
for his dealer. So we wrote drugs into our contract.

Before we left, we worked out who would play which
parts, assigning roles. *Ghost Train* was going to be directed
by Malcolm McKay, a young director whom we hadn't met
before but whose actress-girlfriend had been appearing in
Ghost Train. That connection made Malcolm the perfect
fit. The appointment of Malcolm also freed up Johnny to
concentrate on *Cuckoo's Nest*, which was where we wanted
to go.

We started work on *Cuckoo's Nest* but we didn't like the
play; it was too thin and we needed to flesh it out. Johnny
and the rest of us agreed that we should re-read Ken Kesey's
book, working through the specific parts that we were playing. The idea was that we'd find tracts of dialogue or action that we liked that could be included in the play. Then
we'd argue, talking democratically about what should and
should not be included.

By this time, Julie Walters and I had been an item for a
year or so. So one Sunday afternoon, we got the bus together
from Liverpool to Aberystwyth for what was to become an
extraordinary season. The others had decided to make their
own way there. Somebody else had gone on ahead to book
a place called Cletty Gegan, a house on the cliffs where we
were all going to live.

As Jules and I boarded the bus, instinctively, I felt something was wrong. Even at that early stage, I knew things

wouldn't turn out quite right. On the bus, we overheard somebody talking about Aber. We assumed they meant Aberystwyth, so we asked the bus driver if he would shout out when we got there. 'Aber, eh?' he said. 'All right, boyo, I'll shout you. That's no problem, you can get off there.' We tootled on and when we got to Aber, the conductor called out the place name and Jules and I picked up our bags and went to get off. We checked our watches but we were an hour and a half earlier than we were meant to be. 'Where's the theatre?' I asked him. And the bus driver looked puzzled. 'Theatre? There's no theatre here. You want Aberystwyth, it's further down the road.' We got back on the bus and carried on. So even on the way there, something was amiss. In retrospect, the seeds for that extraordinary time had already been sown. There were small indicators all along the way.

Jules and I arrived and, by chance, met everyone else in a local pub on the Sunday afternoon. The rest of the cast emerged from a boozy session and wandered down to the seafront. Some madcap, I can't remember who, decided to launch himself into the briny. 'Waaahhhhhhyyyyyyy,' came the shout, as he ran across the dark sand and pebbles, kicking them into the surf. It was freezing cold. 'Come on,' he laughed, manically splashing both arms in the water. 'It's lovely.'

One by one, the cast joined him in the water until almost everybody was submerged. Eventually, I was the only one left. 'Come on, Pete,' someone shouted, but I was implacable. The others were oblivious, laughing and playing in the waves. I stuck out, I was the only one not doing it. I point-blank refused. 'It's bloody freezing,' I called back. 'Forget it.' That was the start of me bucking the trend and it was the beginning of the end of my Everyman years. While everybody ran into the sea, I stayed dry. The incident was a microcosm of what was about to unfold.

Ghost Train was our first play and we duly started re-hearsing. We'd devote ourselves unconditionally to our work during the day but, at night, anything would go. It was a wild time. The plan was to nail *Ghost Train* and then concentrate on *Cuckoo's Nest*, in which I was playing the lead, McMurphy. Matthew Kelly was playing the lead in *Ghost Train* and he performed it with a broken leg at one point, because he'd hurt himself. He played his part on crutches. The show must go on, and all that jazz.

At the Everyman, we had grown accustomed to a climate in which we challenged anything that didn't feel right. So, during rehearsals, I questioned our new director Malcolm repeatedly. He was coming at *Ghost Train* from an im-provisational point of view, initially trying to develop the characters that way, to find out what they were all about. Instinctively, to me, that was not right, it felt wrong. But I went with it.

After a while, the pressure built up. We didn't seem to be anywhere near to a production level, never mind get-ting it on stage. After about three weeks, I stayed up one night and wrote down what was wrong. In my mind, the extraordinary quality of the play was the structure of the plot. It was a thriller, a mystery, a what's-going-on produc-tion. The beauty of it was the way Ridley had hidden the con. The characters were stock characters, they weren't im-portant, they were there to service the plot. There was a silly-arse bloke who was constantly messing about but who then turned out to be the detective who was on the case, and plenty more like him.

Through a dense fog of booze and hashish smoke, I com-mitted my complex theory about what was going on to paper. I'd been well schooled by the likes of Johnny Roche and Ralph Steadman and, despite the drink and dope, I arrived at a brilliantly lucid and logical conclusion as to how the action should unfold. At about four or five o'clock the following morning, I finished my theory, put down my pen and tried to doze off. I'd worked out what I wanted to do the following morning, I would take the theory to Malcolm and the others and say: 'Look, here you are. This is where we're going wrong. This is how we're supposed to play it.' It was important to me, because Malcolm and I had argued about it. He thought I was being obstreperous but I was adamant that I was not. That's the way things were, in the Everyman. We always fought our own corner so that we could get the best possible production on stage. When Malcolm and I disagreed, it wasn't about me having a go at him, it was because I thought we were going at the play the wrong way round.

Before I went to sleep, I considered how the others would react. I thought they'd read it and go: 'Of course, you're bloody right, Pete, that's a brilliant analysis.' But, at that exact moment, I had a Saul of Tarsus moment. It was the start of a hellish episode in which I was overwhelmed by a vicious paranoid psychosis. I thought: 'Oh my God, they've known this all along. The company has known what it's all about. If I go in tomorrow and show them the way I've deconstructed the play, they're all going to go "We know, why didn't you get on board with it earlier?"' I was in a complete bind.

The level of irrational fear grew as I considered their views on other matters. I reasoned that if they'd thought I should have been on board earlier with *Ghost Train*, they'd have thought the same about everything else. They'd have viewed me as being out of step, an outsider. They'd have decided I was the one who didn't understand what they were trying to do. It wouldn't have been me telling them how it should be done, it would be the other way round. It would be them trying to coax me into their way of thinking.

That idea permeated my whole vision, not just of that particular play but of everything we did. It cast a cloud over my relationship with the Everyman Theatre, with Jules and with everything else associated with my theatrical life. Suddenly, I felt like the outsider. The whole inter-reactive relationship between me and those people from the Everyman became black and white. I thought they were all part of an esoteric group, and I was on the outside. They'd known, all along, that the penny would drop with me, that I'd get on board and come round to their way of thinking. I'd been apart from them all. 'He'll get it, he'll spot it, he'll realise what we're about,' was how I imagined their thoughts. 'All of us had to go through this rite of passage, this emotional denouement, and now Pete's got to go through it as well.'

The paranoia came at me with the rat-tat-tat speed of a gun. My mind whirred like a flywheel. I honestly thought that I had to go through some sort of trial, a trial by fire, rather than by jury. I got no more than a few hours' light sleep and, the next morning, I was careful to leave behind the piece of paper with my deconstruction of *Ghost Train*. I tried to be more attentive to other members of the group and to fit in more readily. But when I listened to the other players, they sounded as though they were talking in tongues. They were still speaking English to one another, but I thought every word, every utterance, had been decoded to hide a more sinister meaning. It was frightening. I thought: 'Hang on, they've got a whole way of speaking to each other that I don't understand.' I thought that if I listened long enough and hard enough, I would get into it, I would learn it. During polite conversation – for instance, when somebody asked: 'Would you like sugar in your tea?' I'd give someone a meaningful nod and say: 'Ah, I know what you mean.' And they'd look at me, puzzled, and say: 'We don't understand you, we don't know what you're saying.

We're just asking if you'd like your tea to be sweetened.' And I'd think that was part of the routine. I'd say: 'Oh yes, well you're bound to say that, I understand.' Nudge, nudge, wink, wink. They were actually trying to keep me on the straight and narrow, but I thought they were double-bluffing me.

It was incredibly isolating and distressing. Of course, I couldn't say anything and so I just kept on going. We got the production of *Ghost Train* on the stage and the piece of paper remained firmly in the closet. There were aspects of it that I didn't like, that just didn't fit – one of the guys, for instance, played the character of an old woman in a wheelchair, who shouldn't have been in it. But we got away with it and got it up and running.

We started work on *Cuckoo's Nest*, which, to be frank, wasn't the best script for somebody to deal with while suffering a seismic emotional collapse. I mean, *Cuckoo's Nest*, it's just a mind fuck. It's about the system and about people who are bucking the trend in the system. And I thought: 'Jesus, the reason I'm playing McMurphy is because I'm the one who's bucking the trend. I'm the odd one out. I'm not a member of the combine. This is a reverse situation, a psychological situation.'

I believed that the other players had thought they'd get me to play McMurphy so that I would get the message about them being part of a secret group. I thought their intention was to make me realise that they were all equal, that there were no individuals. I believed our relationships and responsibilities within the group were unlimited. So, for instance, I could be with Jules and Malcolm could be with his lady. But, actually, physically and sexually, if somebody decided to have a weekend with me or Jules or Malcolm or his partner, and we were agreeable, then we could do that, without losing the relationship. The paranoia invaded my sexual view, as well as my psychological, spiritual and theatrical beliefs.

Day by day, hour by hour, minute by minute, life became more tumultuous. By the time rehearsals began for *Cuckoo's Nest*, I firmly believed everybody was on a different wavelength. There I was, playing McMurphy; the very avatar of rebellion, a man born to fight the system. But I was in meltdown. My mind was reeling. I was trying to be part of the group, trying to perform in *Ghost Train* during the evening and suffering psychological collapse.

During that summer season in Aberystwyth, I was commissioned to do my first ever telly. I commuted from Aberystwyth to Birmingham during the day, because we weren't performing until the evening. I did a Mike Stott play on telly, called *Thwum* and my paranoia returned. I was completely naked in one scene and I thought: 'Whoah, hang on, this is how they get an actor. Nationally, now, I'm known nationally as this person who takes his clothes off.' It was a kind of backswing of the paranoia thing. There I was, completely nude and green, a kind of venutian. I thought, 'Is this what the BBC do to new people before they decide where to put them?'

It got to the point where there was bound to be a collision, some sort of dramatic explosion. And the catharsis came during the performance of *Ghost Train*. It was during Act II, I think, and, about ten minutes in, I suddenly saw the light. We had secured our costumes from a store in Aberystwyth and the only pair of shoes that I had been able to find had one raised heel. They'd been designed for somebody with a club foot but I wore them anyway. As with so many aspects of our production of *Ghost Train*, the shoes had nothing to do with what Arnold Ridley wrote. He hadn't written about a character with a club foot. But that didn't matter. We were the Everyman and could do as we pleased.

As the performance progressed, the club foot took on a deeper meaning. To me, it became a symbol that identified me to the audience as The Outsider. As Act II began, I started to believe that my thumping great shoe was a marker, letting the audience know that I was the patsy of our group. It all fell into place. I continued the performance for a while, frantically trying to deduce why I was the odd one out. Questions raced through my mind. Why did we come to Aberystwyth? Answer: Because Aberystwyth was the headquarters of the sect. The people in Aberystwyth were all in on it, they knew the language, they could all talk to each other in tongues.

As the seconds ticked by, I realised that the people in Aberystwyth hated the way society was run and so had devised an alternative society whereby they could talk to each other in a secret way.

And there, during Act II of Arnold Ridley's *Ghost Train*, there was the crash. At that particular moment, I had enough. I thought: 'Oh fuck, the whole of the audience knows that I'm the fucking idiot. I'm on the outside.' And I thought, 'Bollocks to the lot of it.' I wasn't having any more. I spun on my club foot and walked off stage. I hurled my shoes into the bin of the dressing room and took my costume off.

The stage manager came over and said: 'What are you doing, Pete?' And I was still locked into the idea that people were talking in tongues. I said: 'Don't be stupid. You knew this sort of thing would happen. You knew there was going to be a blow up, you knew that I was going to twig it.' I was deadly serious, my face was contorted, I was lost. The stage manager tried to calm me: 'What are you talking about? I don't know what you're talking about.' But, of course, I thought that was part of the game. I shouted: 'Don't tell me lies. I know what you're doing.'

Back on stage, Bill Nighy was trying to keep the show going, filling in for my character. I raged at the stage manager: 'Look, Bill's saying my lines now on stage. He's ready for this. Bill Nighy's saying my lines, you knew that this was going to happen. Well, it has happened and I'm off, I'm going.' And that was it, I left the theatre.

I started walking down the hill from the theatre, into the town, and decided to stop off for a pint, to try to calm myself down. As I was walking, two boys ran by me. One shouted: 'He's left the exchange, he's left the exchange.' And I thought they were warning people. I thought they were in on it too. 'Bloody hell,' I thought. 'They're warning people. I'm the cuckoo who's left the *Cuckoo's Nest*.' I walked on a bit further, trying to pull myself together. I was telling myself that my thoughts were ridiculous, that things had got out of hand, that there couldn't be a conspiracy involving the Everyman and people beyond the theatre.

Then two old ladies stopped me and said: 'Excuse me, can you tell me the way to the Catholic church?' And I thought their question had a deeper meaning. 'Oh yes, oh yes, get lost, get lost. Go and find a bloody Catholic church yourself.' The paranoia raged. I thought the whole town was in on it. I couldn't go to the pub, because I feared I would be mocked. My only hope was to get back to Cletty Gegan, to the house. I had to get back to the house where we were staying, it was all that I'd got left.

I turned sharply and went to the taxi rank. As I was walking towards it, I could see all the drivers talking to each other. There is, I realise, nothing unusual in a rank of taxi drivers standing around talking. But I thought they were talking about me. I was experiencing high paranoia. I ploughed on regardless, determined to get back to the house. I stopped at the front of the queue and went up to a guy: 'Can you take me to Cletty Gegan?' He nodded in the direction of his mate. 'He'll take you, boyo,' he said, pointing in the direction of another cab driven by an older chap. The driver pointed inside: 'Come on, I'll take you back.'

I got in and sat there, struck dumb with fear. I thought he was the one, that he was somehow going to release me from my torment. I thought there was going to be some form of sexual baptism: 'Maybe he's the one who has got to sexually take my homosexual virginity,' I thought. I mean, I knew I was heterosexual. But in my mind, the sect consisted of people who were homosexual, heterosexual and bisexual. I'd never been homosexual before, but I thought that was why I was in the taxi. I thought to be part of the community, I would have to have homosexual encounters, as well.

I peered from the back seat, terrified, looking through the rear-view mirror so that I could see the taxi driver's face. I was resigned: 'Looks like it's you then,' I said. The driver looked over my shoulder: 'What, boyo?' he said. 'What are you talking about?' He hadn't a clue what I was on about and was clearly terrified of me. There he was, this big taxi-driving bloke, who'd seen everything and done everything, and he was frightened half to death of the quivering, hyper-sensitive actor on the back seat. I spoke to him again, but thought he couldn't understand. 'Maybe he isn't the one, after all,' I thought.

Eventually, when we approached Cletty Gegan, he stopped. I couldn't get him to take me down the lane. He pulled up and switched off the engine. 'This is as far as I go, boyo,' he said, as he dropped me off. And I'd been sitting there, starting intently at him, all the time. He must have been thinking: 'What the hell is that guy doing? What is he on?'

Back at the theatre, they'd soldiered on as much as they could to get through that act, but then they'd made an announcement and apologised to the audience. They explained that one of the cast had fallen ill and that the performance had been cancelled.

I had about two hundred yards to walk to get back to the house. As I was walking, I came upon a cow and a bull, blocking the path. I thought they were another sign. I thought somehow, for some reason, they'd been put there deliberately, as a symbol. I thought the bull represented male and the cow represented female. I thought I had to choose. I snapped myself out of it, steeled myself, and whacked them both on the side. I hollered at them to move and they scrambled up the side, making angry noises. I daren't look back. I just carried on walking.

I thought Cletty Gegan would bring relief, but my sense of alienation grew. The things I saw were almost like signs. For instance, there was half a Guinness bottle, on the side, broken, like me. Everywhere else was spotlessly clean, which wasn't how it was supposed to be. We were usually a mess, but everything was well ordered and tidy. The dirty kitchen, which normally resembled a students' kitchen after a dishwashing strike, had been cleaned up. My head was swirling, I wanted to get away, I had to get out of Aberystwyth before something happened. It was terrifically frightening. The whole experience was deeply disturbing. I couldn't understand any of it. Everything I saw and heard was imbued with meaning. At the house, for instance, there was a puppy, a Welsh puppy, that somebody had brought. And it had peed on the floor. And I thought: 'Is that puppy me, are they saying that I'm like a little puppy that's peed on the floor?'

I lay down on the bed and tried to sleep, hoping things would be better in the morning. But as I nodded off, I must have knocked the tape recorder because when I woke up, I could hear Stevie Wonder singing 'Living for the City'. My mind fizzed like a Catherine wheel. I thought the song was a sign, telling me that I'd been planted there, in that house, along with the drugs, and that the police were going to come and find me. So I went. I just bolted. I got out and walked up into the hills. When the group came back, they didn't know where the hell I was, or what I was doing. They saw the signs that I'd been there but had no idea what I'd done next. I was gone for two or three nights, nobody knew where, not even me. I can't remember what happened, those days and nights are a complete blank in my memory. Eventually, I think I must have wandered back down to the house. But, before I did, I remember one incident which happened very early one morning. There was a silver dawn and everything else was black, including the trees. And then it just switched around. And the dawn was black and the trees were silver. It was a complete mirror image. It was a moment of negative/positive. Visually, physically and in my head, I thought that's what the world was saying.

When I emerged back at Cletty Gegan, I still thought I had to be part of the group and I was very humble, very worried about what I should do. The group was also worried and they'd had discussions about how to help. One of the actors' brothers was a psychologist, or psychiatrist, and they'd rung him for advice. He'd asked whether I'd slept and they'd said: 'No, he hasn't slept for two or three nights.' He intended to come to the house and give me an injection, to send me to sleep, but the group rejected that idea. They were worried that it would remind me of a scene in *Cuckoo's Nest*, when the boys, the black boys, come towards McMurphy to give him sedation because they think he is being violent. The group figured that if a doctor came towards me with sedation, or any form of medication, I'd go berserk. So they just kept a close eye on me and kept me in their company. Slowly, they talked me round and nursed me back to some kind of reality. They gradually brought me back to the real world, out of the paranoid world that I had got into. Looking back now, I don't know where I went or what I did. I remember the positive/negative image, but the rest, well, I still just don't know.

I spoke to Bill Nighy, some time after, and he told me he thought it had just got too much for me and that I was protesting about the way we were doing *Cuckoo's Nest*. He thought: 'You know, to be quite honest, Pete's right – why are we doing things in this way? Why is it like this?' To a certain extent, my breakdown had an extraordinary amount of logic to it. I had created a vision of utopia. The sect I'd constructed had been an extension of that, they'd been looking for the good society, looking for the society that really cared about people, that looked after each other. People could be sexually connected, there was no reason why anybody should get uptight about it.

But, of course, I realised that things were not the way I'd been seeing them. People weren't living like that and they weren't talking in tongues. The Everyman cast nursed me back to some sort of stability as the summer came to an end. In a way, it's like a quote from *Cuckoo's Nest*: 'It's true even if it didn't happen.' I remember a conversation involving Jonathan Pryce which typified my view. It took place in the dressing room of the Everyman. He was describing his unease because he thought everyone hated him; he said he was worried about being paranoid.

Someone piped up: 'Jonathan, don't be stupid. You're not paranoid, you're right: everybody does hate you. It's fact.'

The theatre is a fertile breeding ground for that sort of rampant paranoia. It's classic because there's usually a tannoy system in the dressing rooms. You think, 'They're talking about me there', and actually they're not. They're talking about something else, but it's easy to imagine they are, even though it's not true.

So the goodness of the Everyman, with the Bill Nighys

and the Johnny Roches and the Matthew Kellys and the Julie Walters of our company, got me back to some kind of reality. We cancelled *Cuckoo's Nest*, of course, we couldn't go on with that, and we left Aberystwyth. I had enormous gratitude to my acting friends for restoring my emotional health. It was deeply unsettling to have gone through that experience. *Cuckoo's Nest* was performed later, back at the Everyman, though not with me in it. Remarkably, the first two shows that we put on when I joined the Little Theatre Company in Bristol were *Ghost Train* and *Cuckoo's Nest*. Though, I hasten to add, I didn't infer any hidden meaning from the fact.

After Aberystwyth, there was no point in going back to the Everyman, I'd taken it as far as I could. What I am was all there. That was me, Pete Postlethwaite, capable of pushing himself through horrendous paranoia, pushing it that far to realise a role. I might not be a better or worse person than the next man, for going through that. But it's what it is. It's who I am and forged what I became. You stand or fall by your values, beliefs and what you think theatre is. Aberystwyth was vitally important to me. It was also important in being the place where I started the transition to TV. I got an inkling of the new life that was going to take over, of television and films. It was, and remains, a seminal time in my life, a real seminal time.

FOUR

Don't Let Them See the Strings

After leaving Liverpool, I became an actor of no fixed abode. Throughout my late twenties and early thirties, home was wherever I laid my hat; I'd doss down on friends' floors, couches or spare beds, living out of a suitcase and surviving on beer, fags and whatever food I could find. 'Fancy a pint? I'm buying,' was my lingua franca. Maybe I'd throw in a bag of chips as well, if their couch was really comfortable. My peripatetic lifestyle suited me, I hated material possessions and was often found in a 'lucky shirt' from a girlfriend that would be too small, too short and held together by a safety pin. Money was a distraction, it didn't motivate me at all and still doesn't. I had no desire to get a place of my own; home ownership just seemed like a hassle. The few items that I did own were stowed away, including a large, framed poster of John Lennon, which I still have to this day. It's at the bottom of the stairs, near the stereo, I'm sixty-four and I still haven't got round to putting it on the wall. I didn't need anywhere permanent to live, my pictures were somewhere in Bristol and my books were stowed in packing cases. I realised that one day I'd own so many books and pictures that I'd have to get my own shelves and walls, but not yet, not yet. My currency was the kindness of acquaintances, rather than pounds, shillings and pence.

I flitted between Liverpool, Bristol, Soho, Newcastle, Manchester and Edinburgh during those years, appearing in plays for a season, before packing my bags and heading off to my next engagement. I was a minstrel, a regular free-wheeling, gone-before-you-know-it, onto-the-next-role kind of bloke. I was keen to extend myself by working with the best new actors and directors; settling into a comfort zone wasn't for me. My lifestyle allowed me to be increasingly selective about my work and I refused to be typecast or accept any part that wasn't different and challenging. Happiness didn't come ready-wrapped in easy-to-perform, crowd-pleasing gigs; I revelled in roles that were hard work and demanded versatility.

I'd already played in London several times, including a particularly memorable comedy, *Funny Peculiar*, that the Everyman had taken to the Mermaid in 1976. Mike Stott's risqué piece became a huge success, transferring to the Garrick and running for a year and a half. The original production featured me alongside Jules, Richard Beckinsale and Matthew Kelly. It was great fun.

I have great memories from that period. I was asked to appear in David Storey's *Cromwell*, which was directed by Anthony Page. It starred Albert Finney, who sported a wild look as the seventeenth-century Irish peasant O'Halloran. We were booked to perform at the Royal Court Theatre, on Sloane Square, and it was a magnificent experience to line up alongside a strong cast, with Alun Armstrong and Jarlath Conroy. We also did Howard Brenton's *Magnificence* at the Royal Court, playing a group of young activists lobbying against housing policy by occupying an empty property.

Given the shambolic, ramshackle lives that many of us led, it felt like life imitating art.

∾

'Pete, we'd like you to come back to Bristol for a season,' the Old Vic was on the line. 'We're planning a production of *A View from the Bridge*, and we'd like you to play the lead.' It was a marvellous opportunity and I jumped at it. I was captivated by Arthur Miller's Italian-American tragedy and relished the role of Eddie. So in 1978, I returned to the south west and spent two seasons in *A View* and other memorable Old Vic plays like *Titus Andronicus* and *The Man Who Came to Dinner.*

From my experience of the venue, I already knew its exceptional reputation and there were brilliant people there, like the then-unknown Adrian Noble, who was putting a blowtorch to the rule book, and the designer Bob Crowley, who was helping us all to realise amazing artistic visions.

While I was at the Old Vic, a new actor joined the company from the theatre school, just as I had done five years before. He was an intense, leonine young Irishman by the name of Daniel Day-Lewis. Dan Day was majestic, a true demi-God. Right from the start I could see he was something else, he stood out in terms of sheer ability and his astonishing commitment to his art. He brought unique qualities to the stage and was willing to pursue a role further than anyone else I knew. He would dive deeper and treat danger as though it were a friend; he just didn't have any fear. I've always believed that Dan Day is one of the top three actors in the film world, if not the top, in my heart. It doesn't matter what part he is playing, he will push himself to the nth degree, then go a little further. He'll wring himself out like a cloth, until there is nothing left.

The two of us struck up an instant rapport and that bond lasted for many, many years. My respect for him has never gone away, he is a gracious, warm, loving and funny man. Though the two of us are different, we both care passionately about our work and our moral compass points in the same direction. As a youngster, he had been sent to a public school because his parents thought he was wild, while I'd settled more easily into grammar school and had been much less rebellious. His family was steeped in arts and culture, his mother was the actress Jill Balcon and his father the Irish-born Poet Laureate Cecil Day-Lewis. Mine, conversely, had led simpler lives. But for all the apparent differences, Dan Day and I just clicked. He was the master technician, an avowed believer in the Method.

'What else do you do, Dan?' I asked him one evening, trying to get to know him a little better.

'Woodwork.'

'Woodwork?'

'That's right,' And he began a wonderfully aureate description of his passion for joinery.

'So why aren't you a carpenter?'

'They rejected me.'

I laughed out loud. Dan Day had wanted to become a cabinet maker but had been told to forget it, so instead he'd turned to acting. Just imagine how good his cabinets would have been; they'd have been fit for kings. This passion makes perfect sense; he is a craftsman who will spend hours and hours honing a piece until it is impeccable. He attended the Bristol Old Vic Theatre School for three years, at one point becoming my understudy. We enjoyed one another's company and laughed a lot during our time in Bristol, we were brothers from other mothers.

As one of the students of the Old Vic Theatre School, he had free tickets to see all of the productions. Not all of

An early foray into drama came in 1959 when Pete trod the boards at Blythe Hall, Ormskirk.

King Lear. Showing promise as one of the UK's most exciting new repertory theatre actors during the early stages of his career, with Kevin Lloyd.

The Fair Maid of the West, 1983. Pete's mother finally accepted the seriousness of her son's desire to be an actor when he was introduced to the Queen, at the RSC, in Stratford, in 1983.

Theatre was the mainstay of Pete's working life during the first twenty years of his career and he tackled a number of classic plays, including *Who's Afraid of Virginia Woolf?*, in which he played opposite Rowena Cooper, who starred as Martha.

With former Everyman co-star Alison Steadman in a National Theatre production of *The Rise and Fall of Little Voice*, 1992.

On the trail of dodgy videos in *Coronation Street*, with Fred Feast.

Playing a character obsessed with *Casablanca* in Central TV's seven-part drama series, *Tales of Sherwood Forest*.

Returning to the Mayfair Centre, in Church Stretton, which Pete opened, to celebrate the venue's second birthday in 1999. With Kitty Murby (left), Will Postlethwaite, Josie Meredith (far right) and Lily Postlethwaite (front).

A sweet success for youngsters at Longnor School Fete in 1995. With (from left) William Chambers, Will Postlethwaite, Hannah Rooke, Sam Rooke and Sean Morris. Youngsters had to guess the number of sweets.

Holding daughter Lily as he watches Church Stretton light up its festive display just before Christmas in 1999.

Playing Giuseppe
Conlon in a role
that won an Oscar
nomination for
Best Supporting
Actor in 1993.

Pete played the
Carpenter opposite
Peter Ustinov's
Walrus in a 1999
NBC presentation of
Alice in Wonderland.

Pete's great friend, Daniel Day-Lewis, encouraged film-maker Jim Sheridan to audition the actor and select him, rather than a bigger name.

Daniel Day-Lewis first met Pete during his days as a youthful protégé in Bristol, where his older friend was running The Little Theatre. Their reunion, on *In the Name of the Father*, was a spectacular hit.

Finding inspiration from the humanity of his own father, Bill, and from his Catholic upbringing, during scenes from *In The Name of the Father*.

Suspiciously eyeing Gloria Green, played by Geraldine James, in his portrayal of ex-con Len Green, in the BBC series *The Sins*. (BBC)

Playing Danny, the band leader, in *Brassed Off*, alongside Ewan McGregor, in a performance that made him a national treasure. This photograph was taken at the New York premiere.

Lost in contemplation in the Shropshire Hills Area of Outstanding Natural Beauty. His shoulders 'dropped by two inches' whenever he came home.

them were easy to watch, in truth; but the theatre students came along anyway. Their brief was to analyse or criticise the work in the theatre, which was light relief for them; it meant they weren't the target themselves. Thankfully, they decided not to turn their small arms fire on me.

I think that the first time he'd have seen me would have been when I played Apemantus in *Timon of Athens*. The students probably wouldn't have gone to some of the productions had they not got in without paying, but he came along to that more than half a dozen times. I think he was interested in my approach to classical theatre, in the way I wanted to transform those works so that they were relevant in the modern idiom. As actors, we take the Hippocratic oath. The first rule of performing is simple: to tell the truth. That simple instruction should go beyond the stage and inform most of our life, but it is often elusive.

Dan Day got his dearest wish when he was taken on as a full-time professional actor in Bristol. As one of the newcomers, he was given an assorted number of nondescript characters and his first job was to understudy me in *Troilus and Cressida*.

He was very shy around me: he was still only a kid and he gave me enormous respect. The new intake all wanted to make a mark, of course, but they were humble enough to realise that they were there to help, as well. When people got noticed at that stage, it was usually for the wrong reasons. I caught him out perfectly on one occasion, when I crept into the back of the room during one of his understudy rehearsals. I was still rehearsing *Troilus and Cressida* from the book because I'd not yet learned my lines. But he had had fuck all else to do and had learned his already. He was terrifically embarrassed when he realised I'd seen him doing the play off the book, when I was still using mine. After that, in the rehearsals that followed, I'd come off stage and seek his mock approval: 'Is that all right then?' He knew I was taking the piss.

Dan Day and the two other newcomers were an absolute bloody nuisance, at times, because they just couldn't stop laughing. The slightest thing would make them laugh; there was one costume break when I appeared dressed in black leather from head to foot and that was just the end of it, it just kicked off from there, they never stopped laughing all the way through it. They were bursting with energy but failing to channel it, so I asked Richard Cottrell, the artistic director then, if we could put them in a play. He suggested a version of *Funny Peculiar*, which I directed. It gave them suitable employment; and after that it was almost as though they were in my pocket, just waddling around after me like little ducklings.

One of the lessons I hoped they'd learn was to never stop giving. Even if we were doing a production that didn't have the juice, which happened, we weren't stupid; I'd urge them to give and give. Dan Day and I share very similar politics, even though we come from different backgrounds. We both realised then that change was in the air and theatre was no longer just for people who'd been sitting down all day and wanted to go and have another sit down somewhere else. I introduced him to the Northern writers. He'd come from south east London and then ended up working in the south west, in Bristol, so he was reading a lot of Barrie Keeffe's work, like the *Gimme Shelter* trilogy. He hugely admired Barrie and other writers, like Nigel Williams, who wrote *Class Enemy*. But he learned that there was stuff going on north of the Watford gap. When we did *Funny Peculiar* I took them on a field trip, up north, to Todmorden, to introduce them to things up there. That got them tuned into writers like Willy Russell and Alan Bleasdale. They hadn't really got much concept of the North, until then, but suddenly they realised there was a whole new world up there.

∽

During the production of *Funny Peculiar*, we had what felt to some of us like shattering news: the BOV was planning to cease its involvement with the Little after the Christmas show. We were determined to keep it afloat, not least because we wanted to preserve the theatre's proud culture and tradition. The Little's history stretched back more than fifty years. It had opened in 1923, becoming the first repertory theatre in the country to start with direct civic encouragement. Its aim was to stay at the cutting edge and when the Rapier Players had taken over in 1935 they'd tackled then-risqué plays like *Private Lives* and Somerset Maugham's *Sheppey*. The Bristol Old Vic Company had taken it over in 1963, operating a dynamic winter programme before handing the space to amateur groups during the summer. That arrangement had continued until now, when the Bristol Old Vic threatened to withdraw its support for the spring season, unless Bristol City Council agreed to substantially increase its weekly guarantee of £1,980. The Little was costing the Old Vic £1,000 a week in subsidies and that couldn't continue.

A group of us, including the actor David Neilson – a generous and kind man who went on to play *Coronation Street*'s Roy Cropper – peeled off to form the Save the Little Committee. We felt we owed it to the people of Bristol to save the 361-seat auditorium from going dark. With the support of members from the acting and stage management company of the Bristol Old Vic, we made a vow: to maintain business as usual at the Little.

Our campaign needed the support of the public and we

held a meeting. We drew up a petition and wrote down our objections: 'The company of actors and stage management at the Bristol Old Vic registers its strongest possible disapproval, disappointment and despair at the action of closing the Little Theatre for the forthcoming spring season. The meeting holds no faith in the statement that the closure is temporary, and intends to translate this protest into activity that will ensure no loss of either a theatre, jobs for Equity members or the withdrawal of an amenity that the community can ill afford to lose.' Ha, that seemed pretty clear.

Copies were sent to Sir Philip Morris, president of the Bristol Old Vic Trust; its chairman, Sir Alec Merrison; the Trust's board of governors and secretary; councillors; the Arts Council of Great Britain; local and national newspapers; *The Stage* and Equity. We published leaflets urging the public to light a fire under the short-sighted money men who wanted to shut us down. Ordinarily, the people of Bristol might not have been the sort to take to the streets, but we were going to agitate as much as we could. Our leaflets said: 'For sixteen years, the Little Theatre has relied on the support of the Bristol Old Vic and Bristol City Council and it has always played to good and enthusiastic audiences. Now, for the sake of candle-end savings, it is expected to close as a professional theatre after Christmas. Please support the Save the Little campaign.'

The theatre's offices were transformed from being a creative hub into a war cabinet as we drew up plans for survival.

'Here, Pete, it's the latest petition, we've got another two hundred and forty-five signatures.'

'Got that response from Sir Philip yet?'

'C'mon, soft lad, get onto the papers, tell them what's going on.'

In three weeks, we collected eight thousand signatures as public opinion swung heavily in our favour. We assumed the powers that be would back down and let us carry on: would they bollocks. The Bristol Old Vic management remained adamant that the spring season would not go ahead. We met to consider the news: 'Let's take the fight to them. If they won't put on a spring season, we'll do it ourselves.' Spontaneous applause filled the room. The fat lady wasn't going to sing while we could still stop her. The Save the Little Committee decided to form a new company, calling itself 'Little Theatre Co', and the axed spring season was reprieved. Equity gave us £2,500 to cover the initial rehearsal period and the City Council underwrote our debts to the tune of £500. What could possibly go wrong?

We assumed the Bristol Old Vic would help us to stand on our two feet but it was as supportive as a grandmother's stocking. It insisted that our season play out across a remorselessly long period, which meant a stop-start flow of box office revenue and increased wage costs. Those problems were offset, however, by public support and a sympathetic media that rallied to our cause. Though we were almost entirely dependent on ticket receipts, we cajoled the BOV into loaning sound and lighting equipment free of charge, and we were grateful for that. We'd been on the edge of the abyss but somehow we'd pulled away. The members of our company agreed to be paid minimum rates, with no extras; production costs were kept to a minimum and the season would be varied.

The company included Sally Baxter, Henrietta Boxer, Nigel Cooke, Michael Derrington, Peter Fish, Russell Harvey, Mark Lambert, Catherine Owen, Dick Penny, Jill Rolfe, Albie Woodington, and Leo Wringer, with myself as artistic director. I enjoyed stepping up from being a regular member of the company to being the guy who made decisions on the programme. There was more responsibility and pressure, of course, but I enjoyed it. We told people that the

Little Theatre had come to a halt after the last performance of *Ten Times Table* on 19 January and that the Bristol Old Vic board had withdrawn financial support. For our season, the seat prices would be as cheap as the Old Vic's principles, at £1, £1.25, £1.55 and £1.75, with discounts to attract even more people in. Our objective was to put bums on seats, pure and simple.

I had to devise the programme, direct the players, keep an eye on the till and bring our season together. It felt, to an extent, like a natural organic extension of how I tended to work. The Little Theatre forced me to take multi-tasking to new levels, there was so much to think about, so much that could go wrong; it was like dancing the foxtrot with an octopus. Everywhere there were 'what if's; we never knew from one day to the next whether we'd continue. But nor did we care. We were the masters of our own destiny; nobody was able to tell us 'you can't do that' because our names were above the shop door. As a group, we were incredibly tight even though disaster lurked just around the corner. My body was in perpetual motion, occupied by a million tasks. From time to time things went wrong, and then it was like trying to find the faulty bulb on a string of Christmas lights. But we got through it and the work shimmered. By the end of it all, I was burned out: 'Quick. Emergency. Somebody get me a pint!'

I drew up a programme comprising my two old friends from Aberystwyth: Ridley's *The Ghost Train* and *One Flew Over the Cuckoo's Nest*. There was a great sense of personal accomplishment for me in producing great versions of those plays. Back in Aberystwyth, I'd gone into meltdown, so I felt as though putting them on in Bristol gave a sense of closure on that episode. I finally got to finish something that I'd started long before. And though I was swimming against a tide of artistic, financial, logistical and spiritual challenges,

I added a third, *Waiting for Godot*, which would run for a further fortnight.

The programme for our opening production, *The Ghost Train*, read like a political pamphlet that re-affirmed our determination to continue. We asked the Little's former director, Ronald Russell, to write a piece about its history and his article crackled with intent. He said the theatre had been founded by a gentleman called Stanley Hill, who had persuaded local Rotarians to find money to get the venture started. The Little had been nurtured by real theatre lovers. It had gone on to develop a reputation for being modest in price, cosy and intimate, which sounded like pretty worthwhile aspirations to maintain.

Ronald had taken over in 1935 and spent twenty-eight exciting years as director, interrupted only by his war service. The Little, however, had not been cowed by the Blitz. I was captivated by Ronald's recollections:

In the spring of 1941, with a lessening of air raids, it was arranged to re-open on Easter Sunday. Unfortunately, the Germans decided that Good Friday was a suitable day for the last big blitz on Bristol, and although the Little was spared, there was no electric light. Undaunted, however, hurricane lamps were prepared at 4.30 p.m. However, the current was restored and at 6 p.m., the curtain rose to a near full house. Bristol had a Theatre once more, and for the next two years we were Bristol's only theatre.

I followed Ronald's lead and used my programme notes as a rallying call. Facing my typewriter for hours, I wondered how on earth I could follow his polemic. The answer was simple, I couldn't. So I wrote this instead: 'What I can do, on behalf of all of us involved with the Little Theatre Company, is graciously accept Ronnie's best wishes and promise him that if they could keep the Little open during the War, we shall do all we can to keep it open during this spring season.' That seemed to strike the right note. The Huns from accounts had been warned.

Even Arnold Ridley, the eighty-year-old Bathonian who had written *The Ghost Train*, was moved by our campaign and wrote a letter of support. Our production opened brilliantly and was so well supported by the local community that during our second week we enjoyed a 93 per cent attendance, a statistic I only know because I had to keep our records. I've still got the books to this day, they're stashed in a folder in my loft. We surpassed our expectations by regularly playing to full houses and making a £5,000 surplus, before wages. Our production costs were next to nothing because we'd borrowed the set and costumes from Redgrave Theatre, in Farnham; everything had gone better than we could have hoped. One play down, two to go. Crisis, what crisis?

Next up was my nemesis: *One Flew Over the Cuckoo's Nest*. This time, I was planning to see the run through as I reprised my role as McMurphy. I was directing this too, though that didn't suggest control-freakery on my part; I was simply saving a salary by being a two-for-the-price-of-one team member. The play was edgy and the cast exemplary; Nigel Cooke played Billy, Shirin Taylor was Nurse Ratched and Michael Derrington was a shockingly emasculated Dale Harding. The play is dark and enthralling and needed to be played against a suitably harsh backdrop. We used a chillingly simple ward-white set and paid every attention to detail, even finding cut-price ways to heighten the drama by using the safety curtain as a prop. The curtain was normally supposed to be lowered and raised between acts to show the audience that they were safe in case of fire. We flipped that idea by covering it with a striking logo, suggesting it was separating the audience from our allegedly insane world. We played out the drama to a soundtrack of Pink Floyd, Bob Dylan, Randy Newman and Supertramp's killer 'Logical Song'.

During the course of the three weeks, we managed to fill the theatre to two-thirds of its capacity and also took the production to students at Bath University. The reviews were great and raved about the play's verve and wit; even the safety curtain got a look in, apparently we'd used it to make a dramatic point with great intelligence. We couldn't have put it better ourselves. Getting two good productions under our belt was a relief, particularly against the backdrop of financial chaos and disorder. But during *Cuckoo's Nest* we'd achieved something far greater. We'd provided placements for two young men on community service, they'd been written off by the courts as no-hopers, just rough-and-ready prison fodder destined for the scrapheap. We looked at them through different eyes; they were human beings, the same as us, and there'd probably been reasons for their crimes. One of the lads didn't want to know but the other was captivated and became so fired up by the play that he took a non-speaking part. He put in enough extra hours to finish off his order in double-quick time.

'Well done, mate,' we told him at the end of the run. He was the measure of our success, not the reviews or box office takings. We were out there, in the community, making people believe and you couldn't put a price on that.

Finally, we put on a production of *Waiting for Godot*, and immediately ran into a brick wall. Before we even began, we had to decide on the overall design of our piece. How did we, or rather, how should we, 'do' the play? We knew that Beckett saw Vladimir and Estragon as two clowns, but Peter Hall had transformed them into Irish tramps and his motif had stuck.

'Need it stick?' I asked the company. 'Two men waiting. That's all we are told. It could be two astronauts waiting for secondary but vital life-support systems. It could be two monks waiting for enlightenment. Two addicts waiting for their next "fix" ... the list is as endless as the play itself.'

Eventually, we decided that to truly realise the play we had to add as little production as possible. Our production needed to be as open-ended as the author's original script. In the programme notes, I wrote: 'Risking the result of a vague, imprecise production, we have opted more to go for Beckett's own details, "a country road, a tree, evening". We have stood these details next to each other and, we believe, allowed them to speak to the viewer in the way that only the viewer could be spoken to, by that series of inter-related details.'

Taking Beckett to the people of Bristol was a brave move but this time our courage wasn't rewarded by box office records. The audience figures didn't rise much above a third, though there were mitigating factors for the poor turnout. Our run had fallen at Easter, when the university and schools were on holiday, so in terms of scheduling, we'd learned a valuable lesson: Easter and Beckett were like money and morals, they just didn't mix.

We handed out questionnaires throughout the season, like a mini army of market researchers. We wanted to sustain audience numbers and find out more about our constituents. Once we'd analysed our findings, we imagined we'd be able to use our 'publicity machine' like a Tommy gun, blasting the people of Bristol with information; though our posters, brochure and the occasional press release made the 'machine' seem more like a slingshot. In any event, the exercise failed. The results were inconclusive and the only useful thing we were told was that people liked our programme. Somehow, during that spring season, we managed to keep afloat, though it was a close-run thing between surplus and loss. Our original budget had required external funding of £3,500 but we'd slashed our costs and received a £500 City Council surety, which had covered our £433 deficit. We saved on wages, administration, front of house and royalties and made more than we'd hoped from box office. As impresarios, we were more paper doily than D'Oyly Carte. But making money hadn't been our objective. We'd set out to save the Little from going dark and we'd succeeded.

By the time we'd finished our third production, my nerves jangled like a cracked bell. I thought, 'I can't go on with this' and I decided to move on. I'd taken the Little as far as I could. I'd enjoyed becoming artistic director, but all of my ambitions were centred on acting, not directing. Much as I enjoyed being involved in every aspect of the company, my truest love was for performance. There was a bit of panic among the company, but they soon found a replacement and continued for another six seasons. Dan Day joined the company after I left. Emerging writers, like Victoria Wood, and established talents like Alan Bleasdale and Willy Russell also found a home. Willy's *Breezeblock Park* was a hit there and he became a champion of the theatre.

Meanwhile, as for me: 'Any chance of a sofa?' I asked a mate, in Manchester, after receiving a call from the Royal Exchange. My Little Theatre days were over and I was heading back to the north west. Adrian Noble had been asked to produce *The Duchess of Malfi* with Helen Mirren in the title role, Bob Hoskins as Bosola and Mike Gwilym as Ferdinand.

'There's plenty, Pete.'

'Thanks. What are you drinking?'

Helen is a stunning actress and exceptional lady. She has always had wonderful ability and can switch from cold to raging, invincible to vulnerable; her emotional palette and range are extraordinary and it was a joy to play her Antonio. I enjoyed renewing my relationship with Adrian, who was rapidly becoming established as a promising young interpreter of the classics. Bob was a hoot, though I don't think he quite saw the point of iambic pentameter. He kept saying to Adrian Noble, in his rough East End accent:

'Listen, Ade, you've got to cut the verbals, mate. No one's gonna have a clue what's going on, know what I'm saying?'

John Webster would have turned in his grave. But Bob had a point, which I realised later on when I caught up with my mother and father. They'd established a routine of travelling around the country to see me and when I spoke to my mother following the performance she was lukewarm.

'What did you think, Mother, did you enjoy it?' I was still buzzing from our performance, hoping she'd sweep me away in a river of platitudes.

She paused, trying hard to find words that simultaneously conveyed an honest opinion without deflating her youngest son's brio.

'Well, to be honest, Pete, I didn't understand a word that anyone said, but I knew what everyone meant.'

It was the best critique I'd ever had and I understood it implicitly. She became an important barometer for how well I did in a role. It stuck in my mind that if we weren't recognisable people, then we were failing. For all our thespian splendour and polished technique, in *Malfi*, we'd failed to connect with real life. My mother was right, as ever.

I appeared in another play at the Royal Exchange that October, while *Duchess* was still showing, though it was amid more controversial circumstances. *Emperor Jones* was in rehearsal at the time but the lead, Errol John, had a major bust up with the artistic director, Richard Negri. They had a fundamental difference of opinion about the way the part should be played. Other actors tried to mediate, but Errol and Richard were miles apart and there was no way of making progress.

'Pete, would you take the lead role?' asked Richard, there was only one week to go before curtain up.

It was a tough call but I agreed. Though I sympathised with Errol, I felt the production ought to go ahead. Besides, I'd just come from playing the honest and virtuous Antonio, a spot of tyranny as Brutus Jones would get my juices flowing.

୨

Theatre was the mainstay throughout the seventies and I didn't hanker for TV or film. Why would I? The small screen was dominated by light-hearted variety shows and twee, middle-class sitcoms, which weren't for me. I was offered roles but nothing appealed. The sort of rough-house, socio-political drama that I'd revelled in at the Everyman and in Bristol wasn't readily available and there was no way I'd play some middle-of-the-road dullard.

Alan Bleasdale and Alan Dossor changed all that. 'We're doing a play for TV,' said Dossor.

'We've written a character that's perfect for you,' Bleasdale added.

I didn't need to think twice. I was in. Bleasdale's intrinsically Liverpudlian black humour ran right through *The Muscle Market*. I played Danny, a battered out-of-his-depth construction company owner, and Dossor shifted us smoothly from the tough stuff to the comedy, with gun heists that ended with gangsters shooting out TVs and getting showered in glass while I crawled around the floor. Every day the make-up department patched up my face and body with an endless supply of plasters and bandages, and by the end of it I looked like I'd done fifteen rounds with Ali.

The Muscle Market was the sort of piece I loved. It was filled with social commentary, about dog-eat-dog in the market economy and the survival of the fittest. It ticked all of my boxes. All sorts of double-dealing and skulduggery surrounded Danny, who'd slogged away for years to come up the hard way. Then, just as he'd reached the top, he was forced to watch helplessly as it crumbled around him. Danny was like a punchy fighter who never knew when he was down. In one scene, I had to lie on the floor with blood everywhere after I'd taken a beating, but I still managed to gasp out another desperate joke. That, I think, was what Liverpool and its people were all about. There were times when their wits had been frightened out of them, but by God they'd laugh about it.

Bleasdale was constantly reshaping scenes as we went. When someone asked him whether the play would relate to people outside Liverpool, he spat: 'I don't give a toss what they think about it in Sutton Coldfield or Huddersfield. It's a play for this city.'

'What's he about: Danny?' I asked Alan. 'What makes him tick?'

'Danny stands for what's happened to this city. People have been driven from pillar to post and back again in Liverpool. It's the same with Danny, everything happens to him. He is hard, aggressive and bankrupt and he keeps on fighting.'

I was playing alongside another Everyman old-timer, the gorgeous Alison Steadman, and Alan had written a scene in which I had to headbutt her. It was like being asked to rob a nun. 'Alan, is it really necessary? Would Danny really have dropped the nut on her?'

He explained his logic. 'Look, Pete, I hate the gratuitous

violence of *The Sweeney* or *The Professionals* as much as anyone. It's bullshit. The characters got thumped and are up straight away for the next round.'

'But isn't that what we're doing here? I mean, headbutting a woman, Alan – the character wouldn't do that, would I?'

Bleasdale was all for it, saying butting was the first form of defence in Liverpool:

'Pete, you stick the head on somebody and I know it's a horrible image. But it's not about aggression, it's a symbol of self-defeat. Butting is admitting you've reached the point where you can't take any more.'

I had to admire his logic. Bleasdale's point was that Danny and the other people in Liverpool had been screwed by the men in suits and were broken. Danny was impotent and his violence was an admission of defeat. Even though I understood it, I still felt uneasy, and on the night before we filmed the scene, I phoned Jules to tell her. 'Butt her with love,' Jules told me. 'Imagine that your head is kissing hers.' So I did.

Action, Camera, Rolling. Alison wasn't used to doing fight scenes, thank God; I sensed her nervousness. 'Fine,' I thought, 'it's a dance, not a fight. I'll orchestrate the scene like a choreographer.' I grabbed hold of her, and butted her. Bang. Then I kicked her up the backside as she tried to scamper away before turning left. There was a window, which Alison looked up through. I picked up the telephone, an old, heavy Bakelite one, and threw it through the window. Off camera, a big sheet of wood had been placed over her head, so that she wasn't hurt. The toffee clash showered Alison, she cowered beneath the window as I hurled abuse. And that was pretty much it. 'Cut, brilliant.' The scene was a success. I went straight to Alison. 'You okay, love?' 'Fine, couldn't be better. You were an absolute pro.'

Alan wrote *The Muscle Market* in nine days and even

found a way of putting his Auntie Ginny's house on the map. He took us there for a scene in which Danny went back to see his mum. Alan wrote it in the morning, I learned my lines at lunchtime and we filmed it in the afternoon. Boom. Instant TV. I did all of my stunts and there were times when I was half-covered in blood and riding stretched across the top of a double-decker bus, which wasn't the easiest thing in the world to achieve. Of all of us, I think the guy who had the best deal was Tony West, a showbusiness agent. He picked up £25 for driving his car ten yards in a scene.

There was other TV work during the early eighties. I made my *Coronation Street* debut, appearing in episode 2061 as Detective Sergeant Cross. I arrested Fred Gee after he'd been dealing in dodgy videos. I remember sitting in the green room watching *The Nutcracker* ballet with Hilda Ogden before going on. 'Cup of tea?' I asked the actress, Jean Alexander, as she fiddled with her rollers while enjoying a daily dose of Tchaikovsky. A more incongruous moment I'd never known. Much later, Corrie offered me a regular role after Alan Bradley went under the tram at Blackpool. I was supposed to play another evil shark-of-a-man but I turned them down because it didn't feel right. If I'd taken it, I'd have forever been known as 'That guy from the street' and I didn't want to be typecast, much to my mother's disappointment.

There was never any danger of being typecast back at the Everyman and I returned to play in *Lucky Strike*. I was thrilled to be back in Hope Street. Little had changed. I still loved every nook and cranny. Though almost everyone who had been there with me during the early seventies had moved on, walking through the doors was a transportive experience. I felt myself carried back to those wonderfully ramshackle and fearless years. And I relished the piece; it had the sort of quick-fire, rat-a-tat-tat dialogue that you'd expect gangsters to play out across smoky, Godforsaken barrooms.

This is how it went: a man rushed into a deserted warehouse in North Africa, pursued by cops. He had a gun, a briefcase and a gut wound. He waited, tense, gun at the ready, while cop sirens wailed in the background. The guy looked around, tripped over a low stack of bales and dropped his briefcase, spilling thousands of US dollar bills across the warehouse. He rushed to collect his money, his gut wound making it difficult for him to move, then he sat back, produced a pack of Luckys, took one, saw that he had only one match so put it away. The guy looked at the strewn money, heard the police sirens wail again, then made a superhuman effort to collect his money, gun ready to fire. Visions of his unfaithful moll and a partner in crime repeatedly collided in his crazed mind as he replayed those last moments of his life.

I played Eddie the Gun and the piece was brilliant. There were flashbacks, flash-forwards, fantasy sequences, nightmares and surrealist imaginings all colliding to repeat a single scene over and over and over again with variations, extensions, illusions and hallucinations. It was action-packed, with very minimal dialogue and a wall-to-wall ear-shattering soundtrack. The play was a tense seventy-minute knot of jealousy, violence, rage, lost love and lost dreams. Dream on, Hilda Ogden. That, rather than *Coronation Street*, was what I was about.

Professionally, I was happy, but my domestic life was starting to unravel. Jules and I had stayed together since Van Load, back at the Everyman, and shared a ramshackle bedsit, in Soho. I was madly in love with her and we had an extraordinary relationship for six years. At the time it seemed limitless in its capacity for joy and sorrow, but we seemed to be in terminal decline.

I had great respect for her ability as an actress and comedienne and we had a lot of fun. We worked at the relationship too, but the truth was that we were probably incompatible. Though I was older than Jules, she was far in advance of me emotionally. The demise of our relationship coincided with her success in *Educating Rita*, although that was not the cause of it. Willy Russell's piece was sublime, a perfect fit for her. She'd wanted to escape her surroundings, like the character in the play. Education had given Rita the means to achieve that and drama had done the same for Jules. I encouraged her to take the part and it was soon a major West End hit. It was wonderful to see how successful Jules became: she enjoyed an inexorable rise. Willy wrote a screenplay and soon she was starring with Michael Caine, Michael Williams and Maureen Lipman. She adored every moment and deserved her Golden Globe and an Oscar nomination. But our time was through. I wished her all the best. I was thrilled for her, genuinely so. It had been quite a sobering experience, seeing things change so quickly, but Jules deserved every bit of it. Ultimately, we were just so different, that's all. Any recognition I've been lucky enough to get has been a slow process. I'm the slow burn, rather than the dazzling pyrotechnic. I've been pretty steady throughout, even though other people's perceptions of me have changed. A lot of the demise of that relationship was due to my inadequacy really, I think, my insecurity and her security to a certain extent. It was emotional insecurity, rather than the pressures of our respective careers. She was a lot more sorted than I was at the time. She had gone through far more, strangely enough, although she was slightly younger. I was not prepared for all that a relationship entailed. We remained friends, though we went our separate ways.

For a long time after that I didn't want to be tied down, and it took me two years to get over Jules. I didn't want to have a significant other in my life, I was happy to divide my time between different cities and the addresses of understanding friends.

Occasionally I recalled my escape from teaching with great relief. I knew I wouldn't have been able to stick it at the reform school, or Loreto. The staff-room attitude and the teachers' petty rulings made schizos out of the Loreto girls. Their skirts had to be measured so that they weren't above their knees, which caused all the girls to hitch them right up to their knickers the moment they were out of sight of the teacher. I'm forever glad that I got out of that atmosphere. In the theatre, there were no conventions or rules. People accepted you for who you were.

The Bristol Old Vic came a-calling again and I returned there for a further season before accepting an offer to appear in Britain's great cauldron of classical theatre: the Royal Shakespeare Company. For me, as an actor, the RSC was Britain's greatest stage. It was far more important than the West End; it was the epicentre of drama. My decision to move there had been a long time coming. They had repeatedly offered me contracts, and each time I'd turned them down. I always felt as though it was something that I needed to do, but I wanted it to be on my own terms. I didn't want to go there for the sake of it, I wanted to go there because I felt I had something to contribute. More than a decade of repertory theatre work had given me the confidence finally to accept the RSC's offer, and so, suitcase packed, I headed to the birthplace of the Bard.

FIVE

Little Red Rooster

෴

I arrived in Stratford-upon-Avon during the early eighties and at times it seemed to exist simply for the benefit of the theatre. There was a great community of actors, seventy or eighty of us, not to mention the directors, technicians, writers and crew. People like Michael Gambon, Mark Rylance, Bob Peck and my Everyman friend, Antony Sher, found themselves at the centre of a creative storm. Suddenly, I was in a world where cliché didn't exist, where people genuinely cared about their art. I remember walking through the town one morning, past the statue of Shakespeare. As I turned to look over my shoulder, the Bard's eye flickered: I'm sure he winked at me.

The world I was joining was different from the one I'd left. I was in for hard work, but it would be worth it. They showed me a schedule and it was insane. Each day, we were to start rehearsals at 10 a.m. and go through until 5.30 p.m., then we'd have a couple of hours off before the performance. Normally, I'd blanch at that sort of workload; not because of any intrinsic laziness, far from it, but because being plugged into the socket for so much of the time wouldn't allow me to step back, reflect and grow into the roles. Now, it was different: there was no choice, no opt-out clause. The RSC worked to a strict, formal structure and we all bought into that. 'Long hours? Pah. Make them longer.' I was being paid for what I enjoyed doing. Besides, most people in life were far worse off, working just as hard but in jobs that didn't give them any sort of enjoyment.

I did a newspaper interview at the time, which proved prophetic. The interviewer asked me how I felt about being at Stratford and which roles I'd most like: 'I think the one part I would really like to play is King Lear. At the moment, I am understudying the part and we do have a full rehearsal of understudies, so that has given me the chance to tackle it. But I would like to play it as my main role.' During that first spring/summer season, our programme comprised *Macbeth*, *Much Ado About Nothing*, *King Lear* and *The Tempest* in the main house, while at The Other Place there was *Arden of Faversham*, Henrik Ibsen's *Peer Gynt* and Edward Bond's *Lear*. The RSC had links with theatres in Newcastle and London, so at times we'd appear in Stratford before heading either north or south. On other occasions, we'd travel even further. Edward Bond's *Lear* was particularly well received and the British Council supported us in taking a production of it to Berlin.

Back in Warwickshire, many of us felt as though Stratford were our own invention, a village that we could redefine and reshape. It was to become the main focus of my life for the next five years. Relationships at that time seemed to be unwaveringly intense. As a group we'd been thrown together in a very beautiful environment and friendships seemed to be either long lasting or absurdly short term. The assistant director, Nick Hamm, was about ten years younger than me and we seemed to click. He was a sprog director and was told to direct us in an understudies' production of *Macbeth*, while Howard Davies directed the performance proper. In all understudy productions, we were promoted to a better role, so in Nick's rehearsals I played Macbeth. Our job was to carbon copy the play that was on stage; in other words, we weren't supposed to be interpretive or in any way imaginative in what we were doing. We were only required to learn the moves that the actors did in the main production, in case one of them couldn't go on stage. Normally, understudy rehearsals were a pain in the arse, where the director literally said: 'The main actor takes four steps backwards this way, then four steps to the right that way, and then he raises his sword ...'

I thought that was bollocks. I wasn't remotely interested and I wasn't having any of it. We weren't automatons, if we were spending our time working, we needed to explore the work. What was the point of being in Stratford if we weren't going to engage in an extraordinary creative process, re-evaluating everything that was happening, redoing the lot? Nick was new and nobody had told him the way rehearsals were supposed to be. It was only when he was told in no uncertain terms that, actually, that was not how we were supposed to rehearse and that actually we weren't supposed to have our own interpretations that he knew. I think we all nearly got fired, to be honest.

My view of Shakespeare was very different from 70 per cent of the people on stage, but Nick got it and it cemented an enormously powerful relationship. I guess he saw me as a complete rebel in those years. But my rebellion wasn't for its own sake. I didn't want to tread the boards in the same old way. I came from a different form of theatre, I was basically a strong working-class actor, so my approach was different to the people who'd come from a classical environment and had maybe studied at RADA. Unlike many of my contemporaries, I wasn't interested in a 'career in the theatre' or being what every other actor wanted to be. I cared about authenticity. I didn't just want to make things real, I absolutely had to.

I think I developed a reputation for being challenging, maybe even difficult. There were times when I pushed established directors beyond their limit. In rehearsal rooms, I would question directors who'd been doing Shakespeare for quite a while. My view was that they were there to help me achieve my vision of how I wanted to play a role, rather than force me through the same old steps. Life became mercurial. I laughed, partied hard, drank a great deal and did copious amounts of whatever drugs were around at that particular time. We had a great time. There were lock-ins at the Dirty Duck, which lasted for hours, sometimes days. Pressure went with the turf and so I found a place about ten miles outside town, a beautiful cottage, in Ettington, that was covered in rambling roses and honeysuckle. It was my escape. When I needed to stay in town I'd doss down at Nick's flat, and when he wanted to get away he'd come to the cottage. The cottage was at the end of a line of buildings and inside was a mix of the avant garde and the working class. My mother used to send me lots of knick-knacks to furnish it. She'd knit these mini tea cosies, for instance, to cover up the toilet rolls: to her, leaving an uncovered toilet roll on display was the height of bad taste. There'd be pictures and sculptures and books lining every wall and shelf, and then tea cosies to cover the loo roll.

I'd passed my driving test in my thirties and bought a 2CV for £700. But my regular income in Stratford enabled me to upgrade. I saw an MGB Roadster for £2,000 and bought it. It was a beautiful machine and I'd put the top down and drive through the Warwickshire countryside at 100 mph with the radio blasting out some raucous song.

We'd spend our non-stage time smoking, drinking and then hurtling through the countryside. One night, the inevitable happened and I had this amazing smash. The car flipped over through the air, literally four times, and ended up in a field, upside down. I think I must have gone over some black ice. I staggered out, unmarked, and the only thing that was still working on the MGB was the stereo: 'Little Red Rooster' by the Stones was blaring out. I think God was trying to tell me something. I managed to get back to Stratford to tell the gang what had happened. 'Get this man a pint,' said one of them.

After this episode, I bought a motorbike and the journey to and from Stratford became even more visceral. Nick and I would be up at the cottage, dropping acid, before heading off to whatever party was going on. How we both lived beyond that period, I don't know. Someone was looking down on us. My constitution was as strong as an ox's and I'd be at the pub, sinking nine or ten pints, before walking home.

That first year passed in a blur. It seemed everybody was acting, directing, working, drinking, smoking, driving, fucking, doing everything, really. It was the most extraordinary journey. The following year brought another filled programme at the RSC and Barbican. It featured *The Taming of the Shrew*, in which I played Grumio to Alun Armstrong's Petruchio and Sinéad Cusack's Katherina. Barry Kyle created a loving, large-spirited and exuberant production.

Mother and Father were both proud that I flourished at the RSC. They saw me being presented to HM the Queen before one of our performances of *The Fair Maid of the West*, at The Swan, in Stratford. I was dressed in fur and enjoyed it. I can remember driving Mother and Father to the theatre and Mother, who was a real royalist, saying, 'Fancy our lad being presented to the Queen.' Afterwards, she glowed like the embers of a fire. 'What was she like? I'm very proud. I'm glad you chose acting, you know.' I smiled. Her opinion that acting was a phase changed overnight. She seemed to think: 'Um, okay, now he's met the Queen, he must be serious – and maybe he's even okay at it. Maybe he won't go back to teaching after all.'

There were other productions in that season, including *Much Ado About Nothing* and Bond's *Lear*, in which I played six different characters, they sure got their money's worth then. The autumn/winter '83/'84 season comprised our production of Edmond Rostand's *Cyrano de Bergerac*, with Derek Jacobi as Cyrano and me as Ragueneau. Of all of the plays, *Cyrano de Bergerac* stood out. We took it to Los Angeles as part of the Olympic Games under the directorship of Terry Hands. It was a sure-footed production from Terry and the shows in LA helped me to afford my first flat, in Hampstead. Up till then I'd been continuing my semi-vagrant peregrinations, renting or sometimes moving in with friends like Nick Hamm.

I met Sean Bean during these years. We had a fantastic time in *Fair Maid of the West*, with Imelda Staunton. He is a decent man, we always know where we stand with one another. 'Sean, that's crap,' I'd say, if he'd done something wrong. 'Pete, that's worse,' he'd reply. The RSC put us in the same dressing room up at Stratford during *Fair Maid*, then we shared a dressing room again when we transferred to the Mermaid, in London. There was a TV and a table in our dressing room, and little else. Beneath the table, we'd keep our stash of beer; we were on the Grolsch when we got to London, but we were always very professional, the work always came first. I remember coming off stage once and Sean was sitting there. 'What happened?' he said; he wanted to know why there'd been long silences during the performance. 'I was listening on the telecom, did you forget your lines?' I laughed. 'No, you daft bugger. The audience were rapt, I was milking the suspense.' We'd sit and talk about all sorts or watch snooker on the telly. I think we stayed glued to the box on the night Dennis Taylor beat Steve Davis in the world final, by potting the last black.

On one occasion, in Newcastle, we did a play called *The Body*, by Nick Darke, which Nick Hamm directed. It was about a group of bored marines guarding nuclear warheads in the Cornish countryside. I was cast in the lead role as a flamboyant, aggressive American marine. It was an overtly political piece; we'd been through Greenham Common, the Falklands War, Thatcher, CND and all sorts of marches. The piece felt more like agit-prop than anything else, it was the sort of thing we'd have done in Liverpool or Bristol. But it was bloody funny too.

One day my brother Mike arrived in Newcastle. He'd become one of the most lovely men ever put on this earth and I loved and loved him. He was an extraordinary guy. I told my housemates that Mike would be staying with us for a couple of days and we decided to take an excursion to a fairground on Whitley Bay; me, Mike and Nick Hamm. We took the afternoon off and went to Britain's northernmost fairground in the middle of winter: it didn't surprise us that we were the only ones there. We lit these huge spliffs and wandered around before coming to the ghost train.

'How much, mate?' I asked, and the guy gave me a look that suggested we were mad.

'It's not even bloody switched on,' he said, before climbing into his booth to give it some juice. 'Get in,' he said, as the karts swung through black doors and stopped next to us.

So there we were, three big guys squashed into these tiny karts, as high as kites, ready to ride the ghost train.

'You're off,' said the guy, as he pushed the button, and we disappeared into the gloom. It was the most frightening experience of our lives. We thought we'd been possessed, demons and spirits seemed to lunge at us on a ride that went on for hours. We didn't think we'd ever emerge from the darkness. When we came out, ashen-faced, the guy was waiting by the doors.

'I'm so sorry about that,' he said. Silence. We looked at him supine, our hearts were in our mouths. 'That must have been really boring.' What did he mean, boring? We'd been frightened half to death. Mike was looking at Nick: 'Jesus, that was terrible.' But the guy on the ghost train carried on: 'I forgot to turn the electrics on inside, so none of the ghosts were working. Do you want to go around again?' Did we buggery. Our cannabis-addled imaginations had given us the most terrifying experience ever. We staggered onto the beach and started running up and down, eating fish and chips, laughing at what had just happened.

∾

I enjoyed the challenges of reinventing Shakespeare and throwing myself into works by contemporary writers – Edward Bond, Howard Barker and Arthur Miller. And I liked to blur the boundaries between actor and character. In *The Body*, for instance, I'd make members of the audience uncomfortable as I'd point my rifle at them and unnerve them with invective. But that in itself wasn't enough. We were in the maw of that mammoth company but wanted to define ourselves as we saw fit, rather than be defined by it. I yearned for the sort of challenges I'd enjoyed in Liverpool and Bristol, when the actors had broken through the boundaries of what was possible. I wanted to take the democratic ideas that Alan Dossor and co had instilled in me and push it even further. A group of us – I think Barry Kyle was the brains behind it – came up with an idea, the Not the RSC Festival, which was commissioned by the Almeida, in London. The committee invited any member of the company who wanted to do anything to submit their plans. Absolutely no censorship would be exercised. Whatever anyone wanted to do would somehow be incorporated into the bedlam of our mad two weeks. Lunchtimes, evenings, afternoons, mornings and late-afternoon slots were rapidly filled with plays, workshops and discussions; the monster began to grow.

Beside the current shows for that season – *Richard III*, *Hamlet*, *Red Noses*, *Henry V* – and the shows in The Pit – *War Plays*, *The Dream Play*, *Today* and *Golden Girls* – plus the new incoming shows of *Love's Labours Lost* and *Desert Air*, both of which had cast changes, the resident acting committee was tackling fifty pieces of work. Fifty. Five O. Holy moly. They'd be performed by more than a hundred members of the company, at the Almeida Theatre in Islington, over a ridiculously crammed fortnight. To fit everything in, we scheduled them at all hours. There were numerous performances through the afternoon, evening and night. Somehow, we shoehorned it all in using all manner of venues and spaces.

The work would be completely voluntary and in many cases valiantly original. Actors were to direct, write, sing, dance and mime in cases where they had never done so before. At least twenty pieces were new to London, some would even be world premieres. The range was unbelievable, matched only by the subtle determination of the company to do it elegant justice.

The problems were legion. For a start, whom should we cast in our productions? That in itself was hard enough, it was a minefield of negotiation, reminiscent of picking sides in a football match at grammar school. Nobody wanted to be the last choice. There were other considerations. Where and when would we rehearse? How would we get our casts together all at the same time? Was there a piano at the Almeida? Who would design, light and provide sound for our shows? When would there ever be enough time to do it all? Were we completely insane to have gotten involved in the first place?

I had agreed to have a stab at Robin Hooper's stylish and original *Astonish Me!* a play about Cocteau and his quest for genius and fame. The search for the cast began. Copies of the script were given to possible and potential players who were, first, available at the right time and, second, wanted to be part of the venture at all. Of course all the other 'directors' were frenetically doing the same thing and offers were cascading on actors like ticker tape, they'd never had it so good. The complications and intricacies of trying to cast reminded me of that dreadful Rubik's cube, it seemed impossible to match the colours to various facets of the infernal thing. Mad incidents would occur ... Richard III, the 'bunch-backed toad' (Sher) would meet me (dressed as Hastings) accidentally in the lift and say 'What about Henry Goodman for Stravinsky?' 'Great idea,' I'd reply, and beetle off to the Tower to be beheaded.

At last we had the casting of *Astonish Me!* resolved but for one part – Serge Diaghilev. We seemed to be in a hole. 'Why don't you do it?' gleamed Sher from under his hump as we passed in the corridor – there was no alternative and I agreed. Indeed an internal irony accompanied the decision – Diaghilev, most famous of the all-time great Theatrical Entrepreneurs, seemed wickedly parodied by my fearful attempts to produce Robin's one-hour show at the Almeida! Ironic, indeed. In true Hydra style, the solving of the problem of casting only served to sprout even more problems. My cast were not exclusively mine and all of them were involved in one, two, three and even four other projects at the same time. Penny Beaumont was even performing in the first half of the very double bill of which *Astonish Me!* formed the second half – and she was playing Cocteau's mum. I had also agreed to do *Temptation*, a one-man show by Nick Dear about a disillusioned teacher trying to commit suicide. Madness!

Where to rehearse was also a problem and in the end we never rehearsed in the same place twice. People's homes, odd corners of the theatre, dressing rooms, corridors and even a pub garden at various times helped us to knit the productions together. Had it not been for the intrinsically ad-hoc feel of the Festival among the company I fear tempers would have flared more readily, but, as it was, if a call was missed or a venue misread, we all took it as part of the general chaos, shrugged shoulders, grinned at each other despairingly and moved on. The Ballets Russes itself could not have supported and driven me on with more vigour than the now finally assembled cast of *Astonish Me!* in those hairy days prior to 30 July: the First Night. The intensity and sheer volume of work made my time at the Little seem like a night shift at a care home. One of my clearest memories is of driving my little black Mini through a storm that felt like a manic car wash, my head overloaded with ideas. The wipers were on andante, not coping with the deluge; visibility was wetly nil and the petrol gauge was flirting maddeningly with red. It seemed like an apt analogy for the situation at the Almeida, where full-scale preparations had thundered upon us with a rage equal to the surprise monsoon. *Astonish Me!* was on in thirteen days' time. Ha. And I'd turn base metal to gold, learn how to fly and play rugby for England during my lunch hour. Easy.

I pulled over and bought more cigarettes. Cigarettes. Damn it. The production called for 'lovely black cigarettes'. Balkan Sobranie Black Russians would have been the obvious choice. But there was a problem: Tony Sher, playing

Jean Cocteau, and Philip Dupuy had both given up smoking, an integral part of the action. The solution came in the form of Honeyrose Herbal cigarettes: gak, that would mean rehearsing in a hazy atmosphere of garden sheds and rotting compost ...

In mounting the production I hit on a major stumbling block: playing Diaghilev and trying to direct at the same time was like attempting to make a blancmange from the inside – a horrible and unproductive experience.

We developed a kind of communal directorial responsibility whenever we came to those scenes involving Diaghilev, with whoever was not involved keeping an eye on things from the stalls, as it were. I think it fair to say that people in those scenes suffered most from this haphazard way of working.

Dateline: 25 July. There were five days to go. Somehow the textual and internal work on the script was being accomplished and that side of the production seemed to have found its own pace and progress. Now – how to mount it? The given logistics of the Festival were bound to make certain demands on the style and look of the finished product, and I dearly hoped we could and would turn those to our own advantage. We knew for a fact that we would get barely two hours to 'tech' it, that is, set up whatever design we arrived at with set, lights and sound, before dress rehearsing on the very morning of the first night. Moreover, we realised we had only an interval to set the whole thing up before curtain up. The budget for each show was limited to £50 at most, and all props, costume and make-up had to be found, begged or stolen by the cast themselves. All of those factors vitally influenced the eventual design and pointed to an overall artistic brief – absolute simplicity. That was – don't do anything! But Robin's play was a fine mixture of surreal elegance and surprising voltes-faces – it had to be astonishing.

The Almeida had a lovely feel to it, it felt naked and boasted a beautifully curved brick back wall. We added a large empty picture frame, made with love by Ronnie Locke of the RSC stage staff, and painted bright red a small table, an easel and a wicker chair, a large theatrical cane skip and a borrowed bicycle with a functional bell. To take the production into the Cocteau/Parade style it demanded we took the make-up to bizarre new lengths. We whitened our faces and, in black, painted spectacles on Stravinsky, a monocle on Diaghilev and even, on stage as part of the action, a moustache on Etienne. So a style formed as much out of necessity as artistic invention.

Limitations once resolved took on an apt splendour. What we couldn't do proved to be a bonus. High up and to the left on the back wall of the Almeida was a large rectangular white space. With half an hour to go before we went up on that first night I fell on an idea. The opening of the play sees Cocteau at an easel (white) sipping a cup of coffee (black). He lifts the spoon from the cup and sees that it is a brush – he paints a profile on the canvas. Eureka. Why shouldn't we mirror that image and write large on the white space behind us? I suggested it to Tony, who was already made up as Cocteau and was painting glasses on Henry Goodman in the dressing room. He followed the flow of the idea. I approached Graham, the sweating stage manager, and asked for a ladder. He wanted to know what for (twenty-five minutes to curtain up). I explained. 'Can't paint on that,' he said. 'The first half of the double bill uses it for a back projection and Ken Branagh's late-night *Tell Me Honestly* won't want a profile on it.'

Stymied!

'You could paint it on same-sized paper, attach it there and take it down afterwards.' Fifteen minutes to curtain. There was no time and anyway the idea would be messy.

At that precise moment, I noticed that Graham was fiddling with a roll of thick black gaffer tape even as we spoke. Bingo! What if we taped the profile on the space and removed it before Ken's show? 'Yes, that'll work.' Ten minutes to go. Tony got to work with tape while in full costume, from the rickety ladder, and the image completed the overall design like a Cocteauesque dream. Simplicity in set design, light and sound was all very well but the actors, poor things, had to act the piece within that concept and in such a minimalist, albeit elegant design, that they would have nothing to hide nor bolster them. That too led to the style in which Robin's play was eventually acted.

As actors it was all we had and it led us to a style of playing that called for a simplicity on the line, clarity of thought and intention, and a stripping away of anything that smacked of cinéma-vérité realism. Like Picasso, eventually drawing with pure light in the air, the actors worked towards a truth that allowed the text to paint itself before the eyes of the audience in a magical pattern. The pattern seemed to echo both the curling snake of opium smoke and the dance of the drama we were desperate to capture.

There was something very special in embarking upon such an unknown journey. I'm sure in one way it could have been unproductive, dissatisfying and disappointing. It was with glee, therefore, and some little pride I discovered that *Astonish Me!* – and in fact, the whole two weeks – was a rich, hectic, deeply satisfying and rewarding adventure for all those lucky and mad enough to have been involved. I imagined that in attempting to touch the moon and falling somewhat short, we'd been on the right side of a fifty-fifty chance of at least rubbing shoulders with proper stars. Well, that's how it seemed to me.

The Not the RSC Summer Festival had run on a wing and a prayer. It reminded me of Alan Dossor's early ideas about the democratisation of theatre. There'd be similar, smaller events in New York and Newcastle. I'd loved the idea that actors could have more control over their work, which seemed innately healthy. Those of us who also directed did so in a non-dictatorial form: anyone could make a suggestion. The festival was about giving actors the opportunity to make a political and artistic statement. As actors we are able to influence people and the way a production is interpreted, but the process only works if people come along so that we can begin the debate.

The RSC was an important part of my development; not because I wanted to morph into an actor with clipped vowels and the ability to enunciate in received pronunciation. My mission during those years was to challenge convention and bring the work into the modern idiom. Just as I'd done at Liverpool and Bristol, I wanted to kick against the traces and take Shakespearian performances out of one Elizabethan era into another. The experience of Not the RSC had given me my wings; I'd been able to lead a group of actors in a reasonably anarchic celebration of theatre. But though I enjoyed being part of the RSC – or, as we called it, The Family – it had finite possibilities. I had already begun to lay the groundwork for a very different career and it was time to take my leave.

SIX

Forget Me Not

❧

With my cap pulled down low and my collar pointed high, I ventured to the picture house in Warrington. My first major film, *A Private Function*, was being screened at the Odeon Film Centre and I was keen to watch it in my home town. My clothes helped me to dissimulate, I didn't want a scene; but I couldn't disguise the scintilla of excitement in my veins. The prospect of seeing myself on celluloid in the place that had fuelled my boyhood dreams was thrilling.

I'd been building towards my movie debut for some time, with increasingly frequent appearances on TV. There'd been roles in *Soldier, Last of the Summer Wine, Doris and Doreen, Afternoon Off, Horse in the House, Crown Court* and others. But *A Private Function* was one step further, I was being entrusted to deliver on a bigger stage. The producers cast me as a crooked butcher, Douglas J. Nuttol, along-side Michael Palin, Maggie Smith, Alison Steadman, Bill Paterson, Tony Haygarth, Richard Griffiths and Denholm Elliott. Alan Bennett had put the film together and was keen that I appear in it. I'd worked with him before and respected his talent, he was a smashing writer. Alan introduced me to the film's director, Malcolm Mowbray, and that was it: a done deal.

The RSC had given me an eight-week sabbatical to film and I really enjoyed the work, it was a pleasant diversion from the sort of things I usually did. The switch from stage and TV to film seemed entirely natural and shooting the scenes was a blast. My abiding memory of being on set was the constant laughter; the team was like a mini repertory company and we were forever smiling and making jokes. There was a real sense of joie de vivre about our group. The action was set in a Yorkshire town in 1947, while rationing still had a grip. The local dignitaries had decided to hold a party and the main item on the menu was an illegal and secretly raised pig: the possession of contraband meant trouble and hilarity ensued. I developed my closest relationship with a creature who, sadly, is no longer with us. Betty the pig and I became very close.

Alan Bennett was on the set, though he seemed to spend plenty of time going off on a little drive through the countryside. And Michael and Bill were constantly off on some jaunt to places they'd found in the *Good Pub Guide*. Bill Paterson was Morris Wormold, the meat inspector. He told me later that Rachel Davies, who played my character's love interest, had been concerned at having to act out an intimate scene with me. She'd disguised her nervousness brilliantly and not let on to me. Afterwards, she confided again in Bill. Apparently, although I still looked like a trucker, she now considered me far more sensitive.

Before the screening, I went back to stay with my parents, in Padgate. My father was a strong silent man, but without his having to say anything, I could feel his implicit support. My mother was more communicative. 'Enjoy it,' she said, maternally, as I set off for the stalls of the Odeon. By the end of the ninety-four-minute film, I felt elevated; I'd played a lot more in it than I'd thought and I found it weird to see myself up there. I didn't look or sound as I'd expected. I've spoken to other actors about this and they usually agree. The way you imagine yourself is different to the external reality. Your voice sounds different, your physical features seem more pronounced.

There was talk of appearing in more films, but my diary was like the Blue Nile in flood. I had just turned down a part in *The Practice*, Granada's soap opera, because I was tied up with *Richard III* and *Henry V* with the RSC at the Barbican. I was rejecting more work than I could accept. The RSC continued to keep me busy and there were plenty of memorable shows in the following years, like *Every Man in His Humour*, which had a fine cast that included Philip Franks.

So, professionally, things were going well and I was also entirely content with my bachelor life. I'd never been much of a ladies' man, there were plenty of parties and work and I had no desire to settle down. I didn't believe in marriage, for a start. I viewed a marriage certificate as a piece of paper which invited a man to rebel against it. In my mind, a perfect relationship was when two people could create a world for themselves which was unaffected by anything else.

And then came the Sicilian thunderbolt, a coup de foudre. Bang – that was it.

Jacqui Morrish was in a yellow sou'wester standing under a streetlamp on a rainy night in Everton when Cupid fired his bow; she was surrounded by a pool of amber light and wore the prettiest smile, she looked so serene. It was 3 a.m. in the morning and we were on the set of *Coast to Coast*, a programme I was doing with Lenny Henry and John Shea.

I was in the production office when I saw Jax. I put my coat over my head and ran out, then noticed the Sony Walkman that was covered by her bright yellow hat.

'What are you listening to?' I asked.

'Van Morrison: *Into the Music*,' she said.

My heart skipped a beat and I asked if she'd join me for a drink the following night. When we went out, I was struck by her sheer beauty and intelligence. 'I think you'd better live with me for the rest of my life,' I said, within hours of sitting down with her. It was just obvious, so obvious to me. Jax was bemused: 'How can you be so sure?'

I told her: 'We're going to be together. I just know.'

She was attractive, smart, funny, kind and passionate. There would never be another. Jax was the assistant floor manager on *Coast to Coast* and was in charge of the props. She made sure there were things like guns and counterfeit plates for the actors. Although she was in a long-term relationship, she succumbed to my advances and people realised we were serious pretty soon. I knew instinctively that I'd spend the rest of my life with Jax. She was transcendent, all of my dreams made real.

Coast to Coast was a great piece; people still remember it fondly now, particularly on Merseyside. I played a funny character, Kecks McGuinness, who delivered punchline after punchline. The script was a riot and we spent most of our time laughing. Kecks was a wild comic villain in Coke-bottle glasses.

The other principles were Lenny Henry and John Shea, and we were working under the directorship of Sandy Johnson. Lenny and John got on particularly well, and their relationship fed out to other people. Lenny was like a sponge, he was still a pup and he soaked up everything, he just wanted to learn. In a way, John and I were mentoring Lenny, he was the perfect pupil. He was very respectful of us and in return we tried to give him the freedom to express himself and develop his character; we gave him room to do his own thing. My friend Bill Nighy came up from London one evening, and joined John and me for a drink. Bill and John had played brothers in *Hitler's SS* the year before.

John was good fun. In later years, he spoke to me about those days and reminded me of another time when we all sat down together. John was to my left and beside him was Jax, who was dressed in a black leather motorcycle jacket. 'Would you be my minder?' I'd asked her. She'd laughed: 'That would be lovely.' We strolled through the streets of Liverpool to a Chinese restaurant, Jax and I walking together, followed by John and Bill.

We filmed during one of Liverpool's coldest winters on record. On the pier head it was minus fourteen degrees, it felt like a particularly unhappy month in Siberia. A lot of it was shot on a famous art deco council estate and Sandy's team positioned a giant crane inside the well of the housing block. There was an internal courtyard and open stairs, spiralling down. We did a lot of night shoots and the physical environment, in the inner city, was pretty edgy. We were in the centre of a very hard, very working-class area and in a flat at the bottom of the crane was a drug-dealing centre. One night, when we were filming, the catering truck got held up by a guy with a gun. 'Give me some food,' he said, as he rasped at the poor chef, pointing his weapon. We were pretty unconcerned; that sort of behaviour was par for the course in that area, we didn't let it worry us. Besides, we were having too much fun; we were a mad band of brothers, singing and dancing, enjoying heady thrills. The music was sensational, we played out to a soundtrack of soul and punk, listening to tunes like The Pogues' 'Dirty Old Town' on the cold, hard back streets of Liverpool.

My character finally got his comeuppance in one scene when I was coming out of a flat, I think with Peter Vaughan and George Baker. Kecks was killed and the action switched to a mortuary. For some reason, Kecks had no toes and so his name tag was positioned, amusingly, on his groin. 'Do you have to put the tag there?' they asked the attendant, as he lifted the sheet.

After I'd finished shooting my scenes, the production team gave me the ritual send-off, to say goodbye. The next day, they were all back on set, carrying on with the remaining scenes. My work was complete and I was due elsewhere. But two days later, I bumped into the director, Sandy Johnson, in the lift at the Adelphi, in Liverpool.

'What are you doing here?' Sandy asked. 'I thought you'd gone a couple of days back.'

'I'm with Jax,' I told him. 'She's gone, she's gone to see Tim, to tell him,' and I shuffled off. Jax was telling her ex that she'd decided to see me and we were together from that day on.

I stayed in Liverpool for as long as I could with Jax and we found ourselves becoming instantly devoted. Our relationship blossomed and we became inseparable. She became my rock, my stability, my touchstone. My every fibre loved Jax. She made me feel like the most important man on earth; I was safe, warm and happy. She loved me for who I was, there was no attempt to change me or make me a different man, and I adored everything about her. She shimmered, just being in her presence gave me a flash of excitement. For all the drinking and wild times, I'd never slept around; I'd discovered girls quite late on and been smitten three or four times. Casual sex had never been for me, probably because of my latent Catholic guilt. The church had taught me to be fearful and mistrusting of sex, to feel guilty about sexuality, rather than helped me to understand that it could be a pleasant thing. But that's how it was – we are who we are. I felt that was wrong. My sisters, Anne and Pat, both had children before they were twenty. The Pope didn't understand the sexuality of Lancashire girls, or me. You can't say condoms are wrong when you've got a population explosion and HIV.

Jax and I moved in together, but before we'd had time to unpack the kettle we found ourselves at the eye of a storm as a convergence of life-changing events hit us. During the course of a few years, we did all the most traumatic things that you are supposed to do as a human being: we got involved in a new relationship, we moved house, Jax got pregnant, I was diagnosed with testicular cancer, and lost someone whom we really loved.

I was reasonably philosophical about my brush with cancer at the time, although I now realise it was profoundly shocking. For some time before I saw a doctor, my back felt like the bumper of a dodgem car. I'd also been suffering from a swollen testis so I booked an appointment with a doctor in Hampstead. He knew it was serious and on the same day rang the consultant, who saw me the following Tuesday. Three days later I was in hospital and on the Monday morning they removed the offending testis. I swotted up on testicular cancer like a student preparing for an exam. Testicular cancer was known in the trade as the friendly cancer, apparently, because it was one of the most treatable and didn't spread quickly. I was out on the Wednesday, it was like bouff – very quick. I didn't feel in danger when it happened, because it all occurred so quickly and because the operation, a right radical orchidectomy, was absurdly simple. Snip, snip; off you go – it was like they'd just done a spot of gardening. Afterwards, I underwent radiotherapy and happily that particular cancer didn't return. I became very philosophical about the experience, reasoning that our lives follow their course and that's it; the world isn't ours, it's on loan and we have to make the most of things while we're here. I considered myself a lucky bastard to have enjoyed such a blessed career, doing the thing I loved the most, and I realised that things could have been much, much worse. Somehow, Jax and I got through it and I guess we wouldn't be what we are without all that happening.

When Jax found out that she was pregnant with Will, it should have been the most incredible day, but our jubilation was short-lived. My brother, Mike, rang up two hours later.

'Have you got that bottle of brandy that we brought you back from Greece?'

'Yeah, why?'

'Willie's knocked on a go-a.' My father played dominoes and in the game, if you say you can't go but the ref thinks you can, you're out of the game, you've 'knocked on a go-a'. The moment Mike told me, I knew what he meant. At 11.30 a.m., the same time that Jax and I heard about our son, my father left us.

One of the many remarkable things about my father was his death. There's a line from Shakespeare, in *Macbeth*, during a conversation between Malcolm and King Duncan, when Malcolm says: 'Nothing in his life became him like the leaving it.' That was true of my father. He always did the *Daily Mail* crossword with his morning cup of tea and on that particular morning it got to 11.30 a.m. and he had got a clue which read 'Fade (3, 4)'. He wrote 'Die Away' and then he put his head down on the kitchen table. Mother told him to stop messing around and tried to put his pipe back in his mouth, but he'd gone. There was a strange thing about his passing, because when we looked at the crossword he'd left one space unfilled. The clue that he didn't get was this: 'Myosotis, blue flower'. The answer was 'Forget me not'. We've still got the crossword. It was a remarkable way to go, remarkable and heartbreaking. We've never forgotten the method of his passing, nor his humanity, none of us ever will. He was an extraordinary man, my dad, simple, unaffected, sweet and straightforward – you couldn't have been more moved than at his funeral.

Jax was a rock. I remember one moment of darkness when I thought: 'Is this it?' I wondered whether it was my turn to go, thinking: 'Am I the next to leave?' I began getting upset, thinking about Jax bringing up a child without me. But she talked me through it. We all have moments of doubt, whether we've had cancer or not, whether we've lost a loved one or not. We're all going to die at some point; but thankfully it wasn't then, sweet Jesus, it wasn't then. Jax was, and is, the most important person in my life. We've been through a hell of a lot together. Some people can do it on their own. I need support.

Though we'd lived in the city, Jax and I yearned for a life in the countryside. We visited friends at weekends and were first introduced to Shropshire by a college friend of mine, who'd gone there to become headmaster of Cruckton School. He rang me up and asked me if I'd help him out.

'Pete, we've got a new sports hall. Would you come and open it for us?'

Sport had been a big part of my life and I was keen to encourage the younger generation. 'Of course I'll help, no problem.'

Jax and I organised a few weekend visits to Shropshire and that was it, we fell in love with the county before we knew it. We packed up and moved to a shire that felt as though it had been designed especially for us. The gentle rise and fall of its hills, the tranquillity of its wide-open spaces and the curious idiosyncrasies of its market towns were like manna from heaven. Our new house was a beautiful cottage in a small hamlet in south Shropshire. It had plenty of character and there were views over the local hills. We were surrounded by fields of sheep; the contrast between the hurly-burly of my working life and the bucolic bliss of Shropshire couldn't have been more pronounced. We were glad that our child would be raised there; we wanted him to be free to live an instinctive and true life.

Will was born in 1989. Having children was life-changing, even though it happened later for me than for most people. When it was time for his baptism, we encouraged him to do it himself, in a woodland pool, while Jax recited a poem by William Blake.

We didn't imagine we'd have any more children, not after the cancer operation and radiotherapy, but the happy arrival of Lily in 1996 made our family complete. She arrived in a birthing pool before a log fire at our home, in Minton. When Jax went into labour, Will woke up, saw lights and heard wild shouts. I think he thought it was a disco. He joined in: 'I'll help,' he said, as our progeny supervised the birth of his sister. It only took four hours and was one of the most moving experiences of my life. It was beautiful for mother, child and family; it became a spiritual thing. We chose the name Lily because she'd been born in water. She was adorable, round and edible. Lily wasn't planned, but then nothing in my life has been, things just have a habit of coming along. The arrival of Lily was a wonderful surprise, a divine blessing, and Will was immediately fascinated by his beautiful younger sister.

During my years with Jax, my views on marriage didn't alter but my commitment only increased. Long before Will and Lily came along, I knew that she was my soulmate and I wanted to find a meaningful way of declaring my intentions. Though it took many, many years for me to propose, Jax and I did organise a commitment ceremony in Greece, in which we made promises to each other. It was one of the most beautiful days of my life. Our families were thrilled, though I suspect some would have preferred if we'd got married. Wearing a wedding band would have pleased my mother and Jax's mother, Catherine, to name but two. 'So, if you're not getting married, could I call you my partner-in-law?' Catherine once asked.

'I've been called much worse,' I laughed. 'Partner-in-law is fine.'

As time rolled on, even Will caught the bug. He wanted to know why we hadn't walked down the aisle. 'Dad, you're mad not marrying, think of all the presents you'd get.'

'I know,' I replied. 'But how many toasters do we need?'

Those years were pivotal, not just at home but in terms of my development as an actor. My RSC years had come to their natural end, and that meant I was able to accept more of the scripts that I was offered. Jax came with me when we filmed *To Kill a Priest*, with Timothy Spall, Christopher Lambert, Ed Harris, Tim Roth, David Suchet, Joss Ackland and various others. I liked the script a lot because it retold a true story about Father Alek, a charismatic priest who bucked the Polish system back in 1981. Father Alek railed against communism and spoke in favour of Solidarity, earning him the support of the people. The British actors, like Timothy Spall and Tim Roth, developed an instant kinship. Jax and I hung out with Spally and his wife, Shane, who'd been together a little bit longer than we had. We really got on well and had a wonderful, wonderful time on that film, shooting a lot of our scenes in Paris. Spally is a really funny man. It felt like we were fearless, uninhibited buccaneers. We never spoke directly about our love of acting; we were probably too busy drinking, and besides, why on earth would we? Welders don't sit around discussing the chemical composition of solder and we didn't want to wear any aesthetic proclivities on our sleeves. But there was an innate understanding, we shared an appreciation of our craft. We revelled in the notion that the union of our minds could elevate our work ... and then there was the drink.

One night – it was spring, heading into summer – and the two Tims were there: Roth and Spall, along with one or two others. We found ourselves wandering the streets of central Paris, going from bar to bar, and came up to this church. I swear to this day it was Notre Dame de Paris, but I'm not very sure. We were talking and joking, bantering, when Spally said: 'Right, I'm going to walk up those stairs like fucking Charles Laughton.'

'Wait a minute,' I slurred. 'Wait a minute, Spally,' and I leapt into his arms.

We walked up the steps of Notre Dame with Spally screaming, 'Esmeralda, Esmeralda.' It was a choice moment of lunacy; Spally mimicking Quasimodo and me playing Esmeralda beneath the carved stone faces of Notre Dame.

There were other gleeful times. Spally and I gravitated towards the same venues, not by choice, we didn't arrange to meet anywhere; we just found ourselves propping up the same bars and cafés. We instinctively knew where to go to get the best drink and the best atmosphere. We'd forever bump into one another in two particular bars in St Germain. On one occasion, I think we were in Café de Flore, where Sartre used to go, I saw Spally coming up the stairs as I was coming down them from the loo.

'Tim, Tim, I've just quashed a fucking cliché,' I told him. 'I just bumped into Frankie Howerd in the loo and he told me that Jean-Paul Sartre's quote was rubbish. He said it was "Hell is other people", but Frankie told me it wasn't.' I adopted my finest French accent: 'He said: "Hell is no loo paper."' Spally loved it.

We shot *To Kill a Priest* in Paris, Lyon and other parts of France. We relished the exotic locations and buddied up

with Ed Harris and Christopher Lambert. Christopher
had a bit of an entourage, though I'm not sure whether
he chose the hangers-on or not. One morning, in Lyon, I
was with Jax when we bumped into Spally, who was walking down the road, looking a bit green. I'd assumed he was
suffering from the after-effects of the previous evening's
imbibing.

'You all right?' I asked him. And he told me a story about
our previous evening's drinking. We'd been in this chi-chi
hotel and Spally could see that Christopher was picking up
the bill for everyone, not just us actors; the hangers-on were
drinking him dry, night after night. Spally had had enough
and, without telling me or any of the others, he'd gone up to
the waiter. There'd been no fuss, he'd just said, 'Let me get
this, I'll get this,' and he'd signed the bill, without looking at
it. The next morning, Spally looked at his bill and thought,
'Oh my fucking Lord.' He'd paid £300, which would be
nearer £700 or £800 in today's money. It was a considerable
part of his fee. He was wandering the medieval streets of
Lyon looking green from the drink and also from the shock
of shelling out almost all of his wages without even realising. 'You're looking a bit rough,' I told him.

'Yeah, Pete,' he said. 'I just looked at this fucking bill
from last night and it was like £300.'

I stuck my hand in my pocket. I'd got £120, it was all the
money I had. 'Take this,' and I pushed it into his hand.

'Pete, no no no, it's mine.'

'Fuck off, it's out of the question, take it.' And the bill was
settled. It wasn't that I was being particularly generous, far
from it. Spally would have done the same if the boot had
been on the other foot, without thinking twice. He was a
good bloke, a kindred spirit.

Other work soon followed and the film that really changed
the game was *Distant Voices, Still Lives*. It was a BFI

production and the script I received from Terence Davies was unlike any I'd ever seen. It wasn't just the gritty, urbane and vividly realistic dialogue and setting that made it stand out; it was also the way it was constructed. Terry had written all of the shots and music into the script; he was obviously a man who thought visually, it was exciting to behold. I don't imagine any of us at that point were sufficiently familiar with his work to realise the strength of the piece. But, from the off, there was a feeling that we were creating a movie that would transcend other films.

One of Terry's great forces as a director was that his characters were drawn from his real life, he had a route map to their behaviour and the way they'd react in any given circumstance. Terry didn't write himself into *Distant Voices*, of course, it was about his parents and older brothers and sisters, but he identified with my performance of his father and at times was acerbic towards me, as though he were actually talking to his father. 'Terry, I'm not your dad,' I told him, during one shot. He didn't delineate between reality and drama, which made my life difficult but also made the film coruscatingly vivid.

Terry worked in a different way to most directors in that there were no rehearsals, no build-ups. In theatre, we'd have spent hours and hours rehearsing and refining our performances, but Terry just expected us to go. He wanted us to be there, enacting the real visions in his mind. I enjoyed that discipline, that intuitive approach; there was no frustration, I wanted to get it spot on. That's not to say I enjoyed filming; my character was a violent alcoholic and I'd not got anything to draw on to play that. I understood the Catholic environment and the working-class society, but my family was warm, loving and supportive; quite the opposite of what I was being asked to play.

There were times when I hated making it and I ran away

With Baldwin (left) and Gabriel Byrne (right) as Mr Kobayashi in Bryan
Singer's double Oscar-winning *The Usual Suspects*. (Corbis)

Steven Spielberg
described Pete as 'the
best actor in the world'
and persuaded him to
play Roland Tembo
in *The Lost World:
Jurassic Park* for which
he won a Saturn Award
nomination. (Corbis)

Filming high up in the sky as Ray, on Sam Miller's acclaimed debut, *Among Giants*.

Finally taking the role of lead man in Sam Miller's *Among Giants*, with Rachel Griffiths.

Relaxing back stage: Pete started smoking at the age of ten.

Below Officially opening The Old Smithy Village Shop, in Wistanstow, near Craven Arms in 2000. The event was followed by an Easter egg hunt in the church yard.

Below right Taking the floor in a local community hall, at Wistanstow, to address people from his beloved south Shropshire during a fund-raising evening for MENCAP.

As John McKeown in Paul Abbott's acclaimed TV film *Butterfly Collectors*, investigating a murder at a breakers yard. (Granada TV)

This portrayal as Deric Longen in 1999's TV film *Lost for Words* secured a BAFTA nomination for Best Actor.

Pete took inspiration from his own mother when he played alongside Thora Hird in *Lost For Words*. Thora met him for breakfast each morning.

'The luckiest man in Britain', with Italian actress Sophia Loren in the 2002 film *Between Strangers*.

Amid an incredible African landscape, that he later discussed with the
Queen upon receipt of his OBE. Pete flees with Ralph Fiennes in Fernando
Meirelles' *The Constant Gardener*. (Corbis)

With Dahila, played by Jennifer Connelly; Cecilia, played by Ariel Gade and
Mr Murray, played by John C. Reilly in a scene from *Dark Water*, the Walter
Salles film, in which Pete played Veeck.

Receiving an honorary fellowship from Liverpool John Moores University for his outstanding contribution to the dramatic arts in a ceremony at Liverpool's Anglican cathedral, 20 July 2005. The film star was one of the key players in the famous 1970s repertory company of the Everyman Theatre in Liverpool.

Shooting scenes for *Closing the Ring* with Jimmy Reilly, played by Martin McCann, and Grandma Reilly, played by Brenda Fricker.

Richard Attenborough shot gritty scenes for *Closing the Ring*, in which Pete played Michael Quinlan.

Pete on the set of *Closing the Ring*, which was filmed in north Belfast.

from the film when I saw it. My character, the father, was irredeemably bad, he was unlike anything and everything that I had ever known. I didn't identify with his terror, with his emotional imbalance or cruelty. There was a scene in which I had to hit his young daughter with a broom and Terry urged me to do it harder. He had a cage put round the camera so I could hit it with all my force. It would have killed a child and I didn't believe in it, but he was insistent. He was reliving scenes he had witnessed; it was very personal. Sometimes, during a break, he would come and sit on my knee for comfort.

Terry wanted a shift from gentle caring father who could tenderly groom a horse to a violent man who would beat his family. That trajectory, from peace to alcoholic violence, was extraordinary, but it meant that *Distant Voices* was exquisitely presented. The film dealt with neo-realist subjects in a completely different form, using music as well as images. I became friends with one of our production assistants, Olivia Stewart, who seemed to do everything from co-ordinating the work to managing the publicity to driving me from A to B. I'd escape the pressure by running off to the pub, and Olivia was forever driving around to find me. The set was sparse; there wasn't anywhere for the actors to sit, let alone trailers or caravans, so it seemed natural to find a watering hole where there'd be the company of strangers and a warm seat. I'd be sitting in the pub, pint in hand, quietly observing others, when Olivia would rush in: 'Where have you been?' she'd ask, as she put me into the back of the car. It was tiring work and on one occasion after she'd driven me home she looked as though she was on the brink of exhaustion. 'You'd better come in for a cup of coffee,' I told her, as her heavy eyelids fought manfully against a need to sleep. I disappeared to the kitchen and when I returned, steaming mug of coffee in hand, Olivia was flat out. She woke half an hour later, hugely apologetic. 'You looked like you needed that,' I said, as I looked up from my newspaper, sat opposite her. Her coffee was still on the arm of the chair.

After we'd finished the film, it took me a long time to get close to the work. I'd really pushed hard and I was worried, really worried, that my character was too despicable. I was afraid that I'd taken it too far. But my peers didn't seem to think I had; thankfully, their view was that I had played it well. It was *Distant Voices, Still Lives* which kind of put me into another league, so that people really started to notice me. The reviews were incredible and it's revered now as an iconic piece of cinema.

Distant Voices, Still Lives illustrated to me that the lines between film and theatre were just lines in the sand; there to be washed away. I love both forms equally. Effectively, actors need to tell lies; to offer convincing stories. The same process has to take place mentally and spiritually, irrespective of form. There are, however, physical differences between theatre and film. On stage, I feel more in control of what I do than in film, in which I'm at the mercy of directors, producers and editors, who choose which bits to use. On stage, it is down to me and the director.

Film and TV work was following me like gunshot on a firing range and I enjoyed working with Richard Eyre, the artistic director of the BBC drama *Tumbledown*. I played an officer in a parachute regiment. Richard is a great supporter of the rich tradition of British character actors who were often not seen as leading men because they didn't have dreamboat looks. I also played in *The Dressmaker*, with Joan Plowright, Billie Whitelaw, Jane Horrocks and Tim Ransom, based on the novel by Beryl Bainbridge and with music by George Fenton. We premiered it to raise money for the NSPCC. It had been set in wartime Liverpool and was a sumptuous love story about a girl falling in love with an American soldier. We all went along to the Odeon Cinema, in London Road; Beryl, Billy, Joan and Jane, as well as the Liverpudlian, John McGrath, who adapted the novel for the screen, and Jim O'Brien, the director.

Central signed me up for a major TV role, called *Tales of Sherwood Forest*; my first engagement as the leading man. After nineteen years treading the boards, it didn't come a moment too soon. I played Rick Hamilton, a middle-aged man and night owl with a dream of owning his own wine bar. He'd lost his job as a polytechnic lecturer and used his redundancy cash to realise his ambition, taking over a wine bar named Sherwood Forest. Jill Baker played my wife, Jill; David Troughton a zealous detective, and Robin Soans our resident pianist.

Rick's big dream was *Casablanca* and there were fantasy scenes from that movie, when the downtown Nottingham bar became Rick's Café Americaine and its clientele became the customers of the forties' film's famous watering hole. We filmed seven one-hour episodes for the playwright Alan Plater, who described it as 'a romantic, but not soppy, yarn'. Being transformed into Bogart was fun, I wore a wig and white tuxedo. I was a big fan of *Casablanca* and Bogart in particular, he and Lauren Bacall were among my screen idols. I read a lot about Bogart before we started and enjoyed the chance to portray him, even though it was in spoof. I obviously wasn't chosen for the part because of any physical resemblance, they sure didn't choose me as a Bogart looka-like. But I did practise the Bogart drawl. 'Here's looking at you, kid.'

I'd never carried the responsibility of a complete TV ser-ies before and it was a big challenge, to sustain a level of performance over six months. But I enjoyed every minute. It was the first time I'd been so involved; I worked with the producers to develop my character, it became a truly democratic piece. When it ended, I returned to the stage: from Bogart to Shakespeare, as I played in Derek Jacobi's *Richard II* as Mowbray.

TV and film kept me busy as *Distant Voices* opened the door to a new world. There were movies like Franco Zeffirelli's *Hamlet*, with Mel Gibson as the young Prince Hamlet, Glenn Close as the Queen, Alan Bates as King Claudius and a youthful Helena Bonham Carter as Ophelia. Then there was the *Alien 3*, with Sigourney Weaver and Charles S. Dutton. I played the shaven-headed inhabitant of a penal colony. The film was troubled from the start. It was a complicated production, with constant changes and huge pressure from the studios. From my point of view, we kept our heads down and waited and waited and played a lot of Scrabble and then did the job when we had to. It sure did go on for some time. But because there was a good gang of us there, it didn't seem to bother us. We just carried on and got on with it. In fact, about five months afterwards, they got some more money to do additional filming in LA. They called me up: 'Fly out to LA, and shave your head again.' I went and fetched my razor.

Split Second was more fun. We did that somewhere in London. I filmed it with the extraordinary Rutger Hauer, playing his aggressive policeman sidekick. Again, I don't know what drew me to it. I don't even think I saw the finished product, to be honest. *Waterland* came after that, with Jeremy Irons, Sinéad Cusack, Ethan Hawke and John Heard. It was a piece I had to play, I adored the beautiful novel by Graham Swift.

But though theatre was beginning to take a back seat, I still found time for great plays. I teamed up with Bill Paterson for *The Good Person of Szechwan*, at the National. I adored the complexity of Brecht and took to my script with a collection of coloured pencils, annotating the text and making notes to myself about the meaning of the play and the way in which I should approach it. 'What are you doing, Pete?' asked Bill, admiring the rainbow-coloured words on my script. He showed me his. 'Look, I've only scribbled a few notes in the margin.'

The Rise and Fall of Little Voice, a black comedy by Jim Cartwright, was another favourite, and I reunited with Jane Horrocks and my old Everyman friend, Alison 'Lofty' Steadman for a successful run at the National and Aldwych Theatres, directed by the talented and creative Sam Mendes.

We had quite a tough time putting it together. I'd wander into rehearsals and Alison would come over to me: 'Have you heard?' 'Heard what.' Then she'd tell me that they'd rewritten our lines … again. When we agreed to do the piece, we were all sent a script, but when we arrived it had been changed and, to be honest, it wasn't as good as the original. Jim Cartwright was rewriting all the time while we were rehearsing so we were learning on the hoof. I had a great relationship with Alison and our characters were quite intimate. We had to snog, at one point; then we were dancing together, lying on the couch and acting out some emotive scenes. We needed to be able to rely on one another, just as we had done at the Everyman and in *Muscle Market*.We had a great understanding and it gave us the confidence to really go for it. Alison had terrible trouble with one scene, when there was a dead blackout and we had to exit via a flight of stairs. For reasons that only Alison can know, she was petrified of blackouts. 'Don't worry, pet,' I told her, each night, as I lent her my arm. 'I'll grab you, I'll lead you off.' I took her arm and led her to safety. We started *The Rise and Fall of Little Voice* at the Cottesloe, at the National Theatre, and it went on for nine months. We picked up an Olivier Award, it ended up being terrific.

The TV work built like a small mountain, with parts in everything from *Lovejoy* and *Minder* to *Between the Lines* and *Casualty*. I started to feature more regularly in the media and people always seemed to ask me about my face. 'Who first said you look as though you've got a clavicle stuck in your mouth?' asked an interviewer. Yawn. Next question. There were times when I thought I ought to create a library of remarks about it. It was something that the boys and girls of the press were able to get their teeth into. My face had been called everything, from an unmade kingsize bed to Lord knows what. Much of it was nonsense and if there was a point it was probably this: when an audience saw emotions reflected in my eyes, they seemed to think: 'How can someone who looks like a rugby prop forward actually be sensitive?' There was a dichotomy that drew people in.

Directors seemed to cast me as villains, but I avoided many parts that were evil for evil's sake. As an actor, it was vital I found sympathy with my baddies, I couldn't have played them if I didn't have a real connection with them. That was why *Distant Voices, Still Lives* was so tough. If you don't connect with the character, you're on the road to superficiality and audiences always sniff out a phoney; they'll think, 'I don't believe he's inside that character.' I needed characters that I could inhabit, I needed to understand the reasons for their behaviour. Even though it was difficult, in *Distant Voices*, for instance, there was a reason why the father was like that. He'd been made redundant and suffered from terrible migraines. I could sympathise with that, even though the things he did were horrendous.

I always had to tune in with a character's psyche, then it didn't matter whether I said something or remained silent. I realised that film had an extraordinary ability to transmit purity of thought. If you're thinking nothing but the thoughts that are in the character's mind, then that's what the people in the cinema see. I learned to leave Pete Postlethwaite in the trailer. As a person, I tried to make sure I didn't get in the way; only then were the audiences gripped by what I was thinking.

SEVEN

Pete Couldn't Make It, Giuseppe Came Instead

∾

To many people, the Guildford Four and the Maguire Seven were names and numbers; but not to me. Long before *In the Name of the Father*, I'd viewed the Guildford Four as a family; a father and a son, an uncle and a nephew. I'd campaigned, like thousands of others, because there'd been a clear miscarriage of justice. Back in the seventies, detectives had been under pressure to make arrests, so they'd framed a bunch of innocents rather than going after the real bombers. When we campaigned, we just wanted questions answered. Long before the courts freed Gerry and his family, it was clear to me and many others that nefarious methods had been employed.

Giuseppe Conlon was an incredible man. When he was arrested, he had utter faith in the British justice system. Not a day went by when he wouldn't tell someone he and Gerry were innocent and nobody doubted him. When I heard in 1992 that they wanted to make *In the Name of the Father*, a film about freedom, justice and relationships, I wanted in.

Dan Day-Lewis had been cast as Gerry. We went back a long way, and the last time we had met professionally had been in the middle of a stream, on the set of the *Last of the Mohicans* in North Carolina, which I had filmed not long before. Our relationship was as strong as ever. We didn't need to talk regularly or see one another, there was a mutual understanding and we were intrinsically close. I'd played Captain Beams in the *Last of the Mohicans* and though most of my part had ended up on the cutting-room floor I'd enjoyed renewing acquaintance with Dan. It had been an interesting experience working with Michael Mann on that project, he was a guy with high artistic self-esteem, who wanted us to give ourselves totally to what we were doing.

The studios wanted a big name to play Giuseppe in *In the Name of the Father*. They were keen on Michael Caine or Sean Connery, and John Hurt was desperate to play him too. But I needed it more than any of them. As a simple story, the script was untouchable; it was the sort of grittily authentic piece that reflected both my political and creative passions. I also knew how good Dan would be in it; when he was at the Bristol Old Vic fifteen years earlier, he'd created extraordinary work and he'd got a real hunger for this. Dan had always had a very 'Method' approach and when he spoke to me about *In the Name of the Father* it was clear he was going about his latest role in a similar way, he was going to be exceptional. He spoke to the film-maker, Jim Sheridan, about me. Jim was wondering aloud who to cast as Giuseppe and Dan said: 'I know who it is, I know who my father is. It's Pete.' It all stemmed from there.

Jim asked me to meet him, briefly, and we talked before agreeing to get together the following week to put something on film. I re-read the book on the Guildford Four and felt like I had an implicit understanding of Giuseppe, he could almost have been my own dad; the cultural similarities were extraordinary. Initially, Jim was unconvinced and his main concern was that I wasn't ready to portray the declining, unwell Giuseppe because I looked so young and typically worked on a great deal of energy. But I knew it would work and that my characterisation of Giuseppe would be instinctive. I was sure I could do 'poise and quiet grace' just as well as 'thunderball'.

A week later, I went to meet Jim at the Grosvenor House Hotel, in London. I was staying in Peckham, in Friary Road, and on the way there I stopped at the local Oxfam shop and bought an outfit that Giuseppe might have worn. I'd spent the week working on my accent and when I arrived at the Grosvenor, I went to the desk dressed in my seventies' suit, kipper-collared shirt, tie and shoes from the charity shop. 'Giuseppe Conlon, here to see Jim Sheridan,' I said, in an accent so thickly Northern Irish that you could have drunk it.

The concierge checked his list and looked up at me, puzzled, wondering what an out-of-date Irishman was doing amid the china cups and oil paintings at the Grosvenor. 'You're not on the list,' he said, apologetically, hoping I'd take my out-of-place face to the local soup kitchen, instead.

'I'm Giuseppe Conlon,' I said, entirely in character, accent perfectly in place. 'Listen, my friend,' I said, my confidence growing by the second, and I leant in to speak. 'You might not have my name on your list, but you'll have the name Pete Postlethwaite on it. Check again, then call Jim and tell him Pete couldn't make it, so Giuseppe came instead.'

The concierge checked, found Pete's name and made the call. Jim told him to send me up. 'Um, yes, sir, thank you, sir, he'll see you now,' he stammered, and I was shown to the lift.

Jim was a little shocked when I went in in character, he imagined that at some point I'd break off and talk to him as myself, Pete the actor. But I kept up the performance for three and a half hours, during which time Jim realised I was Giuseppe. My approach wasn't entirely for Jim's benefit. If I was going to play the part, I had to test myself, to be sure I could do it justice; there was no greater test than playing it to the guy who was putting the film on screen. I'd stayed in character throughout, even on the way to the hotel and when I came out. I couldn't have cheated on it. The people in the film were living; certainly, members of the family were, and to serve the work I had to give 100 per cent. My preparation was good and the work on Giuseppe's walk and movements paid dividends. It was a mark of how much I wanted the role, and Jim told me it was mine. In many ways, that was a turning point in my life, a big turning point, there's no doubt about it. It was all circumstance and happenstance. If Dan hadn't said I was his father, then ... But he did.

When I read the script it leapt out at me. Sometimes, very, very rarely, I get a script that grabs me from page one, and this was one. Jim had created a role that I just had to do, no question. I just put flesh on the bones, the real truth was in the writing. My portrayal of Giuseppe had to be of an innocent character, whom the audience would grieve for. His only 'crime' was to have been implicated by his son's 'confession', which had been beaten out of Gerry by desperate police. My Giuseppe would have to be searing, compulsive and sincere.

Jim took a very measured approach to the film. He wanted it to be a drama, not documentary, and he was determined that he'd start the film with the bombing; that was quite deliberate. Of course, the bombing didn't start the whole series of events, but it was the right way to start our work. That flash of light didn't illuminate anything, it just killed the five people who were the original victims. We all felt we had a responsibility to all of the victims, not just the Guildford Four but the people who'd suffered from the off. By starting that way, we were reminding people of the gravity of our work and also announcing ourselves as being strictly anti-violence.

Jim spoke about the film as 'faction'. He set out to make a healing film, not a whingeing one about how badly the Irish had been treated. From the get-go, it was clear it would hit a raw nerve in England, people would be uneasy that one of the victims, Giuseppe, died in prison when the police, when in my opinion the judiciary and some politicians must have suspected from the start that they'd been innocent. But the main point of the film was not to put the police on trial or, indeed, British justice. The agenda was to take that complicated story out of the context of a quarter-century struggle and to show that there was still hope. Beyond that, I loved the relationship between Giuseppe and Gerry. I wanted to take the kernel of it and dramatise it, I didn't want to change it. Giuseppe's dying words to Gerry were 'Clear my name'. There was an unbelievably close bond between them. It wasn't that long since my father had died and we'd also had an ineffably close relationship; Bill Postlethwaite had been my hero and he was exactly like Giuseppe. Like many Northern men, my father and I had never discussed our feelings, as such, but I always felt as though he were with me; I always knew that he would be there for me. Bill was very Catholic, very simple; one of those naturally straightforward, honest, unsung heroes. Both men knew exactly what was right and what was wrong. My dad would have behaved in the same way as Giuseppe did, if he'd found himself in those circumstances. They were both morally courageous, they'd breathed the same air. I'd always believed that there was something very spiritual about the men you found in hard, working-class areas, whether north or south, irrespective of religion or creed. I'd always considered them to have great integrity and spirituality. From a personal point of view, it was a chance to do something for my dad. To me, it felt like In the Name of My Father, as much as anything.

Jim wanted to do a story about a good father because there weren't any in Irish literature. 'Joyce had to create a Jewish father, Leopold Bloom, because he couldn't find within his own people qualities he admired and respected,' he said. My aim had been to find someone who appeared fragile but had inner steel. By the end, Giuseppe had made his son confront his own emotions. Giuseppe helped Gerry break the cycle of victimisation, he showed him that it was okay to admit his father had been a good man.

As the work started, Dan and I disappeared into our parts. We spent all day in character and were addressed by the cast as Gerry and Giuseppe. Dan used to describe himself as an impostor, a professional lie teller. He'd say there wasn't much difference between film and theatre, between Hollywood and England, it was all the same. He summed it up with an expression I loved: 'As soon as I hear the director shout "Action!" a voice in my head shouts "Lie!"' Without wishing to descend into actor-speak, his point was that if you tell that lie well enough, you'll get through to another kind of reality, which is even closer to the truth. We had an interesting dialogue about the work. Dan and I both thought the Method was consistently misrepresented, that it isn't about building up muscle, being locked in a cell or going on pub crawls. It is largely an interior process by which one uses one's imagination and personal experience to relate, moment by moment, an absolute understanding of the life you've chosen to take on. What that does if it works – and it doesn't always – is to free you to be spontaneous.

Dan and I both immersed ourselves in the research and we were enormously fortunate that Gerry Conlon and his mother, Sarah, were so accommodating. Sarah made available to me all of the prison letters between her and Giuseppe. He had written twice a week between December 1974 and

December 1979, with Sarah replying to every letter, so there were one thousand or more letters. I also spent a lot of time with her and with Gerry's sister, Ann, getting to know the character, his movements and his idiosyncrasies. Sarah and Ann told me the pace that he'd walk at, how he'd lean over a balcony; every little detail. Gerry was also helpful, he realised how sensitive we were to what we were doing. We knew that we had to get it right and make that transformation.

Jim wanted Gerry to have a Gandhi-type father; he wanted power backed up by gentleness, someone who could be tough but also had something of the poet about him. I threw myself into the work; but for me, the whole point was this: playing Giuseppe didn't feel like acting, it was something I needed to fulfil. I spent long hours perfecting a west Belfast accent during pub crawls with Dan. We'd go out as father and son, as Giuseppe and Gerry. Sometimes, we'd spend the whole evening not saying anything, just drinking, as Dan built up the idea early in the film of Gerry's resentment. We worked hard on our characters; Dan was eating prison food, losing more than two stones and was locked in his cell on set for three days while a group of very, very unpleasant guys threw cold water at him and stopped him from sleeping. He also spent months hanging out with Gerry in London.

Dan and I were interested in observation, most of all, rather than socialising. To us, the entire period of time working on a film had to be continuous, we didn't switch on in the morning and switch off at night. It was almost as if one day, coincidentally, a camera was put in front of us; that's what we tried to achieve. We stayed like that for ten weeks or so.

The film was shot on location in Dublin and Liverpool and at Kilmainham Gaol, Dublin, and Ardmore Studios in Ireland. I spent three and a half summer months on the set in Monkstown, which I'd known since the later sixties, when I was courting a girl from Banbridge, in Co. Down. I took a horse-drawn caravan holiday there. We had no idea about the Troubles at that stage, although I do remember being chased down the streets of Newry because a bunch of us were singing 'Kevin Barry'. We had no idea why – we just thought of it as a traditional song.

Whenever the opportunity arose, I organised for my family to come and spend time with me. That was my idea of the perfect world. But there were occasions when that was simply not possible and I had to remain in character and work. At those times, I was selfish to the work; I detached myself from my ordinary reality and immersed myself in my character. I wouldn't seek anyone's sympathy for having to do that, nor would I describe it as being tough. It was what I did; actors have to act, sometimes they're lucky enough to do that while their family is with them, on other occasions they have to do it alone.

There was light to match the shade on the shoot. Emma Thompson was also there. She is an exquisite actress and was very much part of our gang. I still have a postcard from her, stored away in my attic somewhere. We knew within two weeks of filming something special was happening. The chemistry was perfect. Of course, Gerry and Jim argued when we were shooting. Gerry was frustrated that the film's time constraints prevented certain issues from being explored. 'The movie doesn't really show the loneliness and despair of solitary confinement,' he said. But he understood that Jim had a job to do, too. They both wanted the film to be as good as it could be.

Once we'd finished the work, there was a preview at Universal Studios, in Hollywood. Jim showed a version which didn't have the bombing at the very beginning and the response was telling; there were lots of laughs in the first few scenes as Gerry was making out like some seventies hepcat. The executives thought it was great and for the first thirty minutes, the whole audience fell about laughing. The next night, Jim showed it with the bombing first and the audience didn't laugh once after that. At that point, we knew in no uncertain terms that the film would be a bigger hit commercially without the bombing at the start. So what did Jim do? He stuck to his principles and left it in. He wasn't going to compromise for the promise of a better box office.

From day one, I had felt a burden of responsibility towards the Conlons. Their reaction was all-important to me, and there was a delicate line for us to tread in terms of respecting their wishes and ensuring the impact of our drama. 'I want Sarah to be happy,' I told Gerry, before we went into production. When we went into pre-production the family had the chance to hear our accents; we knew we had to nail those. Gerry and the family didn't come onto the set, I think that would have been too tough for all of us, but he watched the rushes and told Jim whenever he thought we could improve. There were times when it became too much. He got up and left a couple of times, because it was too real, and it also caused him to suffer flashbacks. I'd learned that his father had a perpetual cough, anything would set it off, even being outside in the breeze. He always had his hankie, and those were some of the small details that I refined. He also had an unwavering defiance, even when he was critically ill, and he maintained his innocence at every opportunity. 'That was my dad,' said Gerry, after watching the rushes. I think the family respected our methods. Later Gerry said that seeing the film had been cathartic and had helped him, his mother and his two sisters heal from the nightmare of fifteen years wrongful imprisonment. They became closer as a family. Gerry told me once: 'My family feels like the film is an exorcism of my father's ghost. When he was dying he made me promise that I would do everything possible to clear his name. To a certain extent I think I've done that and my father's ghost is saying, "Okay, go on, have a life."'

When the film hit, the response was electrifying. But we were right about the film being controversial and one incident hit me harder than any other. While we were shooting, the IRA attacked Warrington. The first attack created a fireball at a gas plant and a police officer was shot when he tried to make an arrest. The second attack killed two children on Bridge Street and injured many more. A lot of people from my home town were asking what I was doing working on that film. They thought that, while the IRA was attacking Warrington, I was off on some jolly in Northern Ireland, making a film that glorified terrorism. Even my brother, Mike, was attacked. 'What's your Pete doing over there making that?' Dan and Emma Thompson and I were all criticised for that. But the film wasn't about the IRA at all, it was about a miscarriage of justice and about the issues and relationships that surrounded it. As a proud Englishman, I was appalled that British justice had been miscarried. I wanted a better society, not just for myself, but for my fellow people.

I also got criticised for playing Giuseppe not as he was. I didn't mind that, I'd been taught Giuseppe by his wife, Sarah Conlon, and in a way I knew him from my own dad. But no matter what we did, we were going to be criticised. Our intention was simply that people went to see the film and then asked questions; the facts of the case were in the books. We didn't try to hoodwink people and the biggest compliment to me was that Sarah was happy with my portrayal of Giuseppe. I know she didn't feel short-changed at all.

The premiere was in Dublin on 16 December 1993, a day after the Downing Street Declaration was issued by Prime Minister John Major and the Taoiseach Albert

Reynolds. It was a Thursday just before Christmas in Dublin, at the Savoy Cinema, and we held it in aid of Very Special Arts. Outside, a group of protestors stood with banners saying 'Free the Ballymurphy Seven'. At the end of the screening, Jim Sheridan went to the front of the cinema and called out a litany of names. As he called them, they emerged from the audience and took their places alongside him, shifting from being members of the audience to being on show. First the producers, then Daniel Day-Lewis, Emma Thompson, myself, Bono, Sinéad O'Connor, made our way, one by one, to face the audience at the front. But it wasn't a display of Hollywood in Dublin. The borders of fiction and reality became blurred as others were called. A nun who had campaigned for the Guildford Four was called, then Paul Hill, Paddy Armstrong, Gerard Conlon, Sarah ... Each actor seemed to have been matched by their real-life counterpart, except for me, of course. Giuseppe had died in prison. There could have been no more powerful statement than his absence among us.

The premiere was an emotional night and I remember coming out of the cinema and going with Gerry over to a quiet corner just before we went to Dublin Castle for the after party. I was asking Gerry, again, whether I'd done a good job.

'My father would have been proud.'

Sarah came over and shook my hand.

Gerry couldn't believe the way things had turned out. 'I suppose something good comes out of everything, no matter how bad you might think things are,' he told me. He and Paul, two kids from the wasteland of Belfast, couldn't believe what had happened to their lives. He'd had a film made about his life and Paul ended up living in New York, married to Courtenay Kennedy. Gerry found it hard watching

Dan play him on the screen, but he found it even harder watching me. 'That was rough because you look like my father so much that it broke my heart,' he said. 'The film played down a lot of the brutality, it wasn't nearly as violent as the real thing. I still wake up at nights, screaming, soaked in sweat, back in the middle of it all.'

Gerry and his sister, Ann, came to London for part of the publicity work. It was symptomatic of the way Gerry's life had changed. He was forever buzzing around different countries, meeting different people, campaigning for other innocent prisoners. Fifteen years of his life had been stolen from him and he was making up for lost time.

I was straight back to work afterwards, but the buzz started to grow and there were indications we were going to be nominated for Oscars. I heard the news when I was in Wells playing one of the toughest roles I'd ever accepted, a character called Mitch who plunged the depths of human despair in a blistering TV drama called *Sin Bin*. On screen, I had to give an excoriating performance, but off set I was being carried by angel wings on a flight of inexplicable happiness, as news of my nomination filtered through. When the word came from Los Angeles that I'd been nominated I was on a high, I started screaming along with the agents. It was quite extraordinary to be nominated for my first major film role and I was delighted with the news. It wasn't a total surprise, as there'd been a lot of talk, but I hadn't thought about it too much until it happened.

We'd been nominated for Best Picture; Best Director – Jim Sheridan; Best Actor – Daniel Day-Lewis; Best Supporting Actress – Emma Thompson; and Best Film Editing – Gerry Hambling. I was nominated for Best Supporting Actor alongside the iron-jawed Tommy Lee Jones in *The Fugitive*; the chameleon-like assassin John Malkovich in *In the Line of Fire*; the Nazi commandant Ralph Fiennes in *Schindler's*

List; and the then-newcomer and troubled teen Leonardo DiCaprio in *What's Eating Gilbert Grape*. The papers back home in Warrington phoned up Mike, and got a quote from him saying how much I held Warrington in my affections and that I still visited regularly. He made me sound very glamorous, telling the reporter that my work had taken me around the world, from Russia to the Caribbean: 'And just before Christmas, he was jet-setting backwards and forwards between Los Angeles and New York, but he still finds time to visit his family at home in Warrington, he really loves the town.' It was amusing, seeing myself in the local newspaper again They seemed to be writing about the person I used to be, rather than the person I'd become: 'Mr Postlethwaite, formerly of Gorsey Lane, Orford ...' I'd come a long way.

There were the inevitable detractors. The *Daily Express* wrote that the IRA was 'going to take the glory at Oscars ceremony'. I guess comics are designed to make people laugh, and that one did.

My birthday was around the same time as the Oscars and we were inundated with cards celebrating both my birthday and the nomination. I celebrated by taking Jax to the UCI Cinema, in Telford, to see the film there. I'd seen the film over and over again, but a lot of my friends hadn't. They'd lived through the making of it and now it was nice for them to see the final product.

I received a letter from the Academy of Motion Pictures Arts and Sciences saying that I'd been accepted as a member. Universal International Pictures organised a round of media, which coincided with the day before the film's general release in the UK. On 10 February, a car was dispatched to collect me from my home at 8.30 a.m. and drive me to BBC Pebble Mill, in Birmingham, for 10 a.m. I was to be interviewed on *Good Morning*, with Anne & Nick ('Are you pleased?' 'Very, it's very nice. I'm honoured because it comes from my peers.') between 10.30 a.m. and 12.15 p.m. and then driven to the Midland Hotel, in New Street, for lunch and a round of interviews. During the afternoon, packed tightly into a two-hour schedule, there were interviews with newspaper and radio. On the back of my UIP schedule I wrote a 'note to self', reminding myself why I was there and what I was doing. It read, simply: 'On his day, he is believed.' Then, beneath, I added a tribute to the people who had inspired my performance: 'In the Name of the Fathers – Bill Postlethwaite, Peter Sheridan, Giuseppe Conlon and the woman behind and in front of them – Mary.'

The promotional tour in the USA was equally intense and on one day alone I did fifty-one TV interviews. It was exhausting. Making the film had a major impact on me. It was one of those experiences in which form and content came together to fulfil the different sides of my nature. It was a life-changing experience. I'd gone along for a while on the same plateau and then along came something that caused me to jump up onto a different level. The irony of my nomination wasn't lost on me, either. I'd played baddies all my life then got an Oscar nomination for playing a man without a bad bone in his body and who thought the same way as my father: love God, keep the family together.

There were ceremonies to attend and I went to the Golden Globes in a white tuxedo. I was the only member of the audience not in black and I mingled well that night – with the waiters. When I got the Oscar nomination, I had a telegram from a friend which read: 'Congratulations. Now burn the white tux.'

Amid the many letters and congratulations cards was one from Antony Sher, with whom I'd shared the stage on many occasions, dating back to the Everyman and the RSC. He was typically generous. His letter touched me enormously because, though we hadn't seen each other for a while, it reminded me how strong the bonds between those of us who had been at the Everyman were. It felt like family – we could all share in each other's excitements. It was as though we'd never been apart. I also got a card from Michael Mann. And the nomination heralded the start of my relationship with Steven Spielberg, who wrote to say once he'd seen *In the Name of the Father* he knew that at some point or other he was going to work with me.

Jax and I flew from London Heathrow to LAX in style, with American Airlines sending us first-class seats. We went to the ceremony, but they locked me out at first because they didn't recognise me. I don't know why. A Northerner who looks like a pugilist, surely I wasn't that hard to spot? But I wasn't the only one. My fellow nominee Ralph Fiennes also failed security's 'instant recognition' test, and he was refused admission too, at first. It was quite funny because Ralph and I knew that our awards were fourth on, so they would be happening soon. But the security guys had no idea who we were and they wouldn't let us in. I was going mad because we were getting nowhere. Then Gregory Peck walked by. I recognised him instantly, and he recognised me from the film.

'Hi, Pete, what's happening?'

After I explained, Gregory had a word with the people on the door and they pulled the 'fillers' – the people hired to sit in empty seats – out of our seats and let us in. It would have been wonderful if we hadn't got in because when it came to our categories in the awards, instead of focusing on me and Ralph, the cameras would have been showing some guys from Trenton, New Jersey, or wherever. We entered through Door 12 of the Los Angeles County Music Center's Dorothy Chandler Pavilion, and sat in our $200 chairs in Row C.

I was in seat 40 and we were long after the 5.30 p.m. start time.

The whole event was a gas, it was just outlandish excess. I didn't care whether I won or not, although I thought it went to the wrong person that year – Tommy Lee Jones for *The Fugitive*. He'd done better performances and was nowhere near as good as Leonardo DiCaprio, who was fantastic in *What's Eating Gilbert Grape*. We'd been invited to the Board of Governors Ball at 9 p.m., a $500-a-head event, at the Los Angeles County Music Center Plaza. It was all madness, a beautiful kind of madness.

We stayed at the Chateau Marmont and bumped into everyone. It was amusing to see Sandy Johnson, the director of *Coast to Coast*, who'd been there when Jax and I first met. He was photographing the front of the hotel for *Film Stars Don't Die in Liverpool*. Helen Mirren was throwing a party in the garden of her cottage, which was for lots of Brits. But we skipped that and went someplace else. We had to work too, while we were there. We had to dub *In the Name of the Father* to clean up the language, so that it could be shown on aeroplanes. But essentially it was a week of partying. They say a party's no good if you can remember too much about it, well, happily I can't. But I know we had the time of our lives.

Later, there were other events and we won the Golden Bear Grand Prix Award at the 1994 Berlin Film Festival. The film was shown at festivals around the world, including Italy's Premio Internazionale Cinema e Narrativa, in Agrigento. I won the Italian version of an Oscar for my portrayal and Gerry's book won the prize for literature. We were in Sicily for the awards ceremony, which was held in a beautiful amphitheatre. Gerry and I enjoyed one another's company. 'Playing your father was a privilege and an honour,' I told Gerry. On the foot of one of the schedules, Gerry wrote me a note: 'To Pete, the greatest, a true friend who not only shows love but gives love. Gerry Conlon.'

From that moment on, my life was changed forever. If you get an Oscar nomination people start to say your name, even if they can't spell it. Suddenly, the work I was offered broadened and I got more recognition, people started to wonder why they hadn't heard of me before. I didn't get too excited, I just felt fortunate that I'd never been out of work. People were saying I was a late developer, but the truth was I'd been developing for thirty years. I'd never been conscious of a career plan or analysed my success and it made me a little paranoid that everybody was talking about me. Whatever came following my role, I always tried to give credit to Giuseppe. For years after, when I was in Belfast, I would call and see Sarah.

People identified with my portrayal because everybody has a father. Not long after, a man in New York stopped me in the street, late at night. I could hear heavy footsteps following behind and I turned, ready to surrender my wallet. The guy said, 'Weren't you in *In the Name of the Father*? I hadn't spoken to my dad for thirty years – after I saw that film, I got straight on the phone.' That, along with Sarah's approval, was the biggest compliment of all.

The over-riding point of *In the Name of the Father* was this: when we played Gerry and Giuseppe Conlon, we knew we had a big responsibility; if you take on the life of somebody that is either still living or somebody that has passed away but lives on in the memory of his family, it's almost terrifying. The Conlon family was very, very generous with their time in helping us to achieve a likeness. The very least you can do is to use all of the material available to get as close to their experience of life as is possible.

EIGHT

Shooting the Breeze

❧

The Oscar nomination changed my life; in an instant the Americans decided I was big news. I was buried beneath a mountain of scripts. Flattered as I was by the interest and opportunity, I didn't want to turn my back on Britain and jet off to the States just then, and besides, I was shooting a major British drama at the time.

Sin Bin was a Screen Two production with George Costigan and Kathy Burke, part of a new series of heavyweight productions on BBC 2. It was a penetrating piece by Catherine Johnson. My character, Mitch, was a nurse in a mental health unit who'd seen a colleague batter one of his patients to death. The big difference between Mitch and his colleagues was that Mitch respected the humanity of his patients, whatever difficulties they may have had. There was a terrific subplot too, involving me and Kathy; it was based on a putative friendship that Mitch formed with a patient, Debbie, which had disastrous consequences. Conflicting loyalties was the central theme of the drama and my character had to decide whether to blow the whistle on his colleagues or turn a blind eye. As dark forces raged against him, Mitch was pitched into a battle with the fast-closing ranks of the nursing fraternity. The location for the piece was perfect; we filmed in a disused psychiatric hospital in Wells, a fitting venue for such a dark drama. By the time we stopped work late each evening, we were all drained; it was the sort of drama that wasn't easy to turn off from.

Mitch was a real gift; he knew that family, union and community stuck together when the chips were down. He reminded me of my experiences at the approved school for boys, all those years earlier. I'd been in almost exactly the same situation, witnessing a teacher beat up one of the pupils and then being told to keep my mouth shut. When I'd refused to be complicit in their deceit, 60 per cent of my colleagues had changed their attitude towards me. That experience helped me to fall easily into the role because I empathised with Mitch, I understood his dilemma. The very nature of working in such an intense environment had brutalised and dehumanised his colleagues, which is why they'd closed ranks; but that was a reason – not a justification – for their behaviour. Mitch had been hardened by his work too, but he'd rediscovered his moral compass before it was too late. Mitch was no avenging hero, he simply saw people as humans; an attitude which led him inexorably to the edge of his own sanity. He became terribly mixed up and I found it an exhausting role to play.

It wasn't all grim, however, and there was a lot of humour and light, particularly at the end; but by then we'd dived deep within ourselves and I imagined the audiences feeling as though they'd received a body blow after watching it. It's hard to imagine now, looking back at such an abrasive piece, that the shoot had been punctuated by moments of intense personal happiness as the Oscar nomination began to have its effect.

Sin Bin wasn't the only production that I was already involved in. By the end of that shoot, I'd already started work on two other pieces and was commuting between the set of *Sin Bin* in Wells to Nice, where I was filming the psychological thriller *Suite 16*, and to Norwich, where I was playing Montague Tigg in BBC's *Martin Chuzzlewit*. *Martin Chuzzlewit* was a wonderful nostalgia piece, which David Lodge had adapted from the novel by Charles Dickens. It juxtaposed vanity, greed, selfishness, treachery and murder – yet its mode was light-hearted comedy. My character was a wonderful comic creation and I played it for all that I was worth. It was a talented cast, with Keith Allen, David Bradley, Paul Scofield, John Mills, Julian Fellowes, Tom Wilkinson and Philip Franks, and our adaptation was a Dickensian pastiche that should have been called Three Weddings and a Suicide.

It was a long way from Norwich to Nice but I frequently made the journey to film *Suite 16* with director Dominique Deruddere. It had a minuscule cast and was set largely in the suite of a ritzy hotel in Nice. It intentionally presented itself as a piece of theatre that just happened to have strayed onto the screen. The script had been written by Charlie Higson and Lise Mayer and was a dark intellectual puzzle about the power games played by the two leading characters; a rich paraplegic and a penniless gigolo. The discipline of playing a paraplegic was tough because I couldn't fall back on the normal ingrained tricks that I frequently relied on. I couldn't use body language and gestures, for instance, which were usually instinctive. It was like somebody had told me I'd only got so many colours to paint with; we were ciphers in an extraordinary ritual haiku. One of the things I enjoyed most about *Suite 16* was that it took me close to an authentic theatrical experience.

It wasn't all flying off to glamorous locations. Pretty soon

I found myself bound for Kiev where I was due to brave sub-zero temperatures alongside Sean Bean. We were being reunited for *Sharpe*, when I played against him as the evil Sergeant Hakeswill. Sean and I played characters that both bore grudges; Hakeswill had Sharpe flogged for something he didn't do, so there was no love lost between them. Both were brought up in the gutter and both were determined to make a name for themselves, the only difference was that Sharpe used his talents for good purposes while Hakeswill used his for bad. *Sharpe* was a rollicking, action-packed drama and I shaved my head and got blackened teeth to make me look really mean. The make-up was brilliant. I hadn't realised quite how good it was until Jax and Will walked right past me during one rehearsal: they didn't recognise me. Will was only five, so it was the first time he'd taken any proper notice of what was going on during the filming. He didn't even give me a second glance. When I'd left home to film, I'd got plenty of hair and clean teeth; but when he saw me again I'd got a shaved head and looked revolting. I spent four months filming in the Ukraine and the weather played havoc; it varied from minus thirty degrees to minus eighteen.

Sean is a fascinating man, he has huge charisma and is a great mate. I think of him as having a rock-star quality. He will soak up everything that happens, his eyes like pools; he's watching and learning all the time. I felt incredibly well supported when I played opposite him, as though it were safe to push things a little further, as though he'd come along with me if I wanted us to take a risk. I'd wind him up something rotten during some of the scenes. I'm not sure why, but I could just make him laugh. We'd be in the middle of a shoot and I'd look at him with a dead straight face, but there'd be a twinkle in my eye. 'Pete, stop fukin' mekin' me laff,' he'd say, as he exploded for the nth time. He'd be collapsing with laughter. Sean found me unpredictable, I'm pretty sure of that, but I found him equally supportive and great fun. We were like two blokes that you'd meet in the snooker room of a working men's club, who just so happened to be making TV programmes together.

Eventually, my character was shot, but I think Sean and the directors felt they'd made a mistake. 'We never should have shot you,' Sean said. 'You were Sharpe's best baddie.' For a while afterwards, he talked to the producers and directors to see whether he could persuade them to revive my character by pretending I'd somehow escaped the firing squad, but I was already onto the next project.

∾

Scripts were arriving like a river in flood and I was reading fifteen a month. One stood out. *The Usual Suspects* had the most original, complex and dazzlingly intelligent story that I'd ever seen. Bryan Singer sent me the script and I phoned him back straight away: 'Bloody hell, Bryan, I don't know what the fuck's going on, but it's brilliant.' My policy has always been simple: if the script is good, then you go, that's the next thing to do, you pack your case, you get on the plane and you do the work. All scripts have different selection criteria, but having recently done something as heavy as *In the Name of the Father*, I suppose subconsciously I was looking for a different challenge.

Bryan arranged a meeting and asked: 'Well, Pete, what do you want to play? They're all Keyser Söze.' He gave me the choice. The character I eventually took, Mr Kobayashi, was just another dead fish in a shoal of red herrings. I liked Bryan Singer a lot; he was confident, a real smart cookie. He wanted to make a film completely unlike any that had ever been seen. He loved stories and entertaining people and wanted individual viewers to return again and again to the film, so that they could figure things out. 'I want them to be addicted,' he told me. 'I want to get the plot to unfold in such a way that the viewer will want to come back again after. I want the audience to be able to answer all the questions, if they look hard enough; I want them to be hooked.'

Bryan came to me after watching *In the Name of the Father* because he thought I'd bring a unique physical presence to the film. He was very enthusiastic and we got along well. My character had originally been written for a Japanese guy, but then Bryan realised he wanted to work with me instead. He had this idea that casting was all an illusion, that the way to put a film together wasn't to take the actor to the role; it was also to move the role towards the actor, until the two met in the middle. I think I was part of Bryan's original financing package, along with Kevin Spacey, Chazz Palminteri, Gabriel Byrne and Stephen Baldwin. We were a pretty good line-up and I wasn't the only one with recent Oscar form: Chazz Palminteri had also been nominated for Woody Allen's *Bullets Over Broadway*, so the studios were pleased with the calibre of our mini-company.

Bryan was planning a seven-week shoot and happily I was only needed for half of it. Somehow I managed to cram it into a schedule that was packed tighter than a Mumbai commuter train: 'If they get this half right, we will be onto something.' As far as I was concerned Bryan was only half of the attraction; the writer, Chris McQuarrie, had an equally formidable talent. Chris was from New Jersey and had worked in a detective agency before switching to screenwriting. He'd created the most articulate, tightly packed script imaginable; he'd rewritten it endlessly until every strand connected. He had given the film a demonic theme and at the front of our scripts they'd written an extract from the Rolling Stones' 'Sympathy for the Devil'.

When I arrived in LA, we arranged to go out for a night on the town. I'd been booked into the Chateau Marmont and the following day I was due to film my first scenes. A group of us ended up going out; myself, Stephen Baldwin, Benicio del Toro, Bryan Singer, Chris McQuarrie and Robert Jones, who was the executive producer on the movie. Nights out with Stephen tended to get out of hand and ours was no exception. There came a certain point in the evening when Robert told Chris: 'You need to watch Pete; we need him on set tomorrow. I want you to keep an eye on him.' I'd been feasting on beer like a whale downing plankton. So Chris and I sat and talked; we pulled up some stools and chewed the fat, we were on Sunset Boulevard at the House of Blues. We had a very pleasant, cordial conversation and we kept ordering drinks; it was drink after drink after drink. At one point, Chris stood up and turned around and that was it, I was gone. I'd seen some other people I wanted to talk to, so I upped and went.

The next morning, at 7 a.m., I was in the make-up trailer, as fresh as a daisy, when Chris walked in looking panic-stricken. 'Pete, where did you go? I've been in an absolute fear.' Nobody had seen me leave and Chris had thought he'd take the rap if anything went wrong. He'd apparently walked up and down Sunset Boulevard, all the way to the Chateau Marmont, at 2 a.m. or 3 a.m., looking for me. Eventually, he'd gone home and called my room: nothing. Then he'd fallen asleep, exhausted, before arriving, looking frightened out of his mind, a few hours later. 'There was no way you could even have got two hours' sleep,' he told me. 'I was about to confess that I'd lost you, and here you are, all smiles.' I just laughed. I'd met a group of people and gone for a quiet drink with them; then I got up and worked a fourteen-hour day.

Throughout the filming, the actors repeatedly tried to

change Chris's script. Even Bryan had wanted to change the name of my character. 'Why?' said Chris. 'Well, Pete's got a Japanese name but he's a Brit.' Chris defended it all. He said: 'Think about it in terms of the script; why should we? Instead of changing his name, let's just see what Pete does with it.' I was fascinated by what I could bring to the piece, the opportunities seemed unlimited.

All that Bryan really cared about was that we delivered specific information at specific times in the film, the rest was down to us. It was the same for me, for Kevin Spacey, for Benicio, for us all. Some of the lines needed to be delivered exactly as they were in the script, so that the story made sense, but others were more or less just a guideline. That gave us a lot of latitude and Stephen Baldwin rewrote all of his own dialogue, to make it sound more like something he might say, though he never lost the meaning. Benicio understood very early on that his character's job was to die first, he didn't have a single line of important dialogue in the whole movie so it didn't matter if people understood him or not. My character was a Brit with a Japanese name, but instead of trying to wrestle with that, I decided to create the character who would have those characteristics. On my first day, which I think was also Benicio's first, I went in and delivered my dialogue with a Pakistani-influenced accent. Bryan had no idea I was going to do that. Benicio also had a pretty strong accent and once we'd delivered our lines, Bryan came up to us both, separately, and asked whether we were going to talk that way for the whole movie. 'Yes, unless you want us to do something different,' was the response we gave him. Bryan said: 'No, I'm cool with that. I just wanted to know that that's what you will do.'

My sinister portrayal of Kobayashi grew from there. Part of the magic and the fun was to keep that Japanese name and play it with this strange, Asian accent. It became the one part of the movie where the lies of the film and the reality of the film intersected. The character just emerged, we didn't discuss it or over-think it; it was just a way of adding something really interesting and giving the film an extra layer. We worked really hard and days that went on for sixteen or eighteen hours were not unusual.

When we were on set, I was a stalwart defender of the writing. Whenever you have an ensemble of actors, everybody wants to bring their own thing to it and often I found I had to stick up for Chris's script to prevent it from being butchered. There was a scene where Kevin Pollack had to pull a gun and everybody started to question what was going on. There was also a briefcase in the room: 'What if there's a bomb in the briefcase?' 'What if this, what if that?' I just stopped them: 'Excuse me,' I said. 'Have you read the script? Have you read every line, do you know what we're all doing? Just trust the writing, give in to the writing and try not to change it so much.' Everything was very carefully constructed and if we'd messed with the fabric of that scene, the whole tapestry of the film would have unravelled.

When we shot the big scene in the pool room, where I addressed the guys, it was another long day. There were moments when it seemed like the whole thing would fall apart as people tried to undo the script. At one point, Chris got up and walked off because he thought his work was going to be massacred. But we talked the guys out of making changes and the shoot lasted for about fourteen hours. When Chris eventually saw the rushes, he was amazed that we'd managed to stick to his original vision. It wasn't until we got to the fag end of the day that Bryan told me he'd been filming all of the other guys, not me. 'We've got to go again, Pete. Let's do it.' It had been a very complicated day and a very complicated location with lots and lots of dialogue. Bryan had been shooting covers of all the suspects before he turned around to me. I didn't complain, whatever I might have thought; I've always considered myself lucky to be doing what I do, even when the absurdity of it is baffling. I could have gone through the motions earlier in the day, when the cameras had been trained on other people; but that might have diminished the quality of their performances. I had to be at my best so that the others would give of their best too.

I saw Bryan about a year later and he came up to me and apologised for the way he'd shot the pool-room scene. He said: 'Man, I'm sorry, I was a young director and made a bad mistake.' I'd forgotten about it; the four pages of dialogue had been delivered perfectly well and the movie was a hit. 'I thought we'd parted on bad terms,' said Bryan. 'You were so prepared and thorough and well thought out. That's why I took advantage. I've learned from that, I'm sorry about the way I shot it.' I was in good spirits when we saw one another and mindful that when films are made tensions rise. 'Don't worry,' I said. 'We made a great film.'

The Usual Suspects was one of the best times any of us had on a film. We were united, everybody involved knew that we were working on something really special. On the set, we all supported each other's choices and found ourselves in a remarkably well-coalesced unit. We clicked when the cameras were rolling and in the downtime I spent hours with Chris, just shooting the breeze. He'd be the least exhausted of us all because he wouldn't have spent a day in front of the cameras. When the two of us sat down, we never talked about the movie we were making. When Chris was with the other guys, he'd face a barrage of questions; people would want more details or notes or they'd want to make changes. But I wasn't about that, I just wanted to pass time socially. After a day on set, we'd often end up back at my room at the Chateau Marmont where these parties would just start to grow without warning or forethought. When I'd leave the set, I'd ask Chris what he was doing and he'd say he'd be meeting friends. 'Great,' I'd say, 'bring them back to the Chateau.' Chris would politely decline: 'Oh, you know, you don't really know these people.' But I'd tell him: 'It doesn't matter, just bring them by.' It didn't matter whom Chris invited, we'd all end up drinking, having the greatest conversations ever with a group of really entertaining people.

I don't think any of us anticipated the response to the film. I think the first time Bryan accepted that he'd got something special was when he staged a screening and a guy jumped up during the film and shouted that he loved it. That was the point where he knew the audiences would be enthralled. Chris and Kevin both won Oscars and we were nominated for countless other awards. I got my favourite ever review for *The Usual Suspects*; the *New York Times* said: 'Here's a guy with a false tan, a false accent and a false name – and we still believe him.'

&

The following year was one of the busiest of my life. The world seemed like a giant repertory company. As a boy, I'd acted among classmates in various schools. When I became a professional, my colleagues were the people with whom I shared the stages of Liverpool, Bristol or Manchester. Now, I felt as though I was working in an international company. The work hadn't changed particularly – I still liked gritty stories with a human conscience, primarily – but the world was now my stage.

It was great to reunite with Sean Bean for *When Saturday Comes*. We filmed it around south Yorkshire and I played Ken Jackson, who kept Sean's character, Jimmy Muir, on the straight and narrow. *James and the Giant Peach* came as light relief during an intensely busy period. I narrated Henry Selick's adaptation of the Roald Dahl book, which didn't take long, and I was soon back on the treadmill. *DragonHeart* with Dennis Quaid, David Thewlis and Julie Christie was similarly untroubling; I didn't have to beat my brains out to chase imaginary dragons. I returned to sci-fi, fantasy and horror at various times and found it all quite enjoyable. Acting opposite *DragonHeart*'s incredible monster, Draco, was slightly surreal, given that it was computer-generated. But I was able to square the circle by going back to the first criterion of an actor, really, which is to use your imagination. It's a quantum leap to imagine you're battling dragons, but it's just another interesting exercise in the crazy work that we do. When I first saw the dragon I was stunned by it. I was in awe of what they did and how they did it. To take Sean Connery's voice and give that creature something like Sean's wry Scottish humour was brilliant. The film didn't do brilliantly well but I wasn't disappointed by that. Those movies are what they are and people will have their own opinions about them. I enjoyed my character, the poetry-spinning priest Brother Gilbert, enormously; I'd been on a roll with emotionally draining parts and it was bliss to do a lovely, romantic medieval story that would be enjoyable for the kids. We shot it in Slovakia and, unusually for me, it was a film where they weren't operating on a minuscule budget. The character was quite witty and there was also the financial consideration. I thought: 'All right, if I do that, it leaves me free to do films that don't have any budget as well.' I heard from Steven Spielberg while I was filming *DragonHeart*, I think they were looking through the rushes and Steven must have had me in mind for his own fantasy movie.

I teamed up with Stephen Baldwin again on *Crimetime*,

George Sluizer's British crime thriller that also featured Sadie Frost. Stephen played an actor, called Bobby, who had been hired to play a serial killer. I played a real-life serial killer, whom Stephen became acquainted with as part of his research. It was a peculiar role to play because the key to my work was to always choose roles that I could identify with. My character, who was called Sidney, had turned into a serial killer by chance and Stephen's character had to re-enact the crimes on a TV programme. Initially, I planned to immerse myself into the world of serial killers, but then thought better of it and decided to stick to the script. Sidney was fascinating to play and I didn't really put any critique on him. I thought, 'That's what he does, I don't necessarily know why he does it.' The film could have been better, I thought there was one murder too many, for instance, and I wanted the audience to understand more about the difference between illusion and reality. It was just a bit too gory; I'd have preferred it if it had been getting into people's minds, rather than focusing on what was happening physically.

In contrast, *Romeo + Juliet* was everything that I love about film. It was artistic, creative, populist, non-elitist and romantic. It took me back to the genesis of my career. I'd first experienced a frisson of dramatic pleasure back in the church, when I'd been an altar boy; now I was going to play the priest. It was equally thrilling to be going from the well-worn boards of the RSC to Mexico, where I'd be re-interpreting the Bard's work as part of one of Hollywood's biggest productions of the year.

Baz Luhrmann changed the map with that movie, just like Peter Brook did with his *A Midsummer Night's Dream*, and like Franco Zeffirelli did with his 1968 film version of *Romeo & Juliet*, which was immensely popular. Once you see productions like those, and like Baz's film, you can never go back, you know things won't be the same again. I loved the fact his movie would connect with young people throughout the world, that they'd be exposed to Shakespeare; though it amused me that teenagers across the globe would be in a dreadful state, because there was no happy ending. Baz made a young person's film, full of life and zap and energy, it pulled the text right into the twentieth century.

Originally, Peter O'Toole was in the role but there was some conflict at the studio about that and then Peter had difficulties of his own, so that didn't pan out. I think Baz Luhrmann then got a FedEx from Marlon Brando, who'd heard about the production and wanted to appear in it. He sent Baz five letters, during pre-production, but the final one said that he was no longer available. He'd had family issues, his son was involved in a very tragic situation, so he couldn't appear. I became available, unexpectedly, and Baz found out. He FedExed a script to my home in Shropshire and the next thing I knew I was on a flight out to Mexico to film it. I think there'd been a week between casting and arriving on set. I knew the play inside out, it really only took a day to get up to speed.

So there we were, doing *Romeo + Juliet*, all of us felt very privileged, we felt as though we couldn't have been luckier. Leonardo DiCaprio gave his all in the lead role. The boy could do it, believe me, he was there, lost in the moment. But my gosh, what a weight he had on his shoulders, having so much pressure at such a young age. I was glad that it was him and not me. I'd never really had any great traumas in my career. I felt glad to be nearer to fifty than twenty-one. It had taken me a lifetime to turn the flame up high, while Leonardo seemed to be starting out like that. Leo and I got on very well and he'd come to me to see whether we could do sessions of prep together. With some actors, playing so close to one another can be unhealthy, with too much competition. With Leo, it was like a game of tennis; he'd ping the ball over the net and I'd knock it straight back to him. There was no doubt that he was going to be huge. James Cameron was looking at the rushes of *Romeo + Juliet*, and there was no doubt he was going to be a bright and shining star.

Leonardo used to get frustrated, he'd not really done Shakespeare before and he was only twenty-one when we were shooting the film. He'd look at Baz or the producer, Gabriella Martinelli, and ask: 'Why is it taking me fourteen takes to do a scene and Pete always gets it in one?' Sometimes his doubt would seep across to me: 'Was I okay in that?' But Gabriella would reassure me. 'It was perfect, Pete. Don't forget, this is what you do.' I was grateful for her support. But for all of my Shakespearian experience, I treated the work as though I were doing it for the first time.

There was much to love about *Romeo + Juliet*. It was brilliant that Baz wanted the horses to be cars and the swords to be guns. That sort of modern-day adaptation was thrilling. It was exactly the same approach as the one we'd adopted back at the Everyman. We weren't interested in doing the work in an age-old stereotypical way; we wanted to bring it to the present day and make it relevant to a new generation of watchers. But it wasn't just a hotchpotch, MTV-generation makeover. Baz had put real thought into it.

When he was very young, he lived in a very small town and went to a minuscule school. One day, he picked up a book by Shakespeare called *Measure for Measure*. It was by the most revered author of all time, but Baz didn't get any of it. He leafed through the pages but in resignation put it back on the shelf. Then, when he was fifteen, he had something of an epiphany. He saw another play, but instead of it being set in Elizabethan England, it was set in the Caribbean; it had been transformed to fit the modern idiom. That had a profound influence on him and so he decided that he'd like to do that sort of thing cinematically. He spent about two years working out how he could do it. His big idea was this: if Shakespeare were making film now, how would he go about that? Baz's argument was that Shakespeare used cutting-edge techniques, so he'd simply do the same: he'd translate the play to the modern era. It wasn't about trying to be groovy, it's what Shakespeare would have done himself; he used popular music, new devices and new mechanics, Baz just wanted to do the same. Like Shakespeare, he wanted to use broad comedy before the transition into melodramatic tragedy.

Away from the set, I also found time to switch off. We had what would be considered a pub, and I made myself at home. I had a wild time. But I think Baz would agree that it never affected the work. Some people are wild and it affects the show, it's unfair on others. I had some sort of internal contract with myself; my rambunctious wildness off the set was matched by a professionalism on it. It was a conscious balance. I think perhaps the duty to my art and the craziness off it fed each other, one fuelled the other, as an artist and as a person.

I was immensely proud of my association with *Romeo + Juliet*. Some years later, the RSC put together a survey where they named the best Shakespearian films of all time. *Romeo + Juliet* was number two – and when you're looking at a list that includes the best ever, second place is not a bad place to be.

NINE

Burning Down the Co-Op

∾

Mark Herman told me a funny story when we met for a three-hour liquid lunch in Soho as we reached the mid-nineties. 'When I sat down to write *Brassed Off*, I put a picture up on the wall above my desk,' he told me.

'That's nice,' I said. 'Was the picture of a miner, trombonist or Grimethorpe?'

'No,' he replied. 'It was of you.'

Mark used to work in that way whenever he was writing. He'd decide which actor he wanted to play a certain role and then pin their picture to his wall. He'd write as if they were in the room, speaking the lines, which helped his words to flow. 'It's very rare for me to get the actors I want to play the parts,' he said, as we sat down with our pints. It was equally rare for me to receive a script so perfectly attuned to my spiritual, political and creative beliefs.

'Let me know if you want to play Danny,' Mark slurred, as our meeting drew to a close.

'When do I start?' I told him. 'I have to do it.'

It mattered not a jot to me that Mark's previous film had

been a disaster, nor that I'd been warned not to go near him. My career was seemingly in the ascendant, with a bunch of Hollywood films and an Oscar nomination under my belt; in contrast, Mark's seemed to be heading south. But the script leapt from the page, it was a perfect mix of comedy and gritty realism; it told a hugely important story in a light-hearted, unpreachy way. I loved the entire script and was rapt by the character he wanted me to play, Danny. Danny had to tread a difficult line; he had to have both humour and gravitas. I asked Mark about the other people that he hoped to cast and he explained how he wanted to avoid actors whose profiles were too high because he was afraid that they wouldn't be believable as their characters. He wanted people whose faces might have been known, but not their names. So he cast myself, a youthful Ewan McGregor, who had only been seen in minor movies and *Shallow Grave*, by then, the brilliant Stephen Tompkinson, Tara Fitzgerald, Philip Jackson, Peter Martin, Melanie Hill and Sue Johnston.

I was into it from the off; Mark's film was a devastatingly brutal indictment of the way that Thatcher had systematically destroyed the working classes in mining communities. He was totally committed to the piece and made sure it rang true. Grimethorpe was in a terrible state when Mark arrived to look at the location, but he didn't baulk at that and put his production office straight in there for six weeks of prep. His film was all about those people and it was important to him that we all became part of their community. When we arrived, the locals were exceptionally wary of our intentions, and with good reason. The year before they'd been the subject of a TV programme that had depicted Grimethorpe cruelly and without sensitivity; the programme makers had re-imagined it as some sort of no-go Twilight Zone. Supposedly the crew was giving the kids

five-pound notes to throw rocks at the windows. After a
few weeks, they saw that what we were doing wasn't like
that. We had a great responsibility. We were making a film
about a community that's been ravaged already; you don't
want to go in again and ravage them with a poor, shoddy
film. Mark set about allaying local fears, he worked hard to
reassure the people that we weren't trying to stitch them up.

I arrived two weeks before we were due to shoot, together
with Stephen Tompkinson, who was playing Danny's son,
Phil. Stephen and I had worked together before, on *Tales of
Sherwood Forest*, and it was a great chance for us to renew
our friendship; we got on brilliantly well. We spent every
waking hour developing our characters and going through
the details of Mark's script. I was obsessive about the whole
production, not just my part; I wanted to expose the horror
of what Thatcher had done. Stephen was a joy to be with; I'd
phoned him to see whether he'd come early to Grimethorpe
to get on with the research and he was there like a shot. The
locals were initially trepidatious but to reassure them of our
good intentions we made copies of the script available to
them. We showed the people as much respect as we could
muster. It was easy for me to sit in their working men's club
and drink with them; I enjoyed it, they were my people,
they were just the same as the folk I'd grown up with in
Warrington. Gradually they became convinced that we
weren't trying to exploit them. There was one old boy who
came over when Stephen and I were drinking. He stood in
front of us and eyeballed me, saying: 'Reet, so let me get this
reet. Thou's playing the bandleader, the father ...' I nodded:
'That's right.' And then he looked at Stephen, who was sat
next to me: 'And thou's playing his son.' He seemed to weigh
up the possibilities of our unlikely family, before turning to
Stephen: 'I bet thou's glad thou takes after tha mother, eh?'
We fell about laughing; we'd got what we were looking for,

the humour and the language. Stephen and I had a very productive fortnight. We just drove around, and said, 'hello,' and people said 'hello' back; after that, we were accepted. Then we started going to some of the miners' pubs, listening to their stories.

On the first day of shooting, Mark was nervous but I was absolutely petrified. I cared so much for the project, I wanted it to convey the reality of right-wing Tory politics. It was a huge responsibility. Mark wasn't sure how to pitch it at first, whether it should be comedy or tragedy; the level was hard to find. But I instinctively knew where we should go. The first scene was one where I was in my kitchen and I had to cough. As I raised my hankie, I made a sign like a conductor; that was the sort of thing that Danny would have done.

Stephen and I continued to develop our backstories and we absorbed every little detail of the clubs, the shops, the streets and the people. We'd spend hours talking to them and I'd ride around on my bicycle, familiarising myself with the terrain. Stephen and I realised that we could achieve an enormous amount in the film visually, by exchanging knowing glances. Our actions would speak as loudly as Mark's words. There was a great example in one momentous scene where Stephen noticed me coughing into a handkerchief, leaving traces of coal. His glance conveyed the gravity of the discovery, he didn't need to talk. That's the way that we played it, there was a lot of unwritten dialogue between us. The relationship between Danny and Phil was so strong and loving that they could hardly talk; they found it difficult to know what to say because they didn't want to break each other's hearts. During breaks and lunchtimes, Stephen and I would go through every line, every gesture, to make sure it was right.

There were moments of great hilarity. On one morning,

I think it was a Sunday, other members of the cast turned up and came to the social centre for band rehearsals. Philip Jackson was given a tuba and told to play it; he looked at one of the assistants as though he'd been handed a box of frogs. I was in full band regalia, on my little bandstand, and Philip looked up at me as though to say: 'Eh up, what am I supposed to do with this?' But I was already Danny, with my baton in hand, conducting the players. 'We'll have no messing,' my look told him. 'You're in the Grimethorpe Colliery Band now, so get that bloody tuba on your lap and play it.' The music felt instinctive, it coursed through my veins; I wanted to convince the band and the audience that we were in this for real. I'd had no musical training whatsoever, I couldn't even read music. But I'd been sent the soundtrack, which had been prerecorded at Abbey Road, and I just listened to it over and over again. I had to play it loud and it drove the family mad. They said, 'It's either you or that brass band – one of you has got to go.' I was taught to conduct by John Anderson, a lecturer at City of Leeds College of Music, who also assembled the soundtrack. John made videos of me for the band and I learned the music by heart.

The fact that we got so into the music helped us to connect with the area. When the local people found out that Ewan McGregor could actually play the cornet and that Tara Fitzgerald could play the flugelhorn and that I could actually sort of keep them in time with the wagging stick, then the community realised we weren't there to take advantage of them again. The band was a very unifying thing, it was very communal. We had the real musicians there as well and they showed us how to get it right, they were very patient; they even taught Philip Jackson how to play the tuba … eventually.

The cast and crew were great. As well as Stephen, Philip,

Ewan and Mark, Olivia Stewart was on board, from *Distant Voices, Still Lives*, as was Sue Johnston, whom I'd enjoyed watching in *Brookside*. I had an instant rapport with Sue, we felt as though we'd known each other all our lives – and we very nearly had. Even though we'd never met or worked together, our two families back in Padgate were linked. Whenever I went home, Sue's aunties would tell her that I'd been back, and vice versa. So when we met it was like we were already old friends. We were born within two years of each other and within two streets. Sue was born in Padgate, just at the back of where I lived. We both had roots in the Labour Party. Sue had been on the picket lines with Ricky Tomlinson and I'd been out in support of the miners too. All of us identified with miners as being at the core of the working-class movement; they had been for many years, right from the General Strike. The work they did and their willingness to stand up and be counted meant everything to folk like us. When Thatcher came in, she had it planned, we knew she would try to destroy that union and then the others after it; none were as strong as the miner's union and if she could split that, she could spoil the lot. She stockpiled coal and then she decimated them. That's what happened. Thatcher was completely vindictive, because Grimesthorpe had one of the strongest unions. She made an example out of them.

Many of us had already been involved in the protests against Thatcher, the film was like tying a bow on it. We cared, almost violently, about the decimation of those communities. They tried to say that it was an economic argument, but when that didn't work, they argued that the way forward would be nuclear power. The reason why the Tories gunned the miners in the pit was that they were politically active. They smashed them so they closed down the pits. The Conservatives made war on the unions, and won, in fact. The pit was not only closed down but destroyed, razed. They covered the pits up with concrete, burying a quarter of a million pounds' worth of equipment. So to be among them was a privilege and to film with the Grimethorpe Brass Band was a total honour.

We could see the effects of Thatcher's policies every day. At times, it was like filming in the Wild West, they had big steel bars on the doors and the atmosphere was like a tinder-box. Women used to say that if they'd been told five years earlier what would happen, none of them would have be-lieved it. The film was about people being disenfranchised, about people being used as pawns, not having any say in what they do. Mining is a horrible job but despite that and the awful conditions miners had to endure, there was hon-our, values, a way of life within a real community and this had been destroyed.

The whole experience of filming in Grimethorpe and seeing for ourselves the personal cost was incredible. Grimethorpe had been a town of 200,000 but when we were there only 20,000 were left. All the coal board houses for workers had been covered in iron grilles to stop people from squatting. It was an extraordinary place. Three generations were living with zero prospects.

Just before Guy Fawkes, Mark Herman started talking to a couple of kids and he asked them: 'What are you going to do for Bonfire Night?' I think he imagined they were going to have a bonfire and fireworks, or something similar. The kids said: 'We're going to burn down the Co-Op.' Mark just laughed, thinking they were joking. The day after, when we drove into Grimethorpe, there it was: the Co-Op was smouldering away.

There were moments of great sorrow, when the things we saw broke our hearts. We'd see the young lads, who'd once been miners, and they were addicted to drugs because they'd lost hope. If we needed fuel for our work, they gave it to us. The soul of that place had been ripped out and it really affected us all. To be thrust into that empty, closed-mill community, where people had just vanished and houses had been boarded up, where the people had no hope; it was quite profound. It felt like I'd come home.

I felt very comfortable in that environment. Like the rest of the cast, I felt it was a film about my people, where I came from and where I belonged. The casting had been brilliant because we were all quite similar, there was nobody on the set who didn't care profoundly about the miners. After we'd finished a day's shooting, we'd pootle off to the Swallow Hotel, in Doncaster, where we were staying. We'd go upstairs and have a quick wash and be back downstairs half an hour later, ready to eat or prop up the bar. It felt like we were an on-the-road repertory company. We got to know the town and the town got to know us.

There were plenty of wild times during the shoot. On one occasion we were in Delph and Philip Jackson piped up that Henry Livings lived in the village. I knew a little about Livings, he was a quirky Northern playwright and actor, so I set off to find him. We got there, not too early, and the pubs were already open. Half an hour later, Henry and I were propped up in the local bar and we enjoyed the afternoon getting sozzled. Another time, Sue Johnston ruined the day for Mark Herman, quite inadvertently. Mark was a huge rugby fan and Sue spoiled a game for him on the day she arrived. We were all up in Doncaster and most of us were sat in the foyer of the Swallow Hotel, the wagons were outside for people who needed make-up and wardrobe. The cast and crew were sat in front of the telly, watching a rugby match that had been recorded without us knowing the score. Sue waltzed in, oblivious to our entertainment, and said something like, 'Oh, isn't it great that they won.'

Pete continued his local fund-raising in 2005 by assisting the NSPCC. Here, he is pictured with then Chairman of the Shropshire Branch of the NSPCC, Rose Crocker, at Concord College, Acton Burnell.

With his friend Sara Robinson, the former director of Ludlow Assembly Rooms, a venue with which he had a strong association and was patron.

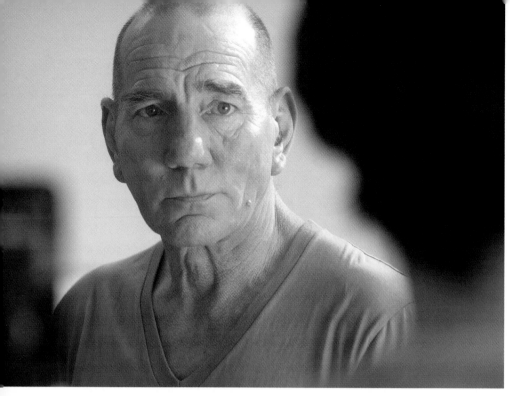

As Hooch in Otto Bathurst's provocative BAFTA-winning BBC series
Criminal Justice. (BBC)

Ben Wishaw is put through his paces as Ben Coulter as he films scenes with
Pete from the production. The newspaper cuttings on the wall would have
been permitted because Pete's character, Hooch, was deemed low risk. (BBC)

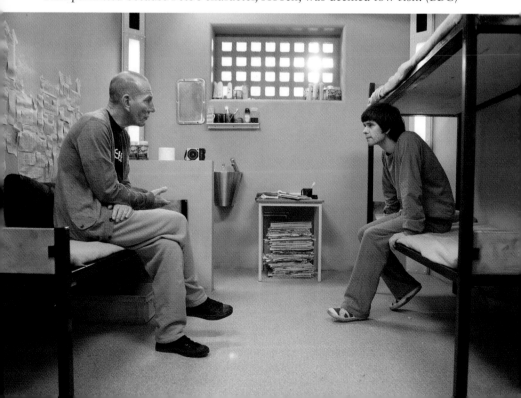

Behind bars in *Criminal Justice*, written by Peter Moffatt, which also won three Royal Television Society Awards and an International Emmy. (BBC)

Pete made an appearance at an arts workshop at Ludlow Assembly Rooms in front of pupils from south Shropshire schools and colleges. He was joined by local pupils (from left), Steve Amos, Imogen Bushell and Lucy Ashley.

On the set of *Solomon Kane*, playing William Crowthorn with Alice Krige as Katherine Crowthorn.

Pete's passion for the environment, inspired by his wife Jacqui, led him to star in *The Age of Stupid*. 'When Franny Armstrong asked me, I couldn't say no,' he said. He arrived for the 'green carpet' premiere on a bike.

Pete's leading role as the archivist in *The Age of Stupid* gave the film a high profile. American President Barack Obama was among the people who asked for information about the movie.

Danny made a new appearance in 2005 when he opened the Church Stretton Food Fayre. Pete helped as many local causes as he possibly could.

Reprising his role as Danny, the *Brassed Off* band leader, to conduct the Grimethrope Colliery Band at Ludlow Festival, in St Laurence's Parish Church.

Top right Ben Affleck pursued Pete for months before finally persuading him to play Fergus 'Fergie' Colm in the hit 2010 film *The Town*.

Right Pete's one-time housemate and long-standing friend Nick Hamm booked him to play a flamboyant gay music impressario in his final film, *Killing Bono*. He was seriously ill when it was made and only able to film for a couple of days. However, he delighted in working with the younger cast.

Hey fiddly dee, an actor's life for me.

The road to home... On the Long Mynd, high above his local town of Church Stretton, enjoying the picturesque views.

And everybody screamed at her, 'No, Sue,' because we were watching it back and didn't know the score.

In the hotel, the fire alarms went off persistently in the night and we'd be thrown out on the streets, freezing. All the local girls would be tottering back from the clubs, half naked, with their mottled legs, and Ewan McGregor would be standing there watching them. The girls would scream: 'Oi mar God, there's Ewan McGregor. Gerremoff, sexy.' And he'd recoil behind a scarf. During the evenings, we found a pub across the road from the hotel that did a quiz twice a week, so we started going. We were unpopular pretty soon, because we won too often. The top prize was a gallon of beer and when we finally finished filming we drank our winnings. We didn't have any money for a wrap party but we'd amassed about fifty gallons of beer from the quiz, so we were fine.

Considering we never got any sleep from the ruddy fire alarms, we were always on it, we were always ready for the work. There were a couple of scenes that really stood out. One was the final scene, where we were driving around London on an open-top bus, with Danny conducting the band. We'd partied hard throughout the shoot and that last day was no exception. On the last night, we'd had to hang around until about 3 a.m. in the morning because we needed them to switch off the lights in the Houses of Parliament before we could film it. We sat around for hours, drinking, and by the time we filmed it I could barely stand. I think there might have been a couple of the actors who hung on to my legs as the bus swung its way round London. I couldn't stand up straight, I kept wobbling over. We'd been kept so long in our trailers and we were saying, 'Let's have a little drink, let's have another little drink.' We were all egging each other on. Danny was supposed to be the one who wasn't drinking and the rest were supposed to be drunk: but the reality was the other way round. No, to tell the truth, I think one or two of the people on the bus might have been just as bad as me. The liquid played an enormous part throughout the film.

Mark was always on the money; creatively, he was exceptional. The editing on the finale of the performance of the *William Tell Overture* was especially rousing. The camera was on a crane and on a track, to track down and crane in. Quite rightly, they used the most extraordinary technique to do the most extraordinary piece of music. The music was like a character; it built and built. They really went to town with that sequence, it was a really excellent piece of film-making.

But the scene that everybody remembers most of all is the one where Danny made his speech in the Royal Albert Hall. Mark thought very carefully about how he wanted to film it and he pointed all of the cameras on the extras, rather than us. He realised that Danny's words would have more effect on them; because they weren't actors, they'd re-act the same way as any human being. The actors had read the script, though they hadn't heard it, but the band and the extras hadn't any idea what was in it. On the first take, Mark was just covering their faces, for the reactions, and it was enormously powerful. It wasn't shot in the Albert Hall, of course, and a lot of the audience were CGI'd into the production later on; but the response of the people who were really there was phenomenal. If you look at it again, you'll see the band members' heads going down one by one when I speak about the havoc that had been wrought with their lives. You see them, especially the young lads, identifying with what Danny says. There was absolute silence in the auditorium, it was the most extraordinary moment and it was a privilege to act it. At the end they got up and applauded without any prompting from the director. All theatre and film is artifice, so to get a moment where it seemed real was absolutely amazing. After we'd filmed a couple of takes, we spoke to members of the band. They told us that in real terms they'd actually won the national championships and two days later their pit was closed. They said they wished they'd done what Danny did, and turned down the cup. We felt proud to be among them.

The premiere was in Leeds and my family came along for it. They made a little *Brassed Off* suit for Will, which he loved, and the whole evening was wonderful; Will even got up with the band. It was a great celebration of the work that we'd completed and a celebration of the Grimethorpe Brass Band. Much as we cared about the film, we didn't really think it would be enjoyed by anyone who lived more than five miles from Barnsley. I mean, it's a hard sell: 'Come and see this new film, it's about miners and a brass band.' The first weekend wasn't good and Channel 4 got very worried about it. But then suddenly it started to roll and it became a word-of-mouth success, the reaction became overwhelming. We knew we had something great, but we didn't realise what the reaction would be or how much of an impact it would have. Eventually they had to stop showing it at Leeds because people wouldn't stop going. I think the video or DVD was coming out, and they were afraid people wouldn't buy it.

The pride I felt for *Brassed Off* has never left me. American actors would hesitate to make a film like that because they might be branded as a leftie, even though it's okay for them to blast people out of the sky with big guns. There's such immense competition in America that if you make a wrong career move you can lose two or three years. That's why they're frightened and constantly looking at their backs wondering, 'How will I appear in this?' rather than 'What's my job here?' You can feel the monkeys on their backs going, 'Am I going to get enough close-ups?' You've got to stick your head up now and again, and *Brassed Off* and *In the Name of the Father* were political. I do feel politically committed. I do believe we had to do something drastic to remove that dreadful lady.

The reaction from the wider community was also profound. The band Chumbawamba got in touch because they wanted to use a sample of Danny's speech in their single, 'Tubthumping', the bit where he said: 'I thought it was music that mattered. But does it bollocks! It's people that matter.' It did really well during the nominations season, picking up the Peter Sellers Award for Comedy at the Evening Standard Film Awards. It was a great night.

There seemed to be no end to the letters that I received from viewers. One woman wrote to me to say she'd never known her husband cry in thirty-five years of marriage until they went to see it, but he just sat there and blubbed. Once, on the way to the station, two girls came up and said 'Are you *Brassed Off*?' And I said: 'No, I'm all right as it happens.'

I was flown out to America to promote it and the schedule was intense. Take, for instance, Thursday, 22 May 1997 to Friday, 23 May 1997. I received this itinerary from Sekita Ekrek, executive director of publicity and promotions at Allied Advertising, in Washington DC. My Delta 1418 flight from Atlanta arrived at 6.01 p.m. in Washington and from there I was met by Sekita before being driven to the Four Seasons Hotel, 2800 Pennsylvania Avenue, Washington DC. I was woken the following morning and driven at 10.15 a.m. to AP Studios, 1825 K Street NW Suite 710. Between 10.30 a.m. and 11 a.m. I recorded a taped radio interview with Michael Weinfeld, from AP Radio, before departing for NPR Studios, 635 Massachusetts Avenue. From 11.15 a.m. to 11.45 a.m. there was a taped radio interview for Pat Dowell's NPR *Morning Edition*. Then it was back to the hotel for an early lunch, before being driven at 12.45 p.m. to the Cineplex Uptown Theater on 43426 Connecticut Avenue. Arch Campbell conducted a TV interview between 1 p.m. and 1.30 p.m. for WRC-TV/NBC. Then it was back to the hotel for a forty-five-minute interview between 2 p.m. and 2.45 p.m. with Gary Arnold, from the *Washington Times*. A telephone interview followed immediately afterwards with Mike Ollove from the *Baltimore Sun*, before a further print interview at the hotel from 3.15 p.m. to 3.45 p.m. with Max Alvarez. The second that finished, I was driven back to the National Airport to make a 5 p.m. flight on Continental 320 to Kennedy Airport. There was, quite literally, no time to pack or unpack, no time to catch breath. The schedule was so intense that I wrote down the Christian names of my interviewers on the back of Sekita's schedule: Michael, Pat (f), Arch, Gary, Mike, Max. My schedule during that pro-motional tour comprised similar days across the USA. At the Hyatt Regency Kauai I wrote down a few thoughts: *1 – Cities. 2 – People in charge of me. 3 – People they made me meet. Impressions – people and cities. 4 Incidents – Why am I here. Differences, similarities, colours, connections.* My schedule comprised New York, LA, Seattle, San Francisco, LA, Houston, Atlanta before arriving in Washington.

For all its success, *Brassed Off* didn't make me a big star, thankfully. I'd have hated it if it had. I couldn't imagine getting to the point where I couldn't just go into a pub and have a pint. I like being about. I don't know how people can concentrate on their work when they've got all of that going on. *Brassed Off* was filmed on a shoestring, but the money didn't matter to any of us. Does twenty million bucks look any different to one million bucks? Tom Cruise has to go through underground car parks to get to his penthouse; imagine that, what a life, it doesn't seem like much fun to me. I'm much better off popping down to the pub for a quick one, or walking through the Shropshire hills.

Brassed Off continues to reverberate and last year I found out that it had influenced John Prescott's policies, when he'd been Deputy Prime Minister. He said that he'd watched it in June 1997 and it had had a deep effect on him. He wrote about how moved he was, particularly by that final speech: 'The line that got me was: "This government has systematically destroyed an entire industry – our industry. And not just our industry – our communities, our homes, our lives. All in the name of 'progress'. And for a few lousy bob."'

Apparently, he realised that he was the minister in charge, so he sat down with English Partnerships and ordered them to compile a programme targeted at regenerating those mining communities. Around £400 million went into the coalfield communities after that.

It was also a film that my mother loved. When she lay dying, some years later, in 2000, she asked to see a video of that film and at the end she turned to me and said: 'He was very good, wasn't he?' She thought it was my father. She thought she was seeing her lovely Bill again. And perhaps, in her own way, she was.

TEN

Rolling Thunder Hits the Road

∾

How time flies. Ewan McGregor had been an up-and-coming actor when we'd played alongside one another in *Brassed Off*. By the time we filmed *The Serpent's Kiss*, the following year, he was the hottest actor in the UK. *Trainspotting* had been a massive hit and Ewan was lighting up the sky like a Perseids meteor. We talked a lot, in the downtime; he was interested in the way that my life had changed following *In the Name of the Father* because he was experiencing a similarly meteoric rise. *Serpent's Kiss* was shot in a wonderful location in County Clare, on the West Coast of Ireland, and also featured Greta Scacchi, Richard E. Grant and Charley Boorman. It was the first time Ewan and Charley had met and they went on to have a great friendship.

My family accompanied me to the small Irish village of Sixmilebridge, where we were filming. It was bucolic Ireland at its rural best. Our gorgeous daughter Lily had recently been born. Will had new interests of his own, taking a shine to Tracey Seaward, the co-producer on *Serpent's Kiss*; he seemed to spend most of his time attached to her – he'd have been about six or seven at the time – while I went to work. After shooting, we'd avail ourselves of the only amenity in Sixmilebridge, a family pub called Casey's Bar that we'd monopolise most evenings, enjoying poker nights with our pints of Guinness and telling stories until the early hours. The cast and crew mixed together well, which I loved. I'd always been as friendly with the resident chippie as I had with my co-stars. We drank late into the night and the craic was great. There'd be music and laughter; the smiles would still be spread across our faces when we went to work the next morning. One night, Mr Casey brought some puppies into the pub, they'd been born on the nearby farm but they were destined for the river because the farmer didn't want them. Tracey fell in love with one like a thief in the night. 'You should take that home,' I told her, as she played with a gorgeous little border collie. We picked it up and put it on the bar.

Tracey couldn't help herself. 'Could I keep it?' she asked Mr Casey. The landlord nodded his consent. 'What are you going to call it?' he asked. Tracey thought for a moment. 'Casey ... Casey ...' she looked me in the eye as I prepared to anoint the poor mite with Guinness. 'Casey Postlethwaite.' And so we baptised the latest addition to our extended family with a drop of Vitamin G, then raised our glasses: 'To Casey, to Casey Postlethwaite.' Casey wagged her tail like a rattlesnake. When we finished the movie, Casey Postlethwaite followed Tracey home and stayed with her for the next twelve years.

There was great excitement as we sat around the bar one evening; I'd received the news that I was going to work with Steven Spielberg on *The Lost World: Jurassic Park*. The team were thrilled. 'He's the most successful moviemaker on the planet,' said Tracey. I thought about this: 'Then I'd better do a good job, and not bloody well let him down.'

The news from Steven Spielberg was phenomenal. The Master had decided to come out of self-imposed retirement to do *The Lost World* and every actor on the planet wanted to work with him. My agent had told me there was a possibility he might want to cast me, but I was convinced it wouldn't happen, especially after a heart-stopping meeting in London, just before we'd started *Serpent's Kiss*. I'd sat down with my agent and she'd told me that Steven's people had called to see if I'd be interested in the follow-up to *Jurassic Park*. Steven wanted to meet me in Los Angeles to talk. 'If you want to do it, you need to be on a plane in two days' time,' she said. 'Hold on, our Lily's just been born,' I said. 'Let me see the script, first.' 'There's no script, Steven won't send out the script, you have to go to see him,' she explained. I didn't think twice. 'Look, I'm sorry, but Lily's less than a week old. My family comes first, I can't leave them to jet off to LA.' My agent told me I'd be walking away from one of the biggest movies of all time. 'Look,' I said. 'Tell him thanks, but no thanks; I can't do it.' It wasn't a moral stand, I didn't do it for effect; there were more important things than films, including my family. As I left her office and walked along Charing Cross Road, I didn't know whether to slash my wrists straight away, or wait until I got home.

Four days later, my phone went. 'Pete? Pete, it's Steven, Steven Spielberg.' He'd called me to talk. I apologised for what had happened earlier and said I was sorry that I couldn't do his film. I told him my family was the most important thing in the world; they had to come first. He listened, then chuckled. 'You getting any sleep yet?' To my surprise, Steven was more interested in Lily than the film. He'd recently adopted a baby and understood my behaviour. We spoke man-to-man, he was incredibly gracious. 'How about I send a copy of the script over by courier? If you like it, we'll do it. It's up to you,' he said, and he was as good as his word. I read the script with the relish of a bridesmaid catching a bouquet; it was a cracking yarn, more like *Indiana Jones* than *Jurassic Park*. The character Steven wanted me to play, Roland Tembo, was wonderfully well developed. He was an ambivalent character, even though he was in the pay of the avaricious Ludlow, who would be played by Arliss Howard. Tembo led an expedition to ransack the island but underwent a sea change towards the end and realised that Ludlow was not particularly wholesome. But much as I liked it, the idea of being away from my family gnawed. We spoke again: 'Steven, my family are my stability. They are always there for me and I couldn't do what I do if I didn't know that.' I'll never know why Steven was so understanding – perhaps he just understood my priorities – but he waited until I was ready. We organised for the whole family to fly out together, the deal was agreed with the minimum of fuss. We took a house in Benedict Canyon, and I came home to them each evening after filming.

While Jax, Will and Lily enjoyed their new home, I immersed myself in one of the most thrilling and exciting creative experiences of my life. The high-blown pressure of shooting *The Lost World* was like playing against the house in some high-stakes casino. The images in *Jurassic Park* had been extraordinary, it had been a rollicking adventure and it had grossed almost $1 billion. Steven was intent on replicating his success. We needed this film to do well. Steven was a lovely, witty, sanguine chap; he'd seen it all, done it all and shot everything there was to shoot. Monster movies weren't the sort that I'd rush out to see, ordinarily, but doing one with Steven changed the game; if I wanted to be in a major motion picture, I might as well work for the Boss.

Steven was steeped in the world of film, in what it did and what it could do. He was very hands-on and was particularly good with actors. He gave us extraordinarily lucid notes that would make me think: 'Why didn't I think of that?' or 'Thank you very much, that's an exquisite idea.' Steven loved what he did and his enthusiasm and rhythm of work were fantastic, everyone worked at quite a lick. We'd improvise on set, which was great and there wasn't much hanging around, which was a bonus. I don't know why I was surprised by his powers of perception and articulacy. His passion was storytelling and his relationships with the actors were wonderful. Any ideas we threw in were caught and returned, we got on extremely well. At heart, Steven was still a little child. In order to do what he did, he had to maintain that child within.

There was a week when Steven was away from the set, he had to go to New York to see his family, but he spoke to us via satellite. It was quite interesting, we were going in for the morning and Steven would be on the monitor, in his kitchen, in the Hamptons, saying, 'Good morning guys, how you doing?' He'd offer directions via satellite and we'd be, 'Good, we'll get on with that now then.' During Steven's absence, we were put through our paces by the first assistant director and screenwriter, David Koepp; though by that time we all knew what we were doing. The scenes were wild; we shot the cliff scene in the mud and rain in the universal lot. It was the sort of hyper-real madness that could only happen in Hollywood.

Steven was an exceptional man in other ways; he was very caring, very accurate in his work and very sensitive towards the crew, it was fantastic working with him. But he wasn't the only one who blew me away. Stan Winston was the genius behind the animatronics and I had to pinch myself every now and then to say: 'No, Stan's dinosaurs aren't real, they're models.' At one point, I was staking out a baby T Rex; I kept my eye on it all the time because it kept turning round, looking at me. I said to Stan, 'What happens if I put one of my fingers in its mouth?' Stan looked at me and spoke slowly and deliberately, like a policeman with a drunk driver: 'It will go through your fingers. One word: don't.' We were working with full-scale models and they terrified the life out of me because they were so real. When we started, Stan warned us that we had to switch off our mobile phones in case the electronics affected the dinosaurs and made them do things they shouldn't have done. 'What, they could come to life?' Stan laughed a sinister Mr Hyde laugh, then shrugged his shoulders. I was in awe of Stan and his crew, he was one of the reasons I enjoyed *The Lost World* so much. I was like a kid in a toy shop; I wanted to see how they did that sort of thing. Being chased by the T Rex was crazy, it reminded me of my mother chasing me with a dishcloth back in Warrington.

Having my family alongside me was a blessing; their companionship compensated for being away from our home in Shropshire, where I'd have been propping up the bar with a pint of Boddies and twenty Embassy fags. Will loved it. He went from being in a small village school to a six-hundred-pupil school in Beverly Hills. They made him the pupil of the week at one point, although the girl who told him couldn't pronounce his name 'Poossterlfwaite. Er, well done ... Will.' Our house had a swimming pool, so that we could cool off at home, and it was fun while it lasted. I tried to avoid much of the brouhaha that went with being in the biggest movie in Hollywood. A film crew was a film crew, whether it was a $70 million film or a $1.2 million film. Ultimately, good movies are as much to do with people like the camera focus puller and the lighting man as they are the director or actors. A lot of my early scenes didn't make the final cut because Steven got rid of some of the character development, which was disappointing. I understood why he did it; in movies like that, the actors are almost incidental to the dinosaurs. I think Steven chose to make *Jurassic Park 2: The Ride*, and sacrificed character development for the actual adventure. Later, he was very generous about me in the press and came out with the fabled line, 'Pete Postlethwaite's the greatest actor in the world.' I laughed: 'It sounds like an advert for a lager. Pete Postlethwaite: Probably the best actor in the world.' Then I thought about what Steven had really meant. It would have been something like: 'Pete Postlethwaite *thinks* he's the best actor in the world.'

I found myself defending blockbusters to suspicious critics. My choice of roles had always been very catholic, my decisions were based on who was doing a project and their reasons for doing it. Tembo had been an engaging character to play; he was the last of the classic hunter-philosophers, he'd tracked prey on foot all his life but had given it up. Then one of his old trackers found him in a bar and said: 'How about bagging a T Rex?' It was a good, light-hearted story that would help people escape for a couple of hours, and there's nothing wrong with that.

But the success of the film brought the inevitable detractors and I'd been lambasted at the Sundance Film Festival when *Brassed Off* was shown. People were enraged that I was working with somebody as populist as Spielberg, hands were thrown into the air in mock disgust. 'How could you?' they'd say, as though I were having an affair with the vicar's wife. But that was just the snobbery of small independent filmmakers. I countered like so: 'It's perfectly possible to make a really bad low-budget movie.' When people suggested that Hollywood was bad, or that money brutalised artists, I rejected that argument too. My experience was that Hollywood was caring. I didn't have the face of a God or a celebrity lifestyle, but I still earned respect. For all the fun we had, I was glad to get home and I didn't ever want to relocate to California; it wouldn't have been right, would it? I mean, I drank, I smoked, I didn't do exercise and I spoke like a welder ... I got enough of America when I was working. I always wanted to come home.

When we were doing interviews to promote the film, a lot of writers asked if I wished I'd found success earlier in my career. At first, I thought 'maybe', but after spending time in Hollywood, I'm glad that I didn't. Hollywood was like something out of *Alice in Wonderland*; it was a maze with smoke and mirrors distorting everything. Things were not always as they seemed. Spielberg called me a regular guy and I think that's why we got on; he was one of the best parts of it. I think he simply meant that I turned up on time and always did my best. Then again, for the money they paid, that's the sort of attitude they should have got from everyone.

If I'd been a superstar at twenty-one, like Leonardo DiCaprio, I'm not sure that I would have treated it with the same sanguinity, if that's a word. There were times when the big studios felt as though they were based in crocodile country and I was always very careful about my choices. During 1994 to 1997, I must have shot around fifteen films; I think only Harvey Keitel worked harder.

There were occasions when I was away from the film set, of course. I landed myself in hot water when I hooked up with another former Warrington resident just before we released *The Lost World*. On *TFI Friday*, I sat down across the table from Chris Evans, whom I remembered from years earlier, when he'd been a busker on the streets of Warrington. Trouble was, they'd left me in the green room for hours on end with Mariella Frostrup plying me with drink, so by the time I went on air I was more than a little inebriated. My appearance caused a bit of a ruckus and my mother disapproved, as did the rest of Warrington. I thought Chris and

I had displayed huge affection for the town by saying what we'd really thought of it. We'd been quite tongue-in-cheek, but our remarks didn't go down well and there was a twenty-four-hour furore. You have to remember that, despite the fuss, I was still going back to Warrington an awful lot and I loved the town as much as any man. I think I'd been talking about the changes they'd made, ripping the heart out of it; that had been my point. It was the same logic that you'd apply to acting, where an agent says you should change your name: 'Oh, really? Then what should I be? Pete de Niro? Pete Hoffman?' I wouldn't want to change my name and nor did I want to see my home town bespoiled; Warrington had always given me a sense of identity, a sense of belonging. It was where my stock lay, where my body was made. My Northern roots had helped me to stay an ordinary man, a private man, a normal dad. Some of the best times of my life were spent with our Mike, in the club, at Warrington, where we'd go for a Sunday lunchtime pint and a few games of pool. Even then, my mother would still be telling me off when I went to see her. 'When you go to America, you're not wearing jeans, are you?' she'd tut. Brilliant, she was in her eighties and she was worried that I'd create the wrong impression among the most powerful nation on earth by wearing denim. But much as I loved Warrington, I needed to move on. Had I not escaped, I think I would have been married with four or five kids by the age of twenty-three.

Straight after *Lost World*, Steven wanted me to work with him on *Amistad*, with Morgan Freeman, Anthony Hopkins, Djimon Hounsou and Matthew McConaughey. *Amistad* was a complete contrast, a film that was all about the spoken word rather than the special effects. *Amistad* had been the name of a Portuguese sailing ship where the slaves mutinied. It was based on an international incident involving Spain, America and England that happened in

1839. There was a series of trials that eventually went to the Supreme Court because no one knew what to do with the slaves. Were they cargo? Or where they people? It was a different kettle of fish to *The Lost World*. Steven spent more time working with the actors; he loved the nuances in our dialogue. It struck me as ironic that a few years earlier, at the Oscars, when we were ignored for *In the Name of the Father*, Steven had swept the board with *Schindler's List*. It was his Bar Mitzvah that night. Steven was very un-prima donna-ish and I loved him as a bloke, as much as I loved him for the thrill of his art. I flew to Hollywood thinking the man was a myth, but came away realising he wasn't. He liked his pretzels with mustard, the same as anyone else.

Still, after *Amistad*, the choice for me was simple. Should I a) act in Hollywood's biggest film of the year, help gross squintillions at the box office and be part of a team that won four Oscars and received six further nominations; or, b) do a wild, unrestrained and financially unrewarding Shakespearian play with some of the best mates I've ever had in provincial British towns. On a scale of One to Bard, I plumped for the guy from Stratford.

I'd been talking to two great friends, Dick Penny and George Costigan, about a production of *Macbeth* that we planned to take on the road. Steven Spielberg wanted me for *Saving Private Ryan* but I had to tell the Boss I was busy. After all, who needs Oscars when you've got Shakespeare and the real, living theatre? With years and years of friendship on the clock, Dick, George and I combined, along with Dick's partner, Steve Rebbeck, to produce *Macbeth* out of Bristol Old Vic. Ashley Martin-Davis was our designer, Pauline Constable was the lighting tech and we assembled a fantastic cast as we headed into Shakespeare's vision of the hell that ambition can, and will, deliver.

I went back many years with Dick and George. Dick was

a formidably well organised and incredibly caring arts ad-
ministrator whom I had persuaded to join the Little Theatre
Company at the start of the 1980s. He was a huge addition
to the company, the sort of indefatigable dynamo who made
things happen. He was enormously innovative, and a master
of being in the right place at the right time. Amid the anarchic trail blazing of those days at the Little, he seemed to be
the one with his hand on the rudder. Dick was a true friend.

George and I, on the other hand, had begun our friendship at the Everyman. We got on well both before and after
the meltdown that was Aberystwyth. When I returned,
tired and a little wounded from that sojourn to the Welsh
coast, he directed me in Roy Minton's *Death in Leicester*.
Our conversations ranged from that summer season, to how
I'd come close to the priesthood, to being a bus conductor
and how we might have faced the Devil or God, or both or
neither. We talked and talked and fell into what men call
Love-Trust. We enjoyed *Death in Leicester*, unlike the good
burghers of Liverpool who stayed away in droves. My nerves
were frayed for that show and I was kaylied on the opening
night, drinking wildly and just getting myself through the
performance. My drinking hadn't had anything to do with
thirst, I was quenching a fire inside. After that, whenever I
wrote letters to George from the RSC, I signed them: 'Pedro
who loved *Death in Leicester*.'

We all kept in touch and somewhere along the timelines
of meeting Jacqui, dealing with testicular cancer and celebrating the joyous birth of Will, we promised that one day
we'd do *Macbeth*.

I think the point at which we moved our plans on from
being fanciful to real was during a dinner. 'So, have we
lost you to the movies then?' said Dick. They hadn't at all.
Theatre was in my blood, I couldn't wait to return. *Macbeth*
was the perfect play because I was the right age for it; I

yearned for Lear but was still too young. We sat and talked seriously about the idea; sparks flew and we realised we had to do it. We wanted to set it up at Bristol or Liverpool, so that we could go back to our roots. We also wanted to take it around the country, rather than just go to London. Our plans were delayed when I was offered *Jurassic Park* and further delayed when *Amistad* came in. After that, however, when Steven offered me *Saving Private Ryan* I knew that, as far as *Macbeth* was concerned, it was now or never. It wasn't just that I relished the challenge, I didn't want to let George or Dick down. *Saving Private Ryan* was a 'no', Macbeth an emphatic 'yes'.

Much as I would have liked to work with Steven again, he understood the reason for my decision and I think we were both slightly sorrowful that we couldn't continue to make films together. He went ahead with Tom Hanks. I managed to surprise him when he was shooting on location in England. They sent a car to pick me up and I arrived on set, interrupting Steven when he was filming one of the big scenes. He didn't even know I was there, so I picked up a loud hailer and bellowed: 'How dare you make a movie without me?' We spent the next hour deep in conversation.

As for *Macbeth*, there is a particular line that Macbeth delivers to the servant who comes with the news that Birnam Wood is on the move that was my inspiration: 'Thou com'st to use thy tongue; thy story quickly.' Fear had rendered the messenger tongue-tied and the reason for that terror was that he had just seen Macbeth strangle his loyal retainer Seyton for bringing him the previous instalment of bad news, that Lady Macbeth was dead. Those were the words that had me hooked. I warned George that I would behave like a megalomaniac bully and I was true to my word. Privately, George seemed to understand this flip side to my personality. Will and Lily were with me when we were in rehearsal at the Old

Vic. They'd ask me questions and I'd answer with lines from the play: 'This supernatural soliciting cannot be ill, cannot be good, if ill why does it.' Will was unimpressed: 'Dad, I think you're becoming a bit too much like Macbeth.'

We rehearsed in Bristol and opened there, playing for a five-week sold-out run. Then we went to the Royal Court, at Liverpool, and carried on around the country's biggest theatres: I called it Macbeth's Rolling Thunder Tour. The box office was 100 per cent, it couldn't have been any better. I was very, very focused and very nervous too. At the outset, I'd wanted our production to be as remarkable as Peter Brook's *Dream*. I wanted it to be looked upon and leant upon like a neighbour's fence in years to come. Of all the tortured souls I'd ever played, no one understood the prickly heat of guilt like Macca. He actually became a monster, Satan's second-in-command. Macbeth realises he's sold his soul to the devil and he can't bear it. I wasn't interested in people wearing Elizabethan costumes mouthing rhubarb, rhubarb, rhubarb; I wanted our play to reflect the problems in Algeria – throat-slitting, or Bosnia – ethnic cleansing. That particular play seemed resonant for the times. We were on the edge of the twenty-first century, a time where paranoia and the decimation of society were the big issues. If *Macbeth* was about anything, it was lust for power and dominance and aggression. In our production, Macbeth became the beast; 666 and all that. One of the reasons George wanted me to do *Macbeth* was my Catholic background. At the end, Macca says, 'Life's but a walking shadow, a poor player that struts and frets his hour upon the stage and then is heard no more; it is a tale told by an idiot, full of sound and fury, signifying nothing.' If that isn't the nadir of nihilism, then I didn't know what is. Off set, my life was entirely different, of course. I'd be getting up early to watch *Teletubbies* with my daughter. Where would I have been without Tinky Winky, Po, Dipsy and Laa-Laa? I got away from the hype by being with Jax, Will and Lily. I even knew which colour and which aerial each Teletubby had.

It was thrilling to be back on stage, hard work but very satisfying. There were populist touches, the newly crowned Macbeths were fanfared to their banquet to the sound of Queen's 'We Are the Champions'. I loved the bizarre mixture of business-suited assassins and kilted samurai warriors. It was wonderful to be away from the high-blown pressure of Hollywood, treading the boards in the cities where I'd begun as a drama student. We visited Liverpool, Belfast, Bradford, Guildford and Nottingham and every performance was spiritually charged. I was a haunted, husky psycho. We wore long red skirts, it was as though we'd been dressed by Vivienne Westwood.

We wanted to do something without being tricksy that would have kids coming out of the theatre saying, 'Shakespeare's not half bad.' And I think we succeeded. We did three matinees per week and after the first five minutes of St Trinian's hell they were there with it, they followed it through. I remember one teenager writing to the Old Vic saying how fantastic the whole show had been. Her letter said: 'I never thought I would have sympathy for Macbeth, until I saw you.' It was manna from heaven. Teachers were appreciative of our work because we were connecting with their pupils. Sue Riley, head of creative arts at Broadlands School, in Keynsham, Bristol, wrote to the *Bristol Evening Post*: 'This production has been a godsend to teachers like myself, who so very rarely are able to show their pupils intelligent and challenging interpretations of Shakespeare's plays. My pupils have not stopped talking about the production.' It was a pleasure, Sue, a real pleasure.

At the RSC, years earlier, I'd once heard somebody say,

'If you dry, make it up, we all do.' But how dare they? How bloody dare they? Shakespeare didn't write a line unmeaningfully. Every word, every breath, every movement of our tour was loaded with meaning. When we were doing the tour, a major Hollywood impresario phoned me up to be in a particular film. He asked my agent: 'How much does it cost to get him out of this piddlin' little play? And then how much does he want on top of that?' I ignored it, there was no sell-out. I'd have been mortified if I'd taken the king's shilling.

We had our problems on tour, including emotional breakdowns and an accident with a sword. The reason for the story of the curse of *Macbeth* is that, in the early days of weekly rep companies, if a company was in financial trouble they'd put on *Macbeth* at short notice to make some quick cash. Without much time to rehearse, things were bound to go wrong. A witch once told me that the reason disaster attends every tour is because in the text there are twenty-two real witch's curses aired every night. Why not believe that? Just because it's stupid doesn't mean it's not true.

I did wake up a bit shivery each morning, thinking, 'Why are we doing this?' Maybe that was the challenge. Many times I was thinking, 'You must be joking.' The Rolling Thunder Tour hit the road in the autumn of 1997. We were doing the publicity just as *Jurassic Park* hit the screens. By that stage in my career, luxury was all about being able to go back to the theatre to work for very little money. At the end of the tour, we had the option of a run in London, but we'd left everything on the pitch; we were too tired to carry on. There was another idea, however, and we considered making a film. We wanted to push ourselves to do something fresh, to take the ideas and see whether they translated into a powerful script. We worked on the project for a year, I was hyper self-critical, and there were endless rewrites before we got to the point where we thought we had the script ready and we pitched to Steve Abbott. At one point, there were meetings in London and Los Angeles and we had it financed; then the studio reorganised and dropped out. Dick, George and I all became busy and shelved our film because it was something that we would have liked to do, rather than needed to do.

∾

I continued to search for new challenges and tried to avoid repeating roles that I'd already played. So I was thrilled to receive a script for Sam Miller's *Among Giants*. I had worked with Sam before as an actor, and he wanted me to take the lead, Ray, in his first feature. I was to star alongside Rachel Griffiths and it was nice being on that trip, not knowing exactly what was going to happen. Of course, being alongside somebody as lissom and alluring as Rachel made it all the sweeter. In fact, I think it was Rachel who got me on board; she'd told Sam: 'We must get Pete to play this part.' When I first read the script, I didn't recognise it as a romance. In fact, Jax pointed it out about two or three weeks later, after she'd read it. She rang me up and said, 'I know why you're doing this.' I said, 'Why?' She said, 'It's a romantic lead.' I hadn't really spotted that. I'd just thought it was a great script with an intriguing story. It had been written by Simon Beaufoy, the guy who'd made *The Full Monty*, and he set it up in windswept Yorkshire. The writer had described it wistfully as a contemporary western, where the characters lived out on the moors in the back of vans and had a very frontiersmen lifestyle. The action revolved around a group of black economy chaps who painted pylons, when into their midst came Rachel. A love triangle occurred between my young mate, me and Rachel. My mate thought he was

going to pull her but she went for me instead. Playing a leading man was a new challenge.

The cinematography was beautiful; the director of photography was Witold Stok, a Polish film-maker who settled
in London and had worked on projects like the BAFTA-
nominated *The Rector's Wife* and *Close My Eyes*. The early
shots didn't work. They'd created a mock-up of a pylon for
me, Rachel and our fellow actor James Thornton. But when
I saw the rushes I didn't believe any of it and, if I wasn't
convinced, the audience wouldn't be either. The producers
went back to the drawing board and agreed that we should
film at height, which meant shooting at either 140 feet up
a pylon or 200 feet up a sheer rock face. The low budget
meant we couldn't afford the cost of blue-screen work or
special effects and there was no money for stuntmen either;
so Rachel and James and I had to do everything for real,
working together hundreds of feet from the ground, often
suspended in space high above the Yorkshire Moors. There
was a double for James on the first climb, but he was so
good that the double wasn't used. There was a double for
Rachel on the plummet down too, when she bungee-jumped
from the pylon, but the rest we did ourselves. Some of the
work was intense; the very end sequence, where the shot
pulled back on Ray underneath the pylon; that was all shot
from a helicopter.

Before *Among Giants*, I'd only ever climbed once before;
I think that had been when I was a student, and I hated
it. I was trained to climb the pylons by a guy called Mike
Brown, a National Grid engineer. I was extremely nervous
at first, but Mike reassured me and by the end I was enjoying it. There were four basic requirements: a head for
heights, nerves of steel, an outward-bound nature and a
strong stomach. It's funny, people saw me in that film and I
was quite trim, so they assumed I must have been working

out. I had friends from America phone up and say: 'Hey, man, have you been pumping iron?' Truth is, I exercised every morning: I got up and raised one eyebrow, then the other.

The most talked-about scene was an erotic one featuring Rachel and me that had been shot in a huge power station cooling tower near Sheffield. We appeared in a naked frolic, with a big stream of water hitting our bodies, it was amazing. I was into my early fifties and there I was, kit off; it felt fantastic. The scene was stunning, one of the most beautiful I've seen on film in terms of two people discovering each other. Obviously, I knew I was no glamour guy, but I had no worries about doing it, it was absolutely right for the film. Special effects had gallons of water splashing around and we were covered in it; it was cold but exhilarating. The day of the shoot was gloriously cloudless and Sam set up a phalanx of music speakers. Then they had the tower lit and put smoke in it; it became like a primordial rock concert played out in some vast, post-modern cathedral. Rachel and I walked into the arena in our dressing gowns, after playing backgammon and drinking Boddingtons all morning; by that time our relationship was so good we could have done anything. I loved the shots; ordinary people have those wonderful moments, you don't have to be an Adonis to have a deeply sensitive scene. When we filmed the nude scene, Alan Stewart, the camera operator, took a steadycam sequence walking backwards in ever-decreasing circles around the two of us. The take was so exhausting that Alan fell to the floor with exhaustion at the end of each six-minute sequence because he couldn't hold the camera up any more. It was stupendous working with Rachel. When you get that honest with each other it can get dangerous, but there was so much mutual trust and respect and all those lovely things that the work seemed very natural. We were

kindred spirits, we thought similar things. Rachel was wonderfully fearless. 'A few years ago, I turned up at a casino
opening naked, except for a crown of thorns,' she told me. I
don't think I'd have been able to do that, I didn't have quite
her body.

It was a dangerous, exciting adventure to be part of
Among Giants; the nudity, climbing, a love story and line
dancing. Besides, it wasn't the physical nudity that frightened me, it was the emotional nudity that was the most dangerous thing of all. But if there hadn't been a deep terror
in what I was doing, then it probably wouldn't have been
worth it. The one thing I had gained from the previous few
years was the confidence to take a risk, to think, 'Fuck it,
failure doesn't matter.'

When the film was in the can, we were pleased with
it; we knew that we faced being hoist by the *Full Monty*
petard but, unlike in that film, the audience actually got a
Full Monty. At the age of fifty-three, it felt great to finally
get the girl. I thought about when Garbo first appeared in
talking movies and they advertised them as 'Garbo talks'.
On *Among Giants*, they should have said: 'Postlethwaite
loves'.

I loved the fact that Sam had taken me out of my comfort
zone and I enjoyed each and every one of the forty-two days
on location. When I'd read the script, I didn't really think of
the physical things I was going to have to do, like climbing
pylons or dancing around in the nude; those things seemed
somehow abstract. They were part of the patchwork of the
film. I'd just thought: 'Okay, we'll do that when it happens.'
The crew probably didn't realise what was in store either.
They had as many challenges as us, they had to climb the
pylons lugging their equipment behind. During one sequence,
one of the cameramen took a Polaroid of me while I was up
one of the pylons. I was wearing dungarees and a woolly

hat, painting the steel, and beside me, in the picture, was a duplicate image, an exact replica. It would have been impossible for that to happen with a Polaroid and I showed it to Will. 'It's obvious, isn't it, Dad?' he said. 'It's your ghost.'

ELEVEN

The Butterfly's Flown

&

There are dramas that come along at the perfect moment. *Lost for Words* was one of those. It was a two-hour ITV film with Dame Thora Hird. The piece was wonderfully engaging and explored the bittersweet relationship between my character, Deric Longden, and his mother, played by Thora Hird, as she declined into dementia. It was thrilling to play alongside Thora, I think it was one of the last things that she did and she deservedly won a BAFTA for it. I was nominated too. *Lost for Words* was a deeply personal choice because at the time my mother was eighty-five and although she didn't suffer from dementia, it reflected many of the aspects of our relationship. She'd have killed me for saying it, but it could have been about us; it smacked of the truth. There was a wonderful balance between tragedy and comedy, it was dreamlike and poignant. I imagined the audience laughing as much crying. Thora was an absolute darling and she'd ring me up at our hotel first thing in the morning to ask what time I was going to take her to breakfast. She was an extraordinary creature, fantastic to work with.

Paul Abbott's *Butterfly Collectors*, which came out around the same time, was a stunning TV drama about a policeman who emphatically hated his job. I played John McKeown, a disillusioned detective who was on the trail of a murder suspect. McKeown was emotionally trapped and spiritually moribund, so he involved himself in the suspect's complex life. He realised that so much of his emotional terrain had been washed away down the years, and that the suspect had far better values. The piece was all about reassessing your life.

It was an apposite project because I'd started to revalue my own life; it had changed irrevocably and whatever I did was news. I remember learning an unpleasant lesson from a journalist once, after I told him I'd love to play Parker in a movie version of *Thunderbirds*. The next thing I knew there was a story in the newspapers saying I'd already been cast as Parker, which was a bit naughty. People seemed to think of me as being the guy who'd never made a dud, though there had been a few over the years including one called *Brute*, which I had made some years before with John Hurt. It was about approved-school pupils being sent out to orphanages in Eastern Europe. It was filmed in Warsaw by Maciej Dejczer, who was a very intense student of Kieslowski. Eventually, it didn't relate to any part of my life. I didn't have any hooks on it, it just seemed as though Maciej hated kids. I thought it was a good script and I suspect my reasons for doing it were that it was there and could be fitted in. But having been part of a film that meant so little to me made me reassess. I started to wonder if I was giving as much attention to my family as I would have liked, so I decided to slow down.

I'd become a bit of a victim of my own success and there were times when the intensity felt like madness as I worked on up to three projects at a time. I remember one occasion when I was doing a couple of films at once and found myself at San Francisco airport thinking: 'Oh no, I should be at JFK in New York.' In actual fact, I should have been in Los Angeles. Having three airports inside my head simultaneously was not a good place to be and I had a stop-this-bus-I-want-to-get-off moment. I took a few months off and enjoyed the time with Jax, Will and Lily. Jax ruled the roost and our nine-year-old and two-year-old were constantly running around. We'd go into the house cleaning sheep droppings off our feet and then clean up after the kids. It felt like I was back to reality; as a family, we had a lot of fun together and I loved them to bits. We were also very much a part of the community in our little Shropshire hamlet. We'd always been very down-to-earth, the village had given us some sort of normality. Whenever I needed to go overseas, I'd try to harden myself to the pain of an enforced absence from my family, otherwise it would have been too much. There's no denying the excitement of flying to Ireland for one week and then America the next; but nothing could ever beat Jax and the kids. I loved the times when we all went away together; seeing Will sitting in a golf cart on Steven Spielberg's knee, being given a personal tour of Universal Studios in Hollywood. But as they got older, I couldn't keep up; I don't suppose any parent can. Sometimes, Lily would look up at me as though to say, 'What is that old man doing here?' Or she'd say: 'Dad! That's not Robbie Williams, that's Steps' or S Club 7, or whoever they happened to be. My family understood that my job wasn't the sort of one I could do at home and there were times when I had to be away and just get on with it. But the best part of going away was always the coming home.

There were times, of course, when coming home was terribly poignant, and around that period my mother died. It was a profound loss, though she had been ill for a while so we had time to prepare ourselves for her departure. She'd survived my father for twelve years, and cancer took her when she was eighty-six. When she died, we were at the house and we waited for undertakers to come so that they could take her away. I was with Mike. He said: 'When they put her in a bag and bring her down the stairs they won't stand on ceremony. I think we should bring her down ourselves.'

I agreed. 'All right, Mike, if it's best that we do it, we'll do it together.'

But when the undertakers arrived, Mike sensed I wasn't ready to see my mother put in a bag. The words he said in those moments will stay with me forever. He was unbelievably empathetic.

'Don't worry, lad. This is just the pupa; the butterfly's already flown.'

The undertakers then zipped her in the bag and we carried her down. Mike's words made me happy for her; there was a sense of freedom: Mother had been liberated. To this day, I still think of my parents all the time and never underestimate their importance. They were everything to me, even though we didn't always agree. Their Catholicism inspired a raging Conservatism and, politically, I had as much in common with them as Adam Smith did with John Maynard Keynes. There were times when my rebellion was overt, particularly during my years at teacher training college. When I'd come home, we'd have fierce arguments, but they were underpinned with love. My mother may have taken years to realise I was serious about being an actor, but when she did so she became very proud. No one could have been more pleased than she was when I was nominated for an Oscar.

The absence of my parents was profound and I missed their constant support and love. But even though I had reassessed my priorities, there would always be the need to act when the right script came along. *The Sins*, in 2000, later nominated for a BAFTA, was certainly one of these. It was one of David Yates' first TV pieces and I played a retired bank robber, Len Green, who wanted to go straight after being released from nick. There was a good cast, with Geraldine James playing my wife, and I renewed my friendship with Philip Jackson, from *Brassed Off*, who played a pub landlord. Some of my recollections are a little hazy and the shoots were quite edgy, even dangerous at times. We worked in a cauldron of creativity and sometimes things got quite near the knuckle, it could be explosive. While we were filming, I had a flat in Notting Hill and Philip used to come round to listen to music and talk. Philip had also recently suffered a bereavement as his father had gone; both of us were devastated by our losses. Actors talk about Northerners and Liverpudlians as being sentimental, but we didn't spend time together because of that; it was just good to get away from the set, reflect on what had happened and switch off.

I hadn't turned my back on films, however, and I lined up in a stellar cast for Lasse Hallström's *The Shipping News*, an adaptation of the Pulitzer Prize-winning E. Annie Proulx novel. Kevin Spacey, Julianne Moore, Dame Judi Dench, Cate Blanchett and Rhys Ifans were among the players who were flown out to New Bonaventure, in Newfoundland, to film amid a bleak canvas of nothingness. The crew was fantastic and had enormous respect for the location. At one point, they built a house in Halifax before disassembling it and shipping it to Newfoundland, where it was rebuilt. Once they'd finished with it, they took it back down and removed every trace. They were very conscious of our environment. Nova Scotia is an immensely beautiful area and the company got along very well. I seem to remember spending a lot of time hanging out with Kevin Spacey, in fleapit bars, where we'd talk all night about great films and theatres – and I'd thrash him at pool. He'd beaten me at the Academy Awards, but I extracted revenge on the green baize. Kevin is a beautiful actor, a man I held in high regard. We hadn't had time to socialise when we'd worked on *The Usual Suspects* but on *The Shipping News* we caught up. His passion for the theatre was just as strong as mine and he was fascinated by the productions that I'd either seen or performed in. He could also drink and there may have been more than one occasion when we crawled back to our rooms, much the worse for wear.

But overall, the emphasis in my career began to move back to theatre, partly through choice and partly because I didn't receive the plethora of scripts, good scripts, that I'd received during the years of *Romeo + Juliet*, *Brassed Off* and *The Usual Suspects*. There'd come a point in my career when I'd become valuable to film-makers, where the backers and producers felt confident about using me because my track record was good. People had never lost faith in me, and for that I was grateful. When I started out, I realised that actors could do anything, providing someone had the bottle to hire them. Thankfully, people had always shown that faith in me. I'd never had to sign on and there had been no shortage of work. Although the offers had changed, I didn't consider myself a better actor than I was ten years earlier. I also remained choosy about my scripts, following Hitchcock's maxim: 'The three most important things about a film are the script, the script and the script.' You can't make a silk purse out of a sow's ear was a phrase that summed up my view of both scriptwriters and the face I saw when I sat down in the make-up artist's chair.

At one stage, I got the opportunity to fulfil one of my lifetime ambitions when I was asked to work with Martin

Scorsese; but I couldn't do it. Martin wanted me to play alongside Dan Day-Lewis in *The Gangs of New York*. He wrote to me saying how good it was that we were going to be working together. The producers tried to persuade all of us to accept less than full pay, just because we were working with Martin. The explanation was 'because everyone wants to work with Martin Scorsese'. It didn't wash with me. It had been the biggest dream of my life to work with him, but I thought it was a bit of a scam and so I said no. It was heartbreaking, really, but I just don't think it was fair. I wasn't doing that.

Theatre, however, threw up constant new challenges. There were new ascents to make, and they were becoming ever steeper. Greg Hersov wanted me to revisit the Royal Exchange in Manchester. We'd first worked together many years earlier, on *Duchess of Malfi* and *Emperor Jones*. We discussed what plays I might do and he was very open. He spent a long time trying to persuade me to do Ben Jonson's *Volpone* and then we talked about *American Buffalo*, which was quite interesting. But I'd got something else in mind. I remembered my experience of playing in *The Homecoming*, back at college, and I wanted to reprise that and take the lead, Max. I'd done it originally with Eamon Boland, a fellow actor, and he came back to play Sam in the new production. During the six months leading up to the show, Greg and I met a lot, or he'd come to stay in Shropshire. We were very meticulous on every area, we were interested in the whole play, not just my character. When we went through casting, I read with the actors and although I didn't see it as my place to say whom I wanted, it meant that Greg could see how people were with me. It was wonderful to return to *The Homecoming*. Back in '66 at college, I'd been twenty years old, playing a character who was seventy, the year after Pinter played it. I'd also directed the play at drama school and it had always hit me right between the eyes, it was an extraordinary piece of writing. Pinter had written it from the point of what an actor could do with that role. He was one of those thrilling playwrights who were about in the mid-1960s that we were discovering fresh from the printers.

It was equally thrilling to be back at the Royal Exchange, a massive Victorian building with a space like a lunar module in the middle of it. I'd always enjoyed being there, playing in the round. I thought it would be brilliantly risky and dangerous to do a play like that, written for a proscenium, in-the-round, and would I hoped capture the extraordinary claustrophobic tension of the piece. I needed to make sure Max took the whole audience with him because it was menacing and funny. I'm not sure how my mother would have reacted to the 'industrial-style' language, had she still been there. She didn't mind what sort of parts I played but she never liked me using bad language on stage. I once told her about one part I was to play and that the language was rather coarse. She said she was glad I'd got the part but I shouldn't swear on stage. 'Tell them you are not going to say it. Just tell them you won't,' she said.

It felt like there was a lot of pressure on me before I started. At times, I thought: 'Why am I doing this? Why do I put myself through it?' I am sure there is an element of sado-masochism in what I do. If it was easy, there would be no point. If it was easy, I would rather stay at home and read a book. *The Homecoming* redefined domestic drama, it was dark and brutal, it was impossible to resist. It dealt with what we really think about marriage and monogamy. To describe it as misogynistic would be too simplistic; it's about people who are lacking in love, who need it tremendously but haven't got the language to ask for it. On a practical level, they don't hug. It's almost a metaphor for humanity; the more speedily we communicate, the less we're talking to each other. Happily, we achieved what we set out to do. It was a hit.

My appetite for the theatre was increasing and I'd also begun working on a project by Justin Butcher, called *Scaramouche Jones*. Justin and the director, Rupert Goold, wanted to put it on and sent it to my agent. I adored it and asked Dick Penny to read it. Initially, Dick didn't like it, but I was certain from the off and eventually the same production team that had worked on *Macbeth* got involved. It spanned the hundred years of the twentieth century and had a cast of one: me. I played a hundred-year-old clown on the last night of his life, looking back at his own story, a story that took in numerous adventures across the globe. Scaramouche was an everyman character, a clown by trade. He had an extraordinary capacity for making people laugh and took the sins of the world on his shoulders, despite being an ordinary clown. Justin's script was phenomenal in its detail, like a baroque cathedral. I pictured it as a massive oratorio with different notes.

Scaramouche was a very ambitious piece of writing and I was daunted by it. I'd done a one-man play before during the Not the RSC Festival in London. It was called *Temptation*, by my friend, Nick Dear. That had been about forty minutes long and the language was simpler. My abiding memory of that piece was the sheer terror of doing a one-man show. Each night, I'd be on my own and when I slipped up on a word it would jar, like hitting a wrong note in a symphony. I worked hard to learn my lines for the ninety-minute *Scaramouche* monologue and found it very rewarding when I could do sections without the book. The trick was to find out exactly what things meant and where the character's head and heart were, what it meant to him spiritually and emotionally. Jax, Will, Lily and I took a break in Minorca and I'd rise early each morning, make a cup of coffee then sit alone by the pool as the sun was coming up, learning my lines. I'd write notes to myself, to help store it in my memory bank.

We opened at the Ulster Bank Dublin Theatre Festival in the Samuel Beckett Theatre, which was a last-minute booking. When I got to Ireland, I still hadn't learned the last twenty minutes, so it was a bit harum-scarum but it went down extremely well. The essence was just to get on and do it, to get through each evening. Scaramouche had seven white masks that had been accumulated at various points in his life and he wanted to rid himself of them so that he could go naked into death. Each night was emotionally liberating and new; I've never been a musician but I imagine if I were to play a piece by Bach I'd interpret the notes in a different way each time I played. That's how I can best describe it. We took it on tour; my choice of accommodation being decided by recommendations in the *Good Beer Guide*. The inns that we stayed at were brilliant because the World Cup was going on so we'd do the show, get back to the pub, have a couple of drinks, get up, have breakfast and watch a World Cup game on the telly at 7.30 a.m. in the morning.

Then, one day: 'Pete, they want to take the play overseas.' *Scaramouche* had mushroomed and we were asked to tour Australia, New Zealand and Canada.

Before flying to Australia, we did a short run in Salisbury, and then boarded the plane to Perth. It was my first time in Australia and heralded the start of an extraordinary series of friendships. On our opening night, a guy came to the stage door in Perth and gave me a film script, called *Liyarn Ngarn*. At the time I didn't take much notice because I was preoccupied with *Scaramouche*, terrified by the prospect of playing to a capacity 1,200-seat theatre. But after the show, I suddenly realised that inside that older man with grey hair was a much younger man I knew from thirty years before.

It was Bill Johnson, who'd been in the seminary with me, when we were both training to be Catholic priests. I had no idea he'd gone to Australia. Luckily he left his phone number on the script.

We spent time together, catching up, and Bill told me about the tragedy of Louis St John, his adopted son. Louis had been one of the stolen generation of Aboriginal children and had been adopted in Alice Springs by Bill and his wife Pauline before he was two years old. On the day of his nineteenth birthday, in January 1992, Louis was walking home from a party when he was attacked and beaten to death. He was only a few blocks from his home in a quiet affluent beach suburb of northern Perth, and two young Englishmen were convicted of his murder. They killed Louis because he was black. Bill suggested I go back to Australia later, which I did, to find out more. He introduced me to an old friend, singer-songwriter Archie Roach, suggesting he also make the journey. A documentary about Louis would have been too expensive to make so we got in touch with the media department at Murdoch University, whose students shot the film with their tutor, Martin Mhando, as director. There was one more important connection: Pat Dodson, one of the fathers of reconciliation in Australia who was a Commissioner into Aboriginal Deaths in Custody, as well as being a former Catholic priest. Pat had recognised me at Broome airport; serendipitously he'd watched *Brassed Off* a few weeks before and quite by chance he came over to talk. We got on, I told him about the project and he agreed to help.

Liyarn Ngarn became incredibly important to me. Within a couple of weeks, the things we encountered were bigger and more important than any of us had anticipated. We had a kind of a plan: the story of Bill's son was the springboard, and the idea for the work was to look at the historical, political and spiritual context of the whole indigenous situation. There wasn't really an agenda, but the deeper we went into the heart of darkness, the more the agenda suggested itself to us. It changed us. I'm still struggling to come to terms with it even now – it's unfathomable. The road was littered with desperation, land dispossession and racism: terra nullis. It was pretty clear that Australia was losing a culture with an extraordinary breadth, depth and colour.

Our editor, David Teale, sifted through more than one hundred hours of film and Archie, Pat and I encouraged him to bring out the emotional side of the story. That was what we wanted. That's what *Liyarn Ngarn* became. People weren't calling it a documentary by the time we'd done, they were calling it a film. *Liyarn Ngarn* literally meant a meeting of the hearts, minds and spirit of the two unique peoples of Australia: Aboriginal and non-Aboriginal. I preferred Archie Roach's explanation. He described it as two stories becoming one, the white fella story and the Aboriginal story, where total respect is given for each side of the storytelling.

There was time for other projects too and at one stage I zoomed off with Paul Hogan and Michael Caton to film the comedy *Strange Bedfellows*, in rural New South Wales. It was the story of two elderly men who discovered there were significant tax advantages to living together as a couple, so they pretended to be gay to fool the authorities.

Scaramouche was also still a work in progress and we took it to Canada, thanks to my great friend, Gabriella Martinelli. I'd worked with Gabriella a few years before on Baz Luhrmann's *Romeo + Juliet* as well as *Between Strangers*, a film with Sophia Loren. Me, a lad from Warrington, filming with Sophia Loren! Karimba. I could hardly believe it. She is fabulous, and wonderful to work with. On the first day of shooting I was in bed with Sophia, who played my wife. She had to massage my legs with oil. I turned and said to Gabriella: 'You do realise, I'm the most envied man in England at this moment.' She laughed. I pushed my luck: 'Sophia, a little harder, if you would.' There was an amazing chemistry between Sophia and me, I adored her. Amusingly, that scene almost didn't happen. I'd been sitting on a bench, watching Sophia work, when a guard came over, put his hand on my shoulder and said: 'I'm sorry, this is a private film set and you will have to leave now. Move away, please.'

'But I'm filming opposite Sophia, I play her husband.'

'I am so terribly sorry, sir.'

Sophia is incredibly beautiful in the most delightful, internal, gorgeous way. It felt as though she wasn't an actress; she couldn't cheat. We had our photographs taken to promote the film and I look at them now and can't believe they're real. They remind me of snaps you take in Blackpool, when you put yourself next to someone famous. 'There's me and there's Sophia Loren.' It's like those tourist things in Spain, when you can make yourself a bullfighter on a poster. When we finished the movie, I told my agent that I would do anything that Gabriella wanted me to do: whether it involved oil and Sophia Loren or not.

Gabriella asked me to return to Toronto for a run in *Scaramouche*. She'd never done theatre before, always film, but she approached the owners of the Wintergarden, who were thrilled to stage a run of about six weeks. I stayed in a hotel nearby, so I could walk to and from work. 'Pete, would you like a driver, or a house somewhere?' asked Gabriella. I said no. We'd do the show and then meet in a pub, right across the street, where I'd order a Guinness and people would gather round. It felt like home, as though we'd transferred Shropshire to Toronto. On my days off, I'd explore the city. At the end of the run, Gabriella gave me a piece of Eskimo art, which was really special. She told me I was one of the greatest actors of the twentieth century; up there, with Olivier and Gielgud. I wasn't so sure about all of that, but the Eskimo art was fantastic.

I'd received my OBE along the way, in 2004. I'd been in Toronto when I took the telephone call asking me to ring Downing Street urgently. They wanted to know whether I would accept it; I think they called on the Wednesday and the closing date was Friday. It was a great honour. The call had been unexpected, it came like a bolt from the blue. I'd no idea where the idea came from, though I thought it was great. I was working on *Dark Water* at the time, a low-key film noir being made in New York and Toronto. The family came with me for the big day and I thoroughly enjoyed meeting the Queen again at the investiture. It was a day my mother would have been very proud of. She had found it life-changing when I met the Queen back at the RSC during the 1980s, so she would have been even more thrilled to have seen my decoration. I talked to HM about my next project, which was to be set in Kenya, a country she knew well. It was something I was very excited about: an adaptation of John le Carré's novel, *The Constant Gardener*. Everything about it excited me – the location, the cast – Ralph Fiennes, Rachel Weisz and Bill Nighy – and the things the film was saying. The integrity of the film matched my activism; Ralph's character turned to his conscience and was seeking redemption; it was almost Biblical.

There was a sad backstory to my part, though. It had originally been given to Tim Spall, but he was too ill to play it, so it was offered to me. The casting director had suggested me to Fernando Meirelles. I've rarely met a man as humble and intuitive. He said he didn't understand why I would take the film. It was as though I needed to interview him, rather than the other way round. But I loved it. Tim had made lots of wonderfully incisive notes, which he passed on to me, and thankfully he made a full recovery. *The Constant Gardener* was a gift and I was able to catch up with Tracey Seaward, who filled me in on the adventures of Casey Postlethwaite. It was a treat to work with her once more. I flew out to Nairobi then went straight to Loiyangalani and enjoyed working with Ralph, who is gentlemanly, motivated and dedicated. The location was the most beautiful one that I've ever visited, we were in this wild, wild landscape and felt as though we were in the birthplace of civilisation. I was there for three weeks and the environment was unspeakably rich and life-affirming. It was quite difficult to get food there, so we appreciated the things we had; we'd just sit there eating in the evening. I worked with the tribespeople and the little girl, Anna. Throughout the shoot, there was an extraordinary discipline and commitment; there was a desire to get it right. Ralph was great fun, we'd sit there laughing in the morning, in our make-up chairs, in the heat. We shared the same approach to the work, wanting it to be exquisite, being prepared to go again and again. There was a real immediacy to working with him, he has great energy and immense concentration. We shot scenes in the most extraordinary light, working in situations that were physically quite challenging. Then, during the evening, we'd have a beer or two, have a laugh and a joke. We'd sit back with our beers and talk. Ralph had a great appreciation of theatre and we talked about the RSC, the plays and directors and actors. Fernando is also a blessed man, he loves people being as natural as possible and his energy fed into the way we responded.

The best part of going away to work was always the coming home. Much as I enjoyed filming in Kenya, it was bliss to return to Shropshire's verdant undulations and, of course, to Jax. My arrival home frequently coincided with a never-ending stream of requests from local community groups and organisations, and I was usually happy to comply. 'Would you launch a new shuttle bus through the Shropshire Hills Area of Outstanding Natural Beauty?' I was asked. 'Yes, as long as you don't want me to be the conductor. "Ding, ding, all aboard the Long Mynd Shuttle."' I was also asked to launch a new cultural strategy for south Shropshire and engage in other campaigns at a local level. I felt it was important to support rural services. I wasn't a city boy, I'd done all that. I think my love for the country stemmed back to those heady, halcyon days of living out in Shakespeare's Warwickshire.

I'd also used *Scaramouche* back home, to raise money for local arts and culture in Shropshire. We helped generate funds for new theatre seating at the local school, which had fostered Will's formative ambition to act, by doing two performances in the school's new auditorium. We also put on a performance at Ludlow Assembly Rooms, to raise money for the Caitlin Kickstart Fund. The fund was named after the Ludlow College student Caitlin Hurcombe, who had died. Her mother had founded it to support other teenagers with artistic ambitions. Caitlin had been in her final year in 1998 when the Government replaced the grant system with a loan system for higher and further education, a policy that was little short of disastrous. She'd taken her life and her mother, Linda, had wanted to do something in her memory and for her friends' futures, something that would have delighted Caitlin as well as her contemporaries. Linda wrote to me to tell me Caitlin's story and ask me to be a patron of the fund. Those shows were a very worthwhile thing and, though it was scary playing in front of my neighbours, the people of Shropshire were invariably supportive.

It wasn't just local groups that wanted me to engage in campaigns. I was once asked whether I was the most traditional leftie in Hollywood. I thought the question was a little ambiguous, so I replied: 'I'm the best traditional leftie in

Hollywood.' I've always been a political man, every breath I've ever taken has been political. I think the Labour Party must have picked up on that because back in 1997 I had got a call from their HQ, asking me to film a Capra-esque election broadcast exhorting people to come out and vote. The election broadcast was directed by Stephen Frears and I played a taxi driver who encouraged people to head for the polling stations. Technically, there had to be a fee: 'I'll do it for a quid,' I told them. Anything to get those Tories shipped out of England.

Even more excitingly, for me, in 2005 Christian Aid asked me to play a part in their Make Poverty History March in Edinburgh and I joined 225,000 other people who were sick to death that the G8 leaders, who were gathered at the near-by Gleneagles Hotel, were ignoring the plight of the poorest people in the world. We wanted more aid for Africa, debt cancellation and fairer trade. It wasn't just about making poverty history, it was about making quite a few things history, like war and greed and capitalism. The atmosphere was electric, absolutely electric. There was a wave of absolute passion and desire; it was phenomenal, phenomenal. I'd never experienced anything like it. I was ushered onto the stage and blown away by the crowd. I raised my cap, tried to get them to pause, so that I could speak. I had my notes in my hand, but I knew what I wanted to say and I spoke from the heart.

'First they ignore you, then they laugh at you, then they fight you, and then you win.' The roar was deafening. 'They're not my words, unfortunately, they're the words of Mahatma Gandhi. But to my mind, that's exactly what to-day is all about. We're gathered here today, bound together by a common humanity, and a passionate desire for justice. But make no mistake about this, we're also here to win. Okay. We have to win. And we won't be ignored. They may laugh at us, but we can say to our political leaders today, give us action and not words. And why? Because we've had enough.' The cheers were loud and long.

I continued: 'We've had enough, we've had enough of press releases and enough of political spin. We've had enough of broken promises and in some cases downright lies. Well, we've had enough. Now is the time for the leaders of the G8 conference, speaking over there in the Gleneagles, to implement policies that are relevant and make them responsible, politically responsible, for the abject poverty, the starvation, the environmental devastation and death that is blighting the lives of millions of our brothers and sisters in the developing world every single day. It's not a laughing matter. It's time for clear justice and not mere charity.

'As Desmond Tutu said: "I'm not interested in picking up the crumbs of compassion from the table, thrown by someone who considers himself to be my master. I want the full menu of rights." And that is exactly what we want for the poverty-stricken: a full menu of rights. And you all know how we can achieve this, in the northern hemisphere and in the south. Campaigns and activists all over the world are calling, not for free trade but for trade justice, for 100 per cent unconditional debt cancellation. And also, not just for aid, but for relevant and specific aid put into the hands of those many thousands who need it and not into the hands of a small elite, who will definitely steal it.'

The organisers were on the stage, urging me to cut it short, to get off and make way for a band.

'I'll cut through right to the end. Nelson Mandela was told he would never see an end to apartheid in South Africa. Well, we all know what happened to that great man. He walked the long road to freedom and he made apartheid history. Our objective here today is crystal clear: make poverty history.'

TWELVE

Your Brother is Still There

∽

The journalists who habitually ask me whether I prefer film, theatre or TV must be blind to the absurdity of their question. They could just as easily ask: 'So, if God tells you he's going to deprive you of A) oxygen, B) food, or, C) water: which one do you choose?' I smile politely at the inanity of their question and tell them I love all equally, though in truth the answer is probably theatre. Being on stage is my Sangreal; it was where I find divine revelation. During the autumn of my career, I played across all three mediums, film, theatre and TV, performing in roles that had political, spiritual and creative meaning.

A film that ticked all of the boxes was a delightfully evocative script for a production by Sir Richard Attenborough. *Closing the Ring* was a wonderful film which was based on a true story about an American fighter plane which crashed into the Black Mountains, outside Belfast. A young lad raced to help the crew and reached the pilot just in time. He spoke to him before the plane burst into flames and the pilot gave the lad a ring off his finger. He asked him to get it to his wife and say: 'Tell her she no longer needs to keep her promise.' The film told an evocative tale of the lad searching out and finding the pilot's wife, who was played by Shirley MacLaine. It was really well written by Peter Woodward.

Nothing could have prepared me for the thunderbolt that struck during filming. I lost my brother, Mike, and it was a devastating blow, a loss of unimaginable proportions that turned my world on its axis. Mike died suddenly, one minute he was there and the next he was not. There was no reason for it, he just got out of bed one morning and collapsed. He was only sixty-one. Mike had been born a year before me and had worked all his life as a builder in Warrington, he'd just begun to think about easing off a little when it happened. The week before he died, he'd complained about a twinge in his chest. I'd asked him if he was going to get it checked out but he said, 'No – I'm not going to spend the rest of my life worrying about death.' None of us expected him to go. He got up at about 5.15 a.m. one day then his wife, Chris, heard a bang; that was it, he'd gone.

Mike had been a real hero throughout my life and I was devastated. Whenever I went back to Warrington we'd meet at St Oswald's Club for a few jars. We'd sit and sup at Ossie's, between frames of pool. He was a very popular guy back home and there was a strong bond between us. He was a Northern, working-class bloke, a builder and decorator, but he was so much more than that. He could perceive how people felt, he was an extraordinary man. Sue Johnston used to tell a wonderful story about Mike and me. Mike would occasionally do odd jobs at her house, when she lived at Cinnamon Brow, next to Padgate. When he'd go through the gate, Sue would look through the window and think: 'Oh, Pete's here, what's Pete doing here?' – then she'd do a double-take and realise it was our Mike. One of the best pictures she had in her mind was of the pair of us going down to the club, at Ossie's, walking along Padgate Lane. There we'd be, in our baseball caps and donkey jackets, looking like a pair of hard-knock builders. Sue would think: 'Right, which of those is a Hollywood film star?' The image just made her laugh. Mike and I loved it at Ossie's, it was where we'd spent our working-class lives, loving one another, spending time. But that was me and him in a nutshell; that image of Sue's summed us up.

Sue had written to me a few years earlier, when I'd lost my mother. I think she'd realised how profound the shock had been back then and her family had also gone to the funeral. We'd seen each other a while after, at the BAFTAs, when the *Royle Family* was up for something. Jax and I joined her table and we'd had a right old night. She understood that losing Mike was an even bigger shock because it was totally unexpected. After Mike had gone, Sue's Auntie Jean, who also went to Ossie's, would look at where my brother used to sit and say: 'It really upsets me because there's no Mike, sitting there.'

He died during *Closing the Ring*, and I had to break off for the funeral. Delivering the eulogy was the toughest performance of my life. When we were filming, Richard could see that I was thinking about Mike the whole time, he sensed my preoccupation. But the group that he'd brought together: Christopher Plummer, Shirley MacLaine, Mischa Barton, Stephen Amell and Neve Campbell, were marvellously supportive; they understood. When I look back on that film now, I watch some of the shots and think, 'I know what I was thinking there.' Lord Attenborough knew too. When he was directing me, he would be saying: 'Your brother was there. That was your brother.'

∾

Ultimately, Mike's passing motivated me to do my next project, *The Tempest*; I needed to do something really important and dangerous to cope with his death. When I was completely immersed in a part, I had no responsibilities to anybody. I was just in that moment, I found solace in being able to become somebody else. As an actor, I had the chance to express emotions that otherwise I wouldn't have been able to. So *The Tempest* came at the right time because I was devastated at losing Mike. A line in the play said: 'Be not afraid: the isle is full of noises': that sealed it for me – on a personal, emotional and artistic level.

Following our production of *The Homecoming*, I'd kept in regular contact with my friend Greg Hersov at the Royal Exchange in Manchester. He had suggested Prospero months earlier and I'd managed to find excuses not to do it; it was simply too frightening a prospect. Until he mentioned it, it was a role I'd not considered. *The Tempest* is one of theatre's great stories, it is an incredible play, but the difficulties involved were manifest. Greg said: 'Well, what do you think? You: Prospero – shall we do it?' I paused, taking in the enormity of the challenge, but he'd already got me: 'Wowee,' I thought. 'Wowee.' For months, I found reasons to avoid any sort of commitment. I filmed *Closing the Ring* and also considered other projects. But *The Tempest* had got me hooked; I was on the end of an interminably long line and, little by little, was being reeled in.

Playing the part of Shakespeare's exiled magician was terrifying, I took myself to one side and reasoned: 'Not wanting to take on such a challenge is simply not a good enough excuse. You need to face challenges.' I realised the very fact that Prospero seemed so difficult was probably the real attraction, so I embraced the fear and thought: 'You're frightened because you can't find a way of doing it. Dig deeper. Work harder.' Without Greg's involvement I'd have said no, but I trusted him implicitly and signed up for the ride. He was a director whose work I really admired and the Royal Exchange was the sort of theatre that added its own magical dimension to any play – especially one as intriguing as *The Tempest*. To my mind, *The Tempest* was all about endings. I didn't think Prospero was some kind of all-powerful magus, he was more of a tired old man, aware of his mortality.

Greg and I developed the ideas over six to eight months. We talked about how the work could be made relevant to modern society and came up with this idea that it should be set on a Roman Abramovich-style superyacht. We'd start it amid a social set whom we christened the Global Arrogance Elite; as the play opened, they'd be being attended to by servants. Then Greg decided he wanted to play music; so he introduced Mantovani's 'Born Free', simply because he liked it. The action would then stop as a pulsating 'bump' thundered through the auditorium, representing the wrecking of a ship: a huge wall of sound would roll angrily at the audience's senses. Greg had an image of a ladder spiralling up into darkness so that Prospero would seem to be walking through space, which seemed crazy. There were so many ideas; all of them were about putting our contemporary world onto Prospero's island. We knew we were onto something, and we took it from there.

Greg and I spent those months talking about the role and developing the ideas and imagery that we'd bring to the stage. We made a collage from Shakespearian sonnets and love plays; featuring words of jealousy and desire and a welter of other emotions. Then Greg had this really fabulous idea: it was the twenty-fifth anniversary of the Royal Exchange and he thought it would be a good plan to get actors who'd previously played there to create an audio decoupage. He approached Bob Lindsay, Michael Sheen, Tom Courtenay and others to each record a line from Shakespeare's twenty-one plays. The decoupage was to be incorporated into the production.

The question that preoccupied my mind was this: 'What is Prospero's staff?' Prospero had magic, but I needed to work out how he invoked it, I needed to figure out what sort of staff he had. Normally Prospero got landed with some director-designer idea, all he'd have to do was make a hand gesture and it would have an effect on people, but I didn't want pantomime theatrics for our production. I retreated to Shropshire to ponder alchemy and the occult and a week later called Greg. 'I think I've got it, kid. I've found my staff.' There was a piece of wood, near to the house, which was perfect. Greg sounded unconvinced: 'Umm, a piece of wood?' 'Yes, don't you see; the staff's been here all along, I just didn't know where it was.' I described the piece of wood I'd found on the farm and Greg became enraptured.

I took my staff to Manchester; it was the perfect size, with a little kink in it, and before taking it to Greg I'd honed it and varnished it. I engraved it with words and motifs, there was stuff from Lily too. It was very personal and when I turned up for rehearsals with this seemingly ordinary stick from a field on our farm, everybody was in awe; they just stopped and stared. Throughout the rehearsals we had an unwritten rule; don't touch the staff. On one occasion, I mistakenly left the staff on the floor and Greg trod on it; everybody lurched as they anticipated a 'snap'. Greg was mortified too, but happily the power of Prospero's magic kept it intact – either that or Greg had been light on his feet. During rehearsals, we decided that instead of break-ing the staff I should hand it to Ariel, as though somebody had taken something valuable from Prospero, like a rib. The whole conception was the antithesis of self-indulgence, my staff was something that had been living, organic; Christ, I'd found it in my own garden. At the end of the run, I gave it to Greg: 'Here, take this,' I said, handing him my magic. I'm pretty sure he's still got it now.

We threw ourselves into rehearsals with abandon. Our homework had been thorough and it showed. I'd been coming into the Exchange each day at 7 a.m., long before anybody else, then the rehearsals would start at 10 a.m. As a company we felt we had the skill, technique, virtuosity and the chops to get it right; we felt people would connect because we'd taken a very human approach to *The Tempest*. I introduced daily Guinness tea breaks, where we'd all sit around and switch off; they were wonderful. We'd all got stories to tell and we enjoyed one another's company. I'd work with Greg until 5 p.m., then he'd do scenes with the others as I knocked off and spent time with people in the workshop or on the door. The Exchange was an inspiring place and I felt privileged to be back there.

The opening night of *The Tempest* sizzled and we got onto a great run. It was as if we were playing a gig every night, the six-and-a-half-week production was amazing. It had initially terrified the life out of me, but pretty soon I was enthralled by every moment. The dialogue and Shakespeare's poetry was superb; it was something else, it was very special. Bob Dylan and Johnny Cash joined me in my dressing room, I'd listen to their music and unwind. And Mike was in the pages of *The Tempest*, as far as I was concerned. As I explored Shakespeare's text, I found new meaning. He was a humanitarian and, like Prospero, he could weigh up people quickly. He had a magic touch, as did all the Postlethwaites.

∾

I completed the thespian trilogy when I returned to TV to appear in *Criminal Justice*, a phenomenal five-part series. This is how it came about: Bill Paterson had approached me a few years earlier to look at a script called *The Bonnie Boys*. Bill had been attached to a film about a couple of comics who had a popular tartan routine. The characters were purportedly big in their day, the late 1960s, but their fame had since shrunk. Bill was attached to it for three years and at various stages had hoped to play alongside Brian Cox and Jim Broadbent. The film was repeatedly delayed and Brian and Jim picked up other commitments; but Bill and I eventually prepared to get started. On the day before our flight to Canada, an email came through saying the funding had collapsed. Bill and I had spoken only that morning and were naturally disappointed, but within days we were signed up to something else. A fantastically creative young director, Otto Bathurst, was putting together a five-part TV serial for the BBC called *Criminal Justice*. The script was sensational, it had been written by a barrister, Peter Moffat, and I had no hesitation in agreeing to do it. It was reminiscent of the time that Mark Herman sent me his script for *Brassed Off*; on both occasions I'd known instantly that I'd wanted in. Peter told me he'd leave the script with me for a few hours, then ring to talk about it. I suppose he'd have been expecting all sorts of questions, but all I said was: 'When do we start?' It is instinctive when something that good comes in.

I spoke with Otto at length and was thrilled to learn that one of his advisors was Erwin James, the ex-con who'd become a *Guardian* columnist. I had massive respect for Erwin's humanity, insight and intelligence, he has an exciting presence and we really got on well. Detail has always meant everything to me and Otto was consumed by the minutiae. We talked through the scenes and there was one that puzzled me, so I questioned Otto about it. My character, Hooch, had lots of newspaper cuttings on the wall of his prison cell. 'How did he manage to cut out the articles from the newspaper, Otto?' I asked. 'If Hooch was inside, he wouldn't have had access to scissors or Sellotape.' The day ended and I sloped off for a pint. The next morning, I had this beautifully written explanation from Otto. He'd spoken to Erwin who'd told him that a prisoner of Hooch's standing would have been friendly with the guards. People like him would have been 'on-side', so if they'd asked to borrow a pair of scissors, they'd have been allowed. Otto had spent an hour having a long, long chat with Erwin and then wrote down the explanation before leaving it in my trailer the next morning. I was tickled pink. The fact that he was putting that amount of energy and thought into the mise en scène added more gravitas to the piece, it gave my character authenticity. Erwin's presence was also hugely important, he would come on set and at times he'd be so blown away he'd be moved to tears. In those moments, I knew we were creating something very, very real. It was compelling drama, about prison politics, the justice system; the whole shebang. The piece was basically saying that the British legal system was flawed. In a court, the prosecution went first and all the defence had to do, ultimately, was disprove the prosecution case: telling the truth didn't come into it, it wasn't part of the equation. The lead character, Ben, had wanted to tell the truth, but his brief wasn't interested. She just wanted to disprove the prosecution's case. The series created the idea that justice was just a game, a commodity that could be bought and sold; the lawyers and barristers and judges manipulated one another just as much as the criminals.

Ben was played by a talented young actor, Ben Wishaw. His character had been implicated in a crime and seemingly sent to prison without cause; there were echoes of *In the Name of the Father*. My character had to protect Ben from all of the bad influences inside, including the guards and the prison's resident thugs. Hooch had been completely corrupted by prison life but recognised that Ben was an innocent abroad. Of all of the characters, Hooch was the most complex because he was compromised. He was a good man, at heart, but was involved in levels of duplicity that tortured his soul. That's kind of what drew me to him: nasty pieces of work sometimes have a big heart and I'd always been drawn to leftfield, complex characters, people who were non-linear. When we started to shoot, I created my own backstory for Hooch, which was very dark. There were echoes of others roles that I'd played because at one point Hooch said: 'Being in here and being a listener is like being a priest. People talk to me like they've never talked to anybody before in their lives.' That was where Hooch found his redemption.

We worked hard and fast. It wasn't like being on a movie set where a director would pamper us before a scene, nor was it like being in theatre where we'd spend weeks in rehearsal. *Criminal Justice* was zippy and quick. In a way, that forced us to think clearly and use all of our energy during the shoot. Filming took place in an old Ministry of Defence facility near Chertsey, in Surrey, and the production team built the stark-looking prison interior from scratch. I think we conveyed a little sense of what prison might be like.

Ben is a stunning young actor, a real chameleon, and he really went through the mill; by the end of it he was physically and emotionally drained. After six or seven weeks, he didn't know what day it was. He was one of those actors who was really prepared to go through it, he was very committed and very genuine. We got on really well, it just clicked.

I had great respect for him, for the fact that he put in such a high level of performance. I'd try to play to him, where I could, making sure I was in the right position to make the scene work for him; Ben was the lead character, not me, so I'd change my position or performance so that he'd take the best shots. We were in these cramped cells, stumbling over each other; there wasn't the time to be nice or polite, we just had to get on with it, squeezing behind cameras, whipping off our clothes, learning new lines. It felt odd when we came to the end of the project. Otto had a saying that rang true. He said working on projects like that led us to develop intense relationships, which were very real and sometimes quite weird. He said: 'It's like kissing a stranger in the dark at a party. When the work is finished, it's like somebody's switched the lights back on and it's time to say goodbye.' But my relationship with Otto continued, happily, and he deserved his BAFTA for the production.

Criminal Justice stimulated debate. There were national newspapers running stories on their front pages saying the whole things was bollocks, while others took the opposite view. People were asking questions about the criminal justice system. Did people behave like that? Did barristers and lawyers behave like that? Is that what prisoners were like? Who was actually running the justice system? TV had created a platform for debate better than any other media, and that piece raised all sorts of issues. It was a really intelligent piece of work.

The Age of Stupid was another seriously intelligent and provocative work that also stimulated debate; not just on the national stage, but on a global platform. Serendipity was at work when it came to casting. Franny Armstrong, the director, contacted me after Googling the words 'Pete Postlethwaite Climate Change'. Apparently, the closest match was a story in my local newspaper, the *Shropshire Star*, which had carried a front-page report about an eleven-metre wind turbine that Jax and I had installed at our home. I was working on *The Tempest* at the time of its installation, but I'd given the newspaper's reporter a quote, saying something like: 'I think we all have a duty to live lives that are more environmentally responsible.' 'Brilliant,' thought Franny, when she read it, 'he might agree to being in my movie.'

Franny had been working on *The Age of Stupid* for three years, initially as a documentary, but she was worried that it lacked any real impact; I think she thought she'd be preaching to the converted, rather than reaching a wider audience. To make the project more accessible, she wanted to add an element of drama, to flip it from being a documentary into something more cinematic. She had discussions with the people in her production office and told them that the actor she most wanted to appear in it was me. They all laughed, telling her there was no chance, and then she Googled, and I said yes.

The environment had long been on my own political agenda, largely because of Jax. Over the years, she'd transformed: when I first met her, she was a rocker, but by the time of the 2010 general election, she was standing for Parliament on behalf of the Green Party. I was as proud as I could be when she decided to stand. She was up against career politicians who'd spent their whole lives living for the chance to be elected; but she was undaunted. She marshalled her arguments intelligently, presented her case with passion and eloquence and picked up votes along the way. And to think: she'd once been a biker on the set of *Coast to Coast*.

Jax had worked over a number of years for an Open University degree in environmental studies. She'd long been interested environmentalism, she was fanatical, to a certain extent; but she had a deep and intelligent understanding of the economics of ecology and why we simply had to find a new way of living. I agreed: we live on a finite planet. We trash it at our peril and our children will not forgive us for the misery they will inherit. It is time to properly value the

Earth and all species that inhabit it. Who will miss us when we're gone.

So when Franny called me, I couldn't say no. I thought I'd just be going to the studios to do a voice-over, but when I turned up she wanted me to act. My character played an old man living in a devastated world of 2055, watching archive footage from 2008 and asking: why didn't we stop climate change while we had the chance? It was shot in seven countries over a period of three years and featured six separate documentary stories. It felt really worthwhile and it was lovely to be on a set where people wanted to be there and doing what they were doing. I was amazed at the set-up and the dialogue was exquisite. The use of the archivist was a brilliant touch, because given the depth and the size of the facts that we were looking at, somehow or other that human element, that person who was looking directly at the camera and was obviously affected by it himself ... well, he was like a mirror to the audience. I thought the audience would look at it and go, 'I agree with him.' I found it very moving. To pack that much information, detail and fact into a film, that was very exciting. It was an extraordinary achievement. It was Spielberg-eat-your-heart-out for the first ten minutes, like Steven on speed. I thought it would make people think, make them debate; it was intended to freshen a few memories among people who should already have known what the hell was going on.

In about six hours, on a one-day shoot, we transformed the film from a low-budget, worthy documentary into one of the most talked about films of the year. It was released in cinemas across the world and had an unprecedented impact on politicians, campaigners and scientists. We showed it at the Houses of Parliament before a meeting on the Climate Bill.

The reaction was stunning and Ed Miliband, who was

then the Climate Change Minister, invited himself to a screening. We decided that was too good an opportunity to miss. I came up with the idea that I'd threaten to give back my OBE if Ed commissioned a new dirty coal-fired power station at Kingsnorth. At the screening, we invited Ed up onto the stage and I stood there, berating him, telling him to stop spinning the news and give us honest answers. I'd had a pint and Ed took the full force of my passionate but good-humoured invective, poor lamb. I could see the terror in his eyes. He looked stupefied. I told him that if he gave permission for the new power station then he was clearly unfit to represent the people of Britain at the Copenhagen climate summit. In front of the audience and the cameras, I told Ed: 'I promise very sadly to return to Her Majesty the Queen the OBE that I was given because I don't believe that I can be a real officer if that is what's going to happen. Unfortunately I would never be able to vote Labour again.' I was happy to be used as a mouthpiece for that film. On one occasion, Jax, my agent, Alex, Franny, myself and a few others were sitting in a House of Commons meeting room, telling MPs and civil servants about the dangers of climate change; I put it all down to the film and the tireless commitment of Franny. Within a month of Ed's attendance at the premiere, he'd re-written the UK's coal policy and decided there'd be no more coal-fired power stations. The Government said new power stations would have to promise to capture and bury 25 per cent of the emissions they produced immediately – and 100 per cent of emissions by 2025. Ha, it was a victory for grass-roots democracy.

We paid every attention to detail in that project. The carbon footprint of the film was ninety-four tonnes of CO_2 and the soundtrack came from bands with an interest in environmentalism, like Radiohead. When we screened the premiere, in London, we made sure it was an environmentally responsible event, with the lowest carbon footprint imaginable. I arrived on the green carpet on a bicycle, to make a point. An idiot from the BBC tried to trip me up, making some ludicrous point about the intrinsic environmental damage that would result in the film being shown around the world. I shot him down in a hail of flames, telling him that I wasn't interested in him taking a cheap shot at me or trying to get a sound bite when we were doing something as important as that. Stick that in your news bulletin, buddy. We took the film to the climate change summit in December and President Obama's people contacted us because they also wanted to see it.

Once we'd started the project, it ran and ran. A group of students at Liverpool's John Moores University were inspired to make a video on water efficiency called *Human After All*, and I lent my support to them.

Of course, by then, there was *King Lear*. Looking back, it's difficult to re-imagine the weight of expectation or level of excitement. I put every atom of my being into making it a success. I remember another interview, a couple of years before I got involved in *Lear*, in which I'd been asked about ambitions. I answered, quite truthfully, that I wanted to play King Lear before I died. That was how much it meant to me. Having played the role, I was thrilled; it had exceeded expectations and been one of the most enlightening performances of my life. Of course I was still hungry to work, there was plenty more to achieve, but I'd reached my Everest and didn't have particular targets in mind.

That didn't mean I had switched off from movies. David Lillard, my American agent, was taking calls during that time. In February 2009, he had heard that Christopher Nolan was going to start casting for a movie called *Olivier's Arrow*, which later changed to *Inception*. My co-star from *Romeo + Juliet*, Leonardo DiCaprio, was already cast and

Christopher's casting director, John Papsidera, was looking at ideas and suggestions for other characters. They wanted to nail down the principal actors first so Christopher wasn't releasing a script; he tended not to meet actors until he'd decided to offer a particular part, and only then would he make the script available. At the end of March, he came back to say that they wanted me to appear. I was already booked to film *Clash of the Titans* for Warner Bros from 15 May for two weeks and then from 2 July for a week and a half. Luckily, *Inception* was being filmed by the same studio and they found a way to make it work. When the offer came through, Christopher's production assistant jumped on a train from London to Shropshire with the script. He waited while I read it and I was immediately enthralled.

'I like the screenplay,' I told David. 'It's a small part, but we should do it.' The schedule was absurd; the studio wanted me to film for a day in the UK in summer and then not again until 18 November, when I needed to be in Los Angeles for a day. David and my British agent, Alex Irwin, both had concerns that it would conflict with other work, but I stuck with it. I was also attached to *Ironclad* at the time, which was pending for August, but we figured I'd be done with that by November. My agents remained unconvinced about *Inception*: not only was it a dreadful schedule but the budget wasn't great, but I was captivated by Christopher Nolan, he is a very exciting film-maker. Christopher was the reason I took it. He tends to work with the same actors frequently, people like Michael Caine, Cillian Murphy, Joseph Gordon-Levitt and Tom Hardy, and I was keen to find out whether we would also develop a longer term relationship. It took ages to agree a fee because there were billing issues due to the size of the cast. But that didn't worry me, money never has; I thought it would be cool to just pop up in the film as a cameo. By the time the film premiered, a year later, the contract had still not been finalised: I never did get around to signing it.

When *Ironclad* didn't work out, it created opportunities for me to appear in two other films. One was *Brighton Rock*, with Helen Mirren, which I'd wanted to do for a long time. I loved Graham Greene's book and I liked what they were doing with the remake. I was cast to play alongside Helen, but as the months went on my health began to stutter and stall like a broken-down car. An ever-lengthening shadow was casting a pall across my life; it seemed as though more difficult times might lie ahead. I'd long admired Helen, from our time together in *Duchess of Malfi* all those years ago, and I'd been looking forward to our reunion. I mean, Helen Mirren, come on: what's not to like? We'd planned to shoot in October in Brighton and London, but complications surrounding my health meant that was just not possible. In my heart, I wanted to go ahead with the project. In my head I knew it was not feasible.

That left *The Town*. My American agent had read the film in March, before I was even offered *Inception*. Ben Affleck had signed on to direct the film and was going to do a rewrite of the script and they were planning a summer/autumn start. By June/July 2009, casting was well underway. Lora Kennedy, the head of casting at Warner Bros, thought I would be great for the part of Fergie. She recommended me to Ben, who really liked the idea, and they sent an offer. Initially, I said no. At that time, I was still planning to work on *Brighton Rock* and it would have conflicted. Three potentially great films were all clustering at around the same time; giving my agents a torrid time. The pieces of the puzzle gradually came together. Unfortunately, it became apparent that I'd have to withdraw from *Brighton Rock*; then *Inception* came in ahead of time which meant I'd have time to work on *The Town* after all.

Ben hadn't found anybody that he liked to play the part of Fergie and we spoke again. I think he came on the phone to me five times, trying hard to persuade me to do it. He was very charming and very accommodating.

'Pete, this would be perfect,' he said.

'Why?'

'You've not been around so much, you've not been as ubiquitous; this is the sort of role that you do so well.'

Ben watched some footage of me and thought I'd gotten a little older and a little skinnier, and thought that would add to the character. 'You'll be much better than if we just hire some regular tough guy,' he said. 'The malice, the danger; it'll come from your soul, rather than your body.' He talked and talked and eventually I came round to the idea. 'You have to do it, you have to, it'll only take a few days,' he said.

Ben was an absolute gentleman. He agreed to change the filming dates so that they dovetailed with the dates on *Inception*. So I flew to Los Angeles in November. It had been a long time since I'd been there and my memories of *The Lost World* and living with the family up at Benedict Canyon all came flooding back. I met my agent, David, and told him all about Jax, Will and Lily, before going onto set with Christopher Nolan. I shot on 4 November and a few days later flew out to Boston, to meet Ben.

One of Ben's biggest worries was that I'd grown a moustache for my part in *Inception*. He wanted me to shave it off; which is another reason why my schedule was arranged for *Inception* to come first. I convinced Ben that a moustached Fergie would be even better. 'Fine,' he said, in agreement. I enjoyed both films; Christopher Nolan and Ben Affleck are extremely talented guys who know what they want. Ben is a serious moviemaker, he wanted to reflect good technique in his direction. He knew when we got it wrong, and needed to go again. But, better still, he knew when we'd got it right, and there was no need to reshoot. I thought the script was good from the off, but Ben elevated what it had to say; he did a fantastic job and I had a really good experience on it.

'I wouldn't have done it if you hadn't talked me into it,' I told him. 'You literally talked me round.'

'I didn't mean to be a pain in your ass,' Ben laughed.

'You were, and I'm glad that you were.' We knew we were making a great film. I would have jumped at the chance to work with either Christopher or Ben again.

In terms of my home life and my career, I was in a good place. I got a huge thrill from jetting off to the States to work with some of the world's best actors and directors. It was remarkably exciting to be able to keep pace with the new kids on the block and play alongside them in creatively inspiring and commercially successful movies. I was able to act in great films, weighty TV productions and dynamic theatre. Me, a boy from Warrington with a trucker's physiognomy. There were moments when it still didn't feel real, when it felt as though my working life had been a dream. I had choices and I still had the energy and hunger to do more. More importantly, I was blessed to have Jax, Will and Lily. Will was starting to carve out his own career as an actor, and by all accounts he was doing well. Lily was happily progressing at school and Jax was in her element at home.

But all the time, the shadows seemed to be lengthening. Happy as I was, I was steeling myself for my greatest challenge of all.

THIRTEEN

I'll Live Until the Hyacinths Bloom

I'm sitting on the terrace of our beautiful family home, in the verdant, rolling hills of Shropshire. It is next to an oak-framed sunroom and I have a plain, utilitarian chair from which I marvel at the Area of Outstanding Natural Beauty. 'Tea?' the call comes from the kitchen; it's Jax, adorable Jax, whom I can describe, without hint of cliché, as my one true love.

Our home lies amid tranquil surrounds and today that seems somehow magical. This place is a victory of substance over style, a testament to the life that Jax and I have led. We're perched on the side of a vertiginous hill and the terrace abuts its sloping contours. Lower down, sheep are grazing in the fields of a U-shaped valley and birds are dancing on the warm, rising currents. Momentarily, a gust of air rolls along the ascending curve of the hill, making me shiver as it passes. I shield myself in my faded, rust-coloured dressing gown; it ain't fashionable, but it fits like a glove. Our ageing chocolate brown Labrador, Fudge, watches me gather the fabric to my chest and nudges at my side, in search of affection. She's eleven and the years have slowed her; grey hairs now fleck her head and face. Food and fuss are Fudge's biggest preoccupations and she seems to have enjoyed plenty of both, over the years. I scratch at the soft skin behind her ears and she nods contentedly, before walking off to rest in our hay barn. Beside me, on the table, lie twenty B&H and I tap at the box, ejecting a ciggie, then place it between my forefinger and index finger and bring it to my lips. I light up, inhale the sweet narcotic smoke and huddle deeper into my dressing gown as I fall into reverie.

This majestic terrace is my haven, it brings peace and tranquillity. I've spent long, loving hours here with Jax and our children. When I'm home alone, I sit in this spot for hours, drinking the view like a fine burgundy: it soothes the soul, we're in the bosom of Mother Nature. But something's not right on this late sunny summer's afternoon. Twelve months ago when I sat in the same spot, I watched with childlike glee as scores of bees darted in and out of the sentry-straight rows of lavender, which separate the terrace from our garden. Today, the lavender grows just as prodigiously, perfuming the air; but during the past hour the erect lilac pods have welcomed only one bee. Where have they gone? Where are all the bees? The breeze seems like an ill wind, it is a wind of change.

The ecology of this idyllic spot is not the only thing undergoing a quiet revolution. For more than a year, I have waged a private battle against ill health. My first intimations of mortality came during *King Lear*. My weight plummeted and the night before we opened ill health fired a warning shot across the bows of my previously good constitution. I'd stopped eating, I wasn't looking after myself properly and I was in a poor state. Physically, as well as emotionally, *Lear* was a real struggle. Happily, once we got through that difficult first week and the production improved, so, apparently, did my health. I was happy at the end, if physically and emotionally exhausted.

A doctor ran some tests and called me in for an appointment. I'd known all was not right, but I'd assumed it would be something simple. 'Eat more greens,' I imagined him saying. 'Stop smoking, drink less, take exercise.' I couldn't have been more wrong. 'I'm sorry to tell you that you have cancer,' said the doctor. 'The tests were positive.'

A large, malignant tumour was growing on one of my kidneys. It was the same size as the blighted organ and urgent intervention was required. It had been there during *Lear*, I'd just not known. Nothing prepares anyone for that diagnosis. I sat there, impassive, watching the doctor's lips move and hearing the words, but failing to compute the meaning. I felt numb, completely shocked, but I deferred my horror and turned to the impact on my family; on my beloved Jax and on Will and Lily, they were at the centre of my thoughts. Throughout our lives together, I'd been the one that had been staunch in the face of other people's problems, I'd been the confidant, the giver of advice. Suddenly, that had changed. Now I was on the ropes, it was me that needed the love and support of others.

The initial shock was replaced by wave after wave of optimism, not to mention a soupçon of black humour. 'I'll beat this bloody thing,' I told myself. 'I'm not going to let this stop me. I'll get the better of it, come hell or high water.' It helped that I'd suffered from cancer before, in 1988–9, an episode that seemed to come and go without much fuss. I'd had a testicle removed but had gone on to father a daughter afterwards; if I could do it then, eighteen years earlier, I could do it again – though at sixty-three, I hoped not to father any more kids. The hospital booked me in for an operation to remove the kidney, a nephro-ureterectomy, to give it its proper name, and the doctors were reassuring in the weeks that followed, telling me I was making good progress. I imagined the operation had been a success, that the tumour had been removed before it had spread. I envisaged returning to film and stage soon after, as though I'd never been away. I did that, of course, managing to work on big budget Hollywood films like *Clash of the Titans*, *The Town* and *Inception*.

I continued to receive scripts. My ever-supportive agents, Pippa and Alex, telephoned me with offers of work. I continued to work in between times, doing my first voice-over work in years and reshooting scenes for *Clash of the Titans*. We were contacted by the makers of that film who said they needed us to go to London to shoot something in greater definition. I was probably in my local when I took the call. 'Bollocks,' I thought. 'Somebody, somewhere has made a monumental fuck-up and it's costing them a fortune to put right.' A car was dispatched to pick me up from Shropshire.

Other work came and went. I received a beautifully written letter from Otto Bathurst asking me to appear in a new production he was planning. I liked Otto, and the script he had posted to me read like a dream. He was working on a very cool pilot, and I went to see him in London. As much as anything, I wanted to show him that I was well enough to do it. Otto met me at Marylebone Station and was waving at the end of the platform as I came striding along it. I had a fag in my hand. 'Pete, what are you doing?' he said. 'You've got cancer.' 'It's not on my lungs,' I said, as I drew on the sweet smoke.

Otto's pilot was a sci-fi, based around a virtual game, where I was the creator of a Second Life. I was kind of like a virtual God; like Steve Jobs meets God with a twist of Denis Leary. I was there for about a week and loved it. I had huge enthusiasm for the piece, I was thrilled that I'd got the chance to work and I did everything I could to nail it.

The nephrectomy was successful, but it hadn't come in time to stop the cancer spreading and scans of my stomach showed small patches of black. Again, the doctors were upbeat, reasoning that a course of chemotherapy would zap the malignant cells. Other projects continued to fall away as my ever-vigilant doctors assumed responsibility for my war against ill health. One project that I had relished was a piece in which I played an old guy who was suffering from Alzheimer's and was about to die. It was the perfect role for me at the time, it would have been improbably cathartic. 'A guy facing his own mortality? No acting required. I'll do it.' I relished the opportunity but, again, my ill health stopped me from taking part.

A role that I did manage to fulfil came from Nick Hamm, my old buddy from our wild days at the RSC. I'd even lived with Nick for a while, in London, until his first wife had told him to throw me out. Apparently, I'd been a bad influence. Wherever did she get that idea? We'd tried to work together on several occasions since then but it had never come off. Nick wanted me to appear in his latest movie, *Killing Bono*, which was based on a rock critic's book about being in a band that faltered in the shadow of U2. It sounded like fun; I'd met Bono a few times some years earlier, on *In the Name of the Father*. The first time I saw him, I assumed he was just some scruffy hanger-on, loitering on the set. I had no idea who he was. He seemed to be surrounded by an entourage and he was talking the talk, like some Mr Big.

'Dan,' I said to Dan Day-Lewis, when I spied Bono's unkempt face and became irritated by his seemingly ingratiating ways, 'who the fuck is that guy, over there? He's pissing me off something rotten.'

'Oh, that's Bono,' he said, nonchalantly.

'Ah, yes,' I thought, 'the singer in the biggest band in the world, the guy who's written part of the soundtrack.' Ho hum. Silly me.

Nick originally asked me to play an underworld gangster in *Killing Bono*, the sort of part that my rock-hewn face was made for and that I'd taken on many occasions. But as my health deteriorated I called Nick to say all wasn't well, that I wasn't sure whether I could do it. He was in his production office when he took the call and I was completely straight with him.

'Nick,' I said, 'there's something I need to tell you ...' and we talked.

With the help of my agents, I'd kept news of my illness out of the public domain. There were two reasons for that. Firstly, as an actor, you can't do a movie unless you're insured; you can't start filming and then die in the middle of it, there has to be a bond. An actor with cancer is uninsurable and if you're uninsurable your career is over. So, from a practical viewpoint, it made no sense to tell anyone. I planned to recover soon and start work again. But beyond that, there was a greater imperative. I didn't see why that part of my life should become public property. I'd never considered myself a celebrity, I didn't even know what the word meant. I'd always been a jobbing actor, nothing more. I saw it this way: if my local butcher was ill, a few people close to him might know, but that would be it. He'd exist in peace, without his life becoming public property, with all the stress that that entails. I saw no reason why I should be any different, and besides, there's no false modesty in saying I didn't think anyone would be interested in whether I was ill or not. I'm just a bloke, a normal bloke, who loves his family, enjoys a pint and happens to have a job that means I'm observed by an audience. Other people have got their own lives to lead and so have I; I don't need other people to worry about me, I can take care of myself. I told Nick that I'd love to play in *Killing Bono* but was fighting cancer. 'Don't worry,' he said. 'If you want to be here, I'll find a way to do it.' And he did.

We realised that if I was going to be on set for eight or nine weeks there'd be insurance issues, but Nick figured that if I was playing a minor role that required, say, two or three days' work, I could be employed on a day-rate basis without needing a bond. I couldn't play the part of the gangster because they couldn't insure me for the full two months. 'Forget about it,' said Nick. 'We're going to write a new part for you. I'll book you in on a day rate, for three days. You up for it?'

Was I ever.

Nick and his writer came up with a character who was a gay patron of the arts, a sort of Derek-Jarman-meets-Karl-Lagerfeld pastiche. We worked out the details on the telephone, with the writer sending me an hilarious script. I'd never played a gay character before but when I got there, Nick seemed to think my gayness was very, very good; not John Inman camp, but reassuringly authentic. 'I've always been a bit of a friend of Dorothy,' I laughed. My innate desire to work wasn't the only reason for being on set, Nick and I shared the view that my character would add comedic value and improve the film. That, fundamentally, was what mattered most. When he'd sent me the script, I'd got it straight away; it was about creative search, about the journey to be somebody and about failure.

I hadn't seen Nick in a long time and when we said hello he tried manfully to hide his shock at my appearance. He failed, of course, cancer patients are finely attuned to the reaction of others. We're like a weather vane that's blown by the breeze of people's responses. I'd anticipated Nick's surprise because the chemotherapy had changed me; physically, I was smaller, even more reduced than I had been during *King Lear*. But I didn't care, I was there to work. I was going to contribute artistically and enjoy the craic. There wasn't the pressure on me that there'd been when I was last on stage in *King Lear*. As an actor, I was almost militant when it came to working in theatre; I guarded my view of a particular performance with ferocious intent and would fight to the death with a director, but in films I rolled with the punches.

When I arrived in Belfast, all of the caravans were parked in the middle of the city and it was minus eight degrees. Nick obviously wanted to make a film called Freezing Bono, rather than Killing him. Nick's kids were in town and they descended on my caravan, along with Martin McCann and Robert Sheehan. One by one, the lights in the other caravans went out but we sat up laughing, joking and smoking endless cigarettes, it was infectious. My van was a beacon of good vibes. Eventually Nick arrived and shooed the others away, we'd got three days' work ahead of us and he wanted to talk me through the shoot. I'd seen my costume, which I loved, and we decided that I should throw myself into the work 100 per cent. So first thing the next morning I was on set doing a rock'n'roll party with cocaine, lots of sex, dancing, jiggery pokery and, I don't know, two or three hundred extras. I was in the middle of it all, in this freezing warehouse in Belfast, with eighties disco music blaring out and everyone dressed in leather trousers and leather thongs walking around kissing each other. It wasn't a big scene for my character, it was a device to introduce him, but by the end of it I was exhausted. The combination of the chemotherapy and biting cold worked like a boxer's jab, dulling my senses. I was so cold and tired that I broke out in shivers and it was a struggle to remember my lines. Nick was onto it straight away, moving my caravan closer to the set and working out a regime so that I could carry on: ill as I was, there was work to be done and I was resolute.

I think Nick felt guilty about having asked me there, he seemed to feel he might in some way be exploiting me. He wasn't, of course, I was there because I wanted to be. Life was short and I wanted to live every moment as though it were the last, I was thrilled that he'd found a way for me to act. I wanted to give a bravura performance, to imbue my character with the humour of the script and to bring out the best of those around me. There were disagreements, of course; I think 'creative friction' is the euphemism for it. On one occasion, Nick reorganised a scene to try and protect me from the pain of the tumour. They'd scripted a piece where I walked towards the camera, with a couple of guys beside me. While I was in the green room, Nick had evidently spoken to his director of photography and reorganised the props. So when I came on, instead of walking to camera, he wanted me to sit in this bloody great chair which he'd plonked in the middle of the set. The director of photography had a sheepish look about him and Nick was trying to bluff it out.

'Pete, you're sitting in that chair.'

I looked at him: 'I'm not sitting in that chair.'

'Pete, just do yourself a favour. Sit in the chair and say the lines and we'll work around you.'

I refused, I absolutely bloody refused. 'I'm not sitting in the fucking chair. It makes no sense, it spoils the scene.' There was no room for sentiment, I was there to work, I wasn't a charity case, I needed my character to improve the film, there was no point in being there otherwise. Nick reorganised the lighting and got rid of the chair, we all knew it would have been ridiculous for my character to sit and film sets aren't places for overt kindness. I didn't care if Nick was trying to protect me from the pain, to hell with it, that wasn't what acting's about. Whether I was weak or not, I was brutal about giving my best. I didn't want a testimonial, I wanted to work. Actor, not cancer victim: that was my mantra.

After that, I enjoyed myself more. They moved heaters around to keep me warm and I revelled in the comic possibilities of my role. I loved being on set, it released me from the invidious futility of cancer. When I was working, I forgot that I was ill, I was soaring through the ether as I'd done for the past forty years. They wrote me a speech for my final scene and there was a hush on set when I delivered it. It went straight to the heart of who I was and what I was about. 'A word for the wise from an old man before you go. Remember only this: the measure of a man is what's left when fame falls away.' It was a poignant goodbye. I'd never been about fame – I couldn't give a shit about it. I was just thankful to be working, to be involved in a great film with a bunch of people I liked and admired.

When I returned home, there was more chemotherapy. The regime was punishing and I didn't always react well. On one occasion, a doctor visited me and asked how I was. I described the sense of desolation and despair following a particularly intense treatment. 'Mr Postlethwaite,' he said, 'you seem to have a very strong exterior, but in fact your body is as sensitive as a seven-year-old girl's.' 'The story of my life,' I thought. 'The story of my life.'

My daily round changed; it was no longer about reading scripts, rehearsing new roles and flying to different parts of the world to work with some of the world's great moviemakers, instead, I was shuttling back and forth from the Royal Shrewsbury Hospital. In a short space of time, I went from being a hirsute King Lear in London's Theatreland to losing half of my hair through chemotherapy. Jax kept me energised, tending to me and keeping me resolutely upbeat.

At times, the treatment seemed to work and it seemed as though we'd defeated it. The doctors believed I was going to be fine and I looked forward to a brief period of convalescence, in which I'd work on this book, while planning my next role. Everything seemed to be falling into place, it felt like the stars had aligned.

But there was more bad news. A new scan indicated that all was not well, there was a shadow on my hip and I needed further tests. 'We'll get to the bottom of this,' I thought, my determination unshaken by the latest setback. 'We're going to beat it.' Throughout the previous year, from my diagnosis of kidney cancer to the unhappy news that the disease had spread, I'd remained entirely positive. I'd not allowed a negative thought to enter my mind, preferring to keep focused on my family and the future. I didn't have a moment of doubt that I'd emerge in good health. But, during the summer, for the first time, I was enveloped in inertia. For the first time, I began to wonder what would happen if I didn't beat it, if they couldn't eradicate the unwanted cells. For the first time, I felt depressed. The consultant said the shadow on my hip was nothing to worry about, but the first round of chemotherapy had not been the out-and-out success that we'd originally believed; there was a three-millimetre tumour that had evaded the chemotherapy.

As summer turned to autumn, my outlook began to change. I started to realise that I'd spent the previous year in denial. During that time, the fact that I had been suffering from cancer had been somehow abstract. I'd been fighting hard, following doctors' orders, keeping off the Guinness and following my dietician's advice. In many ways, I'd been the perfect patient, doing everything by the book and remaining highly motivated. But the news that the chemotherapy had failed sent me reeling. It changed every facet of my life. Let me give you an example; before the summer, each time I'd returned home from hospital I'd gone straight to the cutlery drawer, taken out the scissors and snipped off my patient's wristband before throwing it in the bin. That simple symbolic act reflected my attitude to the illness, I didn't care about it, it didn't mean anything to me. Within days, I'd reverted to my old routine, carrying on with things as normal, looking forward to getting back to work. Now, everything had changed. I suddenly became acutely aware of my own mortality. The things that had seemed important to me before no longer were, the things that I'd worried about melted away. My love for my family, my friendships with actors, my political and environmental beliefs; those are the things that are important. The rest has as much meaning as a mosquito net in Finland. The beauty of nature, my gratitude for the smallest of kindnesses, my appreciation of other people; all of those were amplified. I was grateful for the people who surrounded me, for any piece of good fortune, for the life that I still had.

On one occasion, after returning from hospital, I deliberately avoided reaching for the scissors to snip off my patient's wristband. I was a cancer patient, whether still at hospital or back at home. My children, Will and Lily, were both there and I explained that I still wasn't well, that I'd need another round of chemotherapy. 'I'm not just going to carry on as normal,' I told them. 'This time, when you feel the time's right, when you think I'm okay, you can cut the wristband for me.' They left it for a couple of days and then one afternoon they emerged from the kitchen together, both carrying the scissors and cutting off the wristband between them. It was a moment of brilliance, of heady joy, of unfettered liberation. My kids were setting me free.

During afternoons, when I sat on the terrace, I marvelled anew at nature, observing the insects and birdlife that filled the surrounding skies. When days went well, it felt as though the heavens were opening and angelic choirs were singing. I was humbled by the life I'd led and joyous at the fleeting, ephemeral moments that I'd once taken for granted. Instead of feeling jaded and ground down by my illness, or being enervated by cancer, I focused on the beauty of my world. I was overwhelmed with love and gratitude for Jax, disarmed by the unconditional love and intimacy of Will and Lily.

I spoke to actor friends, renewed long-lost acquaintances and revelled in reminiscence. I revisited the corners of my life. There were plenty of good days. When auspicious news came from the hospital, I received it with the joy of a child on Christmas morning; I was genuinely grateful. When information was more downbeat, I received it stoically and got ready to go again. I spoke to other cancer patients, getting on brilliantly with a guy from Liverpool. We'd both been through the same thing and we supported one another along the way. He had a dark wit too and we spent afternoons chatting on the telephone, finding humour in places that would make most people cry. 'This tumour's funny, I'm splitting my sides because of it.'

'Yeah, it's a fucking killer.'

A further round of chemotherapy with three sessions planned. The first session hit me particularly hard and afterwards I experienced another long dark night of the soul; the physical reaction was frightening, truly horrific. For about fourteen hours, I felt as though I was apart from this world, as though the illness had punched me, knocked me to the ground and rendered me defenceless. In those hours, I went to the darkest places I'd known. Words don't easily convey the desperation or trauma, the sheer terror of it. I felt as though I were in the shadows, trying to find fortitude, resilience and determination from previously untapped reserves. Physically, it felt as though I'd been pummelled by a gang that hadn't known when to stop. I'd been left for dead.

Somehow I found the determination to pick myself up, dust myself down and face another day.

In between times, I recuperated at home. We had a wonderful time at harvest, when a local crew arrived to help with the haymaking. On the terrace, we laid a great table with food and drink and they took their fill. They were like underfed guests at the wedding buffet. 'Come on, tuck in,' I told them, filling glasses and offering more food. I watched proudly, disappointed I'd not got the strength to help them with the haymaking but pleased that I could provide for them at the end of a long, hot day. When they finished, I cleared the table and took all of their plates and glasses through to the kitchen, washed up and tidied everything away. 'Who's done this?' asked Jax, inspecting our immaculate kitchen. She couldn't believe I'd been so domesticated, so attentive.

Before my third and final round of chemotherapy, I returned to hospital for tests. The chemotherapy was planned for a Monday but postponed because of renewed complications. 'Mr Postlethwaite,' the doctor looked at me, compassion writ large, 'the tumour is still growing, a further round of chemotherapy would not defeat it, it is inoperable.' And that was it. The SP was that I might make it to my birthday, I'd got a couple of months to live.

It's time to get serious, if only for a little while. When I was initially approached by a writer who suggested I work on my life story, he seemed to think it might be the tale of someone who'd risen beyond himself, who'd overcome all manner of demons to get some place. He had a hackneyed, cliché idea that my life had been a struggle against all odds, that I was a local boy made good or that there'd been some unknown driving force that had propelled me onto the stage and into Hollywood. That idea was – and is – anathema to me. It's false, fake, a hotchpotch of misrepresentation and beguiling perversion. I didn't act because I wanted a passport to the glitziest, most glamorous places on earth; they've never meant a thing to me. I was never interested in picking up Hollywood's biggest pay cheques or being first in line on the red carpet. This isn't the story of a local boy made good. It isn't the tale of buckets and spades on the beach, flights over the Serengeti, handshakes with the Queen or being at the centre of the over-blown Hollywood machine. My life doesn't come wrapped in shiny red wrapping paper, tied with a neat silken bow.

Before starting this work, I'd spoken to my dear friend Bill Nighy. He'd felt utterly stitched up by the people behind an unauthorised biography because they'd got so much of it wrong, he felt he'd been thoroughly misrepresented and he had no control over the portrayal in the book. I didn't want the same to happen to me. I didn't want people thinking my story was one of egos, heartbreaks or the miasma of a production gone wrong – because it isn't. I long since divorced myself from the politics of my industry. I've always been resolute in the face of that bunkum, I've faced it down. In my early days, when an agent asked me to change my name to a more showbiz-ey moniker, I had a simple solution: I fired him. I changed my agent, not my name. The name Postlethwaite is Anglo-Saxon, it's all to do with the rotation of crops during the thirteenth century. A postle was the fallow field, the thwaite was the fertile one. Did I ever consider changing it? No, of course not.

I have no interest in self-aggrandisement or rewriting my own history; I'm as vulnerable and imperfect as the next man. And I have an instinctive mistrust and dislike of autobiography. It took much persuasion before I decided to commit to this memoir. In doing so, I made three observations. I wanted to be sure that I'd be creatively fulfilled by engaging with the work. I had no desire simply to cash my story in, to commodify my life. As in acting, I didn't want to compromise in the way I told my stories. Secondly, I refused to get carried away and my total investment was £1. That was the cost of the A4 lined notebook that I bought from a shop in Bishop's Castle before I began to write. I wrote on the cover '£1 invested: I trust it will not have been wasted.' You, the reader, will be the judge of that. Finally, the title of the book came to me instantly, or, rather, it came from Lily. She'd been describing the tiny particles of dust that fall to the stage in theatre, glinting and glimmering as they descend from on high as they catch the halogen light and reflect it to the audience. Those particles dance like snowflakes on a windy night. Lily created a new word for them, spectacle, which was a combination of speck and particle. She gave me the title for this book.

My life isn't about transcending difficulty, it's about love and belief; it's about following your heart and never giving in. My life has been about being true to myself, it's been filled with comedy, laugher and the absurd. I've been relentless, I've pushed beyond conventional limits, learned all the time and tried to do the right thing. There's been an unending search for community, from my childhood in the Church to working with a team of actors; I've never sought the leading role. My journey into the theatre mirrored my journey into the seminary, all those years earlier. I loved the company of others, loved being with others who shared a common belief and who wanted to improve things and make sense of the world around us.

A long time ago I realised that acting isn't just a silly game. It has meaning, it has the power to shape and improve lives. But there's one thing that's always been above the creative and political in my life: family. The kindness of my parents, brother and sisters shaped my formative years. And my own family: my wife, Jax, my son, Will, and my daughter, Lily,

have been all and everything to me. They, more than anything, have been at the centre of my universe. They are the
people who catch me when I fall, who right me when I'm
wrong and love me when I'm afraid. My story is a love letter to them; it is a heart-felt, tender evocation to the three
people whom I love more than anything else in the world.

Back at Royal Shrewsbury Hospital, I digested the news
that I was terminally ill. A welter of emotions ran through
me. There was shock, of course, and anger. There was also
a feeling of tedium; I wouldn't escape the endless, mind-
numbing cycle of treatment, hospitals and tests, I wouldn't
be able to take flight on the stage. Jax was ineffably strong;
helping to sustain me, offering her unconditional love and
being there for me in every moment. My children, too, provided succour and unequalled love. But in moments of reflection, in the time between time, I realised there was no
way back from this. The truth was simple and I had to accept it: I was going to die.

It's too cold to be out on the terrace now; winter has fall-
en and blanketed the hills with snow. So here I sit, in our
sunroom, still gazing across the valleys, enjoying the views.
The track from our home down to the road is impassable,
I feel like Nanook of the North, marooned in my beautiful
home. Lily's decided to stay away from school for a while,
to be here with me while Jax runs the ship.

Will and Lily are both very beautiful and I've never tried
to influence them or change them, they've always been left
to make their own decisions.

I'm profoundly lucky to have my family around me. They
are everything to me, absolutely everything. I'm very proud
of Will and Lily, they're incredible young adults.

It's heaven to spend time with Lily and Jax. I still can't
believe the way my family has reacted to the news. It's only
been a week or two and they are carrying on as normal,

making me feel loved and providing constant reassurance. Jax is unbelievable, her selflessness, kindness, humour and patience know no bounds. Lily is just as remarkable. She's fourteen and yet so strong. She asked me how I was this morning and I told her: 'I'm scared. Today is the first day that I've been scared.' There's no point hiding, no point trying to pretend everything's okay. I'd rather be honest, rather give the truth. Lily is here because she just wants to spend time with me. She is so adorable, I really can't describe how much she means to me. I can't believe how she copes with all that has happened. She is strong and caring and kind and loving. I am blessed indeed, she exceeds any hope a man could have.

It's not long until Christmas, and I'll be with my family until then. My birthday is early in the New Year, in February, so that's my target. I want to get to my sixty-fifth and I want the Government to give me my pension, all of it, in one big lump sum. They can pay me in advance because I won't be around to collect it in the normal, weekly instalments. So I'll expect messers Cameron and Clegg on the doorstep, cheque book in hand, come February.

On the little stool, next to my seat, is a list of visitors. There are endless friends who want to come to see me, it's like being backstage on the last night of a successful play. The doctor comes along with care workers. I don't have to get into the surgery, they come to me; not because I'm well known, or anything silly like that, but because that's what they do. Apparently, they don't do this in other parts of the country, but believe me, they should. Morphine dulls the pain, though sometimes the pain in my stomach is like a hot knife.

Funny that I should no longer be acting, yet my life is as busy as it ever was. Visitors, nurses, doctors and carers are ever present; helping me with this, telling me about that.

I'm eternally grateful for their kindness, though I feel bombarded by the information when all I want to do is rest. But that's how my life has always been. Things have moved at an incredible pace and I've just followed the river down to the sea. I've done things now and dealt with it later.

My memory turns to happy times: fans coming up to me, unexpectedly, and engaging me in deep and personal conversations, during which we agree that my career has been a complete fluke, engineered by the gods: or to our small family wedding, which we finally decided to do in 2003, with Will as my best man and Lily as the chief bridesmaid: or to flying to LA for a meeting with Steven Spielberg about *Jurassic Park* 2, and thinking, 'This is a long way from Warrington.'

When I received my final diagnosis, my literary agent visited the publisher, Alan, immediately and apologised that I'd have to withdraw. I'd assumed they would not want to print my story, given that I won't be around when it's printed. But the opposite was true.

'You're not going to believe this,' my agent said. 'I told them your contract hadn't been signed and they can walk away. But Alan was resolute. He said it was a wonderful testimony before and it still is now. Nothing's changed.'

It brings me immeasurable joy that they decided to keep the faith and that's been a common theme of my life. People have believed in me, trusted my ability to convey a particular emotion or tell the truth. I feel very blessed that I've been able to act out my life for others. And I feel doubly blessed to have then created a family of my own, with Jacqui, Will and Lily; because they have been the stuff of my dreams.

I set off on the most incredible journey forty years ago and I've never struggled to get work. There's always been an offer or a script, an idea or a role. There's been some downtime, happily, when I've spent days or weeks or months with

Jax and Will and Lily, but apart from those times I've never really been out of work from the day that my career began. It all seems seamless to me.

I had a letter once from a lad who'd been homeless in the days when we used to do the pub tours of Liverpool, as part of Van Load. Apparently, we were playing in a small community centre and he'd been sheltering in the doorway from the rain. He came inside to dry himself and sat down at the front. He enjoyed the show and afterwards I apparently bought him a pint. 'That was the first pint I'd ever had – and the first theatre I'd seen,' he wrote. 'I've never forgotten either and I wanted to say thank you.' You can keep your Oscar nominations and OBEs, because that's what acting's really about; you can't beat that, can you?

It is time to stop writing now. I have given my all and want to spend the final days with Jax and Will and Lily. There's a Christmas tree for Will to fetch, visitors to welcome and a good time to be had; one last good time. Soon I will be gone, my decline is insuperable, and I accept it with peace and equanimity. I know my family will miss me, and I will miss them. And that, in the end, is all that matters.

INDEX

Abbott, Paul, 212
Abbott, Steve, 206
Aberystwyth, 69–84, 94, 201
Academy of Motion Pictures and
  Sciences, 156
Ackland, Joss, 133
Affleck, Ben, 245–7
Afternoon Off, 123
Age of Stupid, The, 239–43
Agutter, Jenny, 6
Albee, Edward
  *Who's Afraid of Virginia
  Woolf?*, 56
Alexander, Jean, 104
Algeria, 203
Alianak, Hrant
  Lucky Strike, 104–5
Alice Springs, 221
Alien 3, 140
Allen, Keith, 163
Allen, Woody, 166
Alvarez, Max, 189
Amell, Stephen, 231
Amistad, 199–200, 202
Among Giants, 206–10

Anderson, John, 181
Arden of Faversham, 109
Armstrong, Alun, 86, 112
Armstrong, Franny, 239–42
Armstrong, Paddy, 154
Arnold, Gary, 189
Arts Council of Great Britain, 92
Aspen, Sheila, 44
Attenborough, Sir Richard, 229,
  231
Australia, 220–2
Ayckbourn, Alan, 70
  Ten Times Table, 94

Bacall, Lauren, 139
Bainbridge, Beryl, 138–9
Baker, George, 128
Baker, Jill, 139
Balcon, Jill, 88
Baldry, Long John, 41
Baldwin, Stephen, 166–8, 172–3
Baltimore Sun, 189
Barker, Howard, 115
Barnes, Peter
  Red Noses, 116

Barton, Mischa, 231
Bates, Alan, 140
Bath University, 97
Bathurst, Otto, 236–7, 239, 251
Baxter, Sally, 93
BBC, 77, 156, 161, 163, 243
Bean, Sean, 113–14, 164–5, 171
Beatles, 3, 5, 41, 69
Beaufoy, Simon, 206
Beaumont, Penny, 117
Beckett, Samuel, 41
    Endgame, 6
    Waiting for Godot, 2, 95,
    97–8
Beckinsale, Richard, 86
Belfast, 150, 154, 160, 204, 229,
    255
Bennett, Alan, 123–4
Between Strangers, 222–3
Between the Lines, 142
Billingham Forum, 59–60
Billington, Michael, 16
Blake, William, 132
Blanchett, Cate, 215
Bleasdale, Alan, 5, 90, 99
    The Muscle Market, 5, 101–4,
    141
    Scully, 62
Bodinetz, Gemma, 7
Bofors Gun, The, 38–9, 62
Bogart, Humphrey, 139–40
Boland, Eamon, 217
Bolt, Robert
    A Man for All Seasons, 35,
    48–9, 58
Bond, Edward, 115
    Lear, 109, 113
    War Plays, 116
Bonham Carter, Helena, 140
Bonnie Boys, The, 236
Bono, 154, 252–3
Boorman, Charley, 191
Bosnia, 203

Boxer, Henrietta, 93
Boyle-Ryan, Francis, 62
Bradley, David, 163
Branagh, Kenneth
    Tell Me Honestly, 120–1
Brando, Marlon, 174
Brassed Off, 11, 177–91, 197,
    215–16, 221, 236
Brecht, Bertolt, 4
    Coriolanus, 63
    The Good Woman of Setzuan,
    62, 140–1
Brenton, Howard
    Magnificence, 86
Brighton Rock, 245
Bristol
    City Council, 91–3, 99
    Little Theatre, 56, 59, 84,
    91–9, 118, 201
    Old Vic Theatre, 56, 87, 91–4,
    107, 145, 200, 202–3, 205
    Old Vic Theatre School, 3, 38,
    51–9, 88–9
    Theatre Royal, 59
Bristol Evening Post, 55–6, 205
Bristol Road Show, The, 57
Broadbent, David, 2, 35
Broadbent, Jim, 236
Brook, Peter, 173, 203
Brookside, 182
Brother Augustine, 34
Brother Dominic, 35, 58–9
Brown, Mike, 207
Browns Holiday Camp, 22
Brute, 213
Bullets Over Broadway, 166
Burke, Kathy, 161
Burtonwood, 26
Butcher, Justin
    Scaramouche Jones, 7, 219–20,
    222–3, 226
Butterfly Collectors, 212
Byrne, Gabriel, 166

Caine, Michael, 106, 145, 244
Cameron, James, 175
Campbell, Neve, 231
Canada, 220, 222, 236
Cartwright, Jim
 *The Rise and Fall of Little
 Voice*, 141–2
Casablanca, 139
Casey (dog), 192, 225
Cash, Johnny, 235
Casualty, 142
Catholicism, 2, 12, 24, 36, 42,
 128–9, 136, 148, 203, 214
Caton, Michael, 222
Chester, 62
Christie, Julie, 171
Chumbawumba, 188
cigarettes, 118–19
Clash of the Titans, 244, 251
Cletty Gegan, 71, 79–82
Close, Glenn, 140
Close My Eyes, 207
Closing the Ring, 229–32
Coast to Coast, 125–6, 159, 240
Cocteau, Jean, 117, 119–20
Congreve, William
 The Double-Dealer, 60
Conlon, Gerry, 149–55, 159–60
Conlon, Guiseppe, 144-150, 153,
 157, 160,
Conlon, Sarah, 149–50, 152–4,
 160
Connery, Sean, 145, 172
Conroy, Jarlath, 86
Constable, Pauline, 200
Constant Gardener, The, 224–5
Cooke, Nigel, 93, 96
Copenhagen climate summit, 242
Coronation Street, 91, 104–5
Costigan, George, 3, 61–2, 161,
 200–3, 206
Cottrell, Richard, 90
Courtenay, Tom, 36, 45, 233

Coward, Noël
 Private Lives, 91
Cox, Brian, 236
Crimetime, 172–3
Criminal Justice, 235–9
Crowley, Bob, 87
Crown Court, 123
Cruise, Tom, 190
Cusack, Sinéad, 112, 140

Dahl, Roald, 172
Daily Express, 156
Daily Mail crosswords, 130–1
Daily Telegraph, 16
Dark Water, 224
Darke, Nick
 The Body, 114–15
Davies, Howard, 110
Davies, Rachel, 124
Davies, Terence, 136–7
Davis, Steve, 114
Day-Lewis, Cecil, 88
Day-Lewis, Daniel, 58, 87–90,
 99, 217
 and *In the Name of the Father*,
 145, 147, 149–50, 153–5, 252
Dear, Nick
 Temptation, 118, 219
Dejczer, Maciej, 212
del Toro, Benicio, 167–8
Delph, 184
Dench, Judi, 215
Derrington, Michael, 93, 96
Deruddere, Dominique, 163
Diaghilev, Serge, 117, 119–20
DiCaprio, Leonardo, 156, 159,
 174–5, 198, 243
Distant Voices, Still Lives, 11,
 136–8, 140, 142, 182
Dodson, Pat, 221–2
Doncaster, 184–5
Doris and Doreen, 123
Dossor, Alan, 5, 60, 101, 115, 121

Downing Street Declaration, 153
DragonHeart, 172
Dressmaker, The, 138–9
Dublin, 150, 153–4, 220
Dupuy, Philip, 119
Durban, Alan, 68
Dutton, Charles S, 140
Dylan, Bob, 97, 235

Eel Pie Island, 41
Ekrek, Sekita, 188–9
Eliot, T. S.
   Murder in the Cathedral, 2
Elizabeth II, Queen, 112–13, 224, 242
Elliott, Denholm, 123
Equity, 56–8, 92
Ettington, 111
Evans, Chris, 198
Eve, Trevor, 4
Evening Standard Film Awards, 188
Eyre, Richard, 138

Fair Maid of the West, The, 112
Farnham, Redgrave Theatre, 96
Farquhar, George
   The Recruiting Officer, 59
Father Aidan, 32
Father Basil, 31
Fellowes, Julian, 163
Fenton, George, 138
Field, Shirley Anne, 36
Fiennes, Ralph, 155, 158, 224–5
*Film Stars Don't Die in
   Liverpool*, 159
Finney, Albert, 36, 45, 86
Fish, Peter, 93
Fitzgerald, Tara, 178, 181
Formby, St George's School,
   45–6, 162
Franks, Philip, 125, 163
Frears, Stephen, 227

Freeman, Morgan, 199
Frost, Sadie, 173
Frostrup, Mariella, 198
Fudge (dog), 248–9
Fugitive, The, 155, 159
Full Monty, The, 206, 209

Gambon, Michael, 6, 108
Gandhi, Mahatma, 227
Gangs of New York, 217
Garbo, Greata, 209
General Strike, 182
Gerry and the Pacemakers, 41
Gibson, Mel, 140
Gielgud, Sir John, 224
Gilbert and Sullivan
   The Pirates of Penzance, 47, 49
Gleneagles summit, 227–8
Glover, Julian, 59–60
Goodman, Henry, 117, 120
Goold, Rupert, 6–7, 9, 13, 16, 18, 219
Gordon-Levitt, Joseph, 244
Grant, Richard E., 191
Greece, 133
Green Party, 240
Greene, Graham, 245
Griffiths, Rachel, 206–9
Griffiths, Richard, 123
Grimethorpe, 178–9, 182–4, 187
Gronant, 22–3
Groves, Roy, 42–3
Guardian, 8, 16, 236
Guildford Four, 144–5, 147, 154
Gwilym, Mike, 99

Hale, Amanda, 19
Hall, Peter, 97
Hallström, Lasse, 215
Hamm, Nick, 109–12, 114–15, 252–6
Hands, Terry, 35, 113
Hanks, Tom, 202

Hardy, Tom, 244
Harris, Ed, 133, 135
Hart, Christopher, 16
Harvey, Russell, 93
Hauer, Roger, 140
Hawke, Ethan, 140
Haygarth, Tony, 123
Heard, John, 140
Heller, Joseph
    We Bombed in New Haven, 59
Henry, Lenny, 125–6
Herman, Mark, 177–80, 182–4,
    186, 236
Hersov, Greg, 217, 232–5
Heywood, Thomas
    The Fair Maid of the West,
    113
Higson, Charlie, 163
Hill, Melanie, 178
Hill, Paul, 154
Hill, Stanley, 95
Hird, Dame Thora, 211
Hitchcock, Alfred, 216
Hitler's SS, 127
Hogan, Paul, 222
Holman, Robert
    Today, 116
Hooper, Robin
    Astonish Me!, 117–21
Hopkins, Anthony, 58, 199
Horrocks, Jane, 138–9, 141
Horse in the House, 123
Hoskins, Bob, 99–100
Hounsou, Djimon, 199
Howard, Arliss, 194
Howerd, Frankie, 134
Human After All, 243
Hurcombe, Caitlin, 226
Hurt, John, 145, 212

Ibsen, Henrik
    Peer Gynt, 109
Ifans, Rhys, 215

In the Line of Fire, 155
In the Name of the Father, 11,
    144–60, 165, 188, 191, 200,
    237, 252
Inception, 243–6, 251
Ionesco, Eugène, 41
IRA, 153, 156
Ironclad, 244–5
Irons, Jeremy, 58, 140
Irwin, Alex, 242, 244, 251

Jack and the Beanstalk, 32
Jackson, Philip, 178, 181, 184,
    215
Jacobi, Derek, 113, 140
Jagger, Joe, 41–2
James, Erwin, 236–7
James, Geraldine, 215
James, Peter, 35
James and the Giant Peach, 172
Jenkins, Martin, 35
John, Errol, 100–1
Johnson, Bill, 32, 221
Johnson, Catherine, 161
Johnson, Pauline, 221
Johnson, Sandy, 126–8, 159
Johnston, Sue, 178, 182, 184–5,
    230–1
Jones, Robert, 167
Jones, Tommy Lee, 155, 159
Jonson, Ben
    Every Man in His Humour,
    125
    Volpone, 217
Joyce, James, 35, 149
Jurassic Park, 194, 197, 267
    see also Lost World, The

Kafka, Franz
    Metamorphosis, 42
Kaufman and Hart
    The Man Who Came to
    Dinner, 87

Keeffe, Barrie
  Gimme Shelter, 90
Keitel, Harvey, 198
Kelly, Matthew, 3, 6, 73, 84, 86
Kennedy, Courtenaythe, 154
Kennedy, Lora, 245
Kenya, 224–5
Kesey, Ken
  *One Flew Over the Cuckoo's
  Nest*, 70–1, 76–7, 79, 82–4,
  94, 96–7
Kesselring, Joseph
  Arsenic and Old Lace, 59
Kieslowski, Krysztof, 212
Kiev, 164
Killing Bono, 252–7
King, Marcia, 57
Kingsnorth power station, 242
Koepp, David, 195
Kyle, Barry, 112, 115

Labour Party, 182, 227, 242
Lambert, Christopher, 133, 135
Lambert, Mark, 93
Lane, Roger, 50–1
Last of the Mohicans, 145
Last of the Summer Wine, 123
Laughton, Charles, 134
le Carré, John, 224
Leeds, 187
Lennon, John, 69, 85
Lillard, David, 243–4, 246
Lindsay, Bob, 233
Lipman, Maureen, 106
Liverpool
  Alan Bleasdale and, 102–3
  Cavern Club, 41
  and *Coast to Coast*, 127–8
  Everyman Theatre, 2–21, 35,
  60–84, 105–6, 141, 157, 175,
  201
  and *King Lear*, 1–20
  Royal Court Theatre, 203, 205

Liverpool FC, 2
Liverpool John Moore's
  University, 243
Liverpool Poets, 60
Livings, Henry, 184
Liyarn Ngarn, 220–2
Locke, Ronnie, 120
Lodge, David, 163
London
  Almeida Theatre, 116–21
  Mermaid Theatre, 113
  National Theatre, 140–2
  Royal Court Theatre, 86
  Young Vic Theatre, 13, 19, 21
Loren, Sophia, 222–3
Lost for Words, 211
Lost World, The: Jurassic Park,
  192–200, 202, 206, 246
Lovejoy, 142
Luhrmann, Baz, 173–6, 222

McCann, Martin, 255
McCartney, Paul, 5
McConaughey, Matthew, 199
McGrath, John, 139
McGregor, Ewan, 178, 181–2,
  185, 191
McKay, Malcolm, 71, 73–4, 76
MacLaine, Shirley, 230, 231
McQuarrie, Chris, 166–71
Major, John, 153
Make Poverty History, 227–8
Malkovich, John, 155
Mamet, David
  American Buffalo, 217
Manchester
  Loreto Grammar School,
  46–51
  Royal Exchange Theatre,
  99–101, 217–18, 232–5
Manchester Evening News, 49
Mandela, Nelson, 228
Mann, Michael, 145, 158

Mantovani, 233
Marter, Ian, 57
Martin, Peter, 178
Martin Chuzzlewit, 163
Martin-Davis, Ashley, 200
Martinelli, Gabriella, 175,
    222–3
Maugham, Somerset
    Sheppey, 91
Mayer, Lise, 163
Meirelles, Fernando, 224–5
Mendes, Sam, 141
Merrison, Sir Alec, 92
Mexico, 173–4
Mhando, Martin, 221
Michael, Lewis, 57
Miliband, Ed, 241–2
Miller, Arthur, 42, 115
    A View from the Bridge, 87
Miller, Sam, 206, 208–9
Mills, John, 163
Minder, 142
Minton, Roy
    Death in Leicester, 201
Mirren, Helen, 99, 159, 245
Moffat, Peter, 236
Moore, Julianne, 215
Moriarty, Paul, 57
Morris, Sir Philip, 92
Morrish, Jacqui, 135, 156, 158,
    164, 194, 201, 204, 206, 213,
    219, 225, 231
    and environment, 239–40, 242
    and PP's illness, 246–9, 257,
    260–1, 263–8
    relationship with PP, 125–33
Morrison, Van, 126
Mother Victorine, 46–51
Mould, Mike, 61
Mowbray, Malcolm, 124
Murdoch University, 221
Murphy, Cillian, 244
Murphy, Michael, 47

Negri, Richard, 100–1
Neilson, David, 91
New Brighton, 2
New York Times, 171
New Zealand, 220
Newcastle, 86, 109, 114, 122
Newfoundland, 215
Newman, Randy, 97
Newry, 151
Nighy, Bill, 3, 78–9, 83, 127, 224,
    262
Noble, Adrian, 87, 99–100
Nolan, Christopher, 243–4, 246–7
NSPCC, 139

Obama, Barack, 243
O'Brien, Jim, 139
O'Connor, Sinéad, 154
Olivier, Sir Laurence, 224
O'Neill, Eugene, 42
    The Emperor Jones, 100–1,
    217
Olivier's Arrow 243
Ollove, Mike, 189
Open University, 240
Ormskirk, 30
Osborne, John, 36, 41
    Look Back in Anger, 2
Oscar nominations, 155–61, 214,
    268
O'Toole, Peter, 58, 174
Owen, Catherine, 93

Page, Anthony, 86
Page, Louise
    Golden Girls, 116
Palin, Michael, 123–4
Palminteri, Chazz, 166
Papsidera, John, 244
Paris, 133–4
Paterson, Bill, 123–4, 140–1,
    235–6
Peck, Bob, 108

Peck, Gregory, 158
Penny, Dick, 93, 200–2, 206, 219
Picasso, Pablo, 121
Pink Floyd, 97
Pinter, Harold, 36, 41
    The Homecoming, 11, 44,
    217–19, 232
Plater, Alan, 139
Plowright, Joan, 138–9
Plummer, Christopher, 231
Pogues, 128
Pollack, Kevin, 169
Postlethwaite, Anne, 24–5, 129
Postlethwaite, Bill, 2, 22–5, 27,
    29, 37, 42, 53–4, 130–1,
    148–9, 157, 190
Postlethwaite, Chris, 230
Postlethwaite, Lily, 132, 191,
    193–4, 202, 204, 213, 219,
    234
    and PP's illness, 246–7, 250,
    259–60, 263–5, 267–8
Postlethwaite, Mary, 22–7, 30,
    33, 37, 54, 157, 190, 211, 218
Postlethwaite, Mike, 38–40,
    114–15, 130, 153, 156, 199,
    214
    childhood and adolescence,
    24–7, 37–8
    his death, 230–2
Postlethwaite, Pat, 24–5, 129
Postlethwaite, Pete
    Aberystwyth season, 69–84
    approach to acting, 110–11,
    149–50, 172
    appearance, 55, 142
    autobiography, 261–3, 267
    Brassed Off, 177–90
    and brother's death, 230–2
    cancer, 15, 129–30, 201,
    248–68
    car crash, 112
    childhood, 22–8, 42

and drama school, 51–8
early acting experience, 28–9,
    32, 35
and environment, 239–42
and Everyman Theatre, 2–21,
    60–84, 104–5
and family life, 212–13
and father's death, 130–1
friendship with Day-Lewis,
    87–90, 145
and grammar school, 33–5, 45
In the Name of the Father,
    144–60
and *King Lear*, 6–21, 249–50
and Little Theatre, 91–9
love of theatre, 229
and mother's death, 213–14
move to Shropshire, 131–2
and OBE, 224, 242, 268
Oscar nomination, 155–61,
    214
paranoid episode, 75–84
peripatetic lifestyle, 85–7, 113
political commitment, 182–3,
    188, 226–8
and primary school, 28–30
relationship with father, 42,
    148–9
relationship with Jacqui
    Morrish, 125–33
relationship with Julie Walters,
    105–6
and religion, 2, 12, 24, 30–1,
    36–7, 42–3, 128–9
repertory work, 58–60
and RSC, 108–22
and seminary, 30–3, 45
sheet-metal working, 53–4
and sport, 39, 131
and teacher training, 39–45,
    214
and teaching, 45–51, 107,
    162

Postlethwaite, Will, 164, 187, 191, 194, 196, 210, 213, 219
and acting, 226, 247, 264–5
early years, 130, 132–3, 201
and *Macbeth*, 202–4
and PP's illness, 246–7, 250, 259–60, 263–5, 267–8
Practice, The, 125
Prescott, John, 190
Prestatyn, 23
Private Function, A, 123–4
Proulx, E. Annie, 215
Pryce, Jonathan, 3, 83

Quaid, Dennis, 172
Queenie (dog), 26

Radio Merseyside, 14
Radiohead, 242
Ransom, Tim, 138
Rapier Players, 91
Rattle, Sir Simon, 5
Rebbeck, Steve, 200
Rector's Wife, The, 207
Redgrave, Michael, 36
Reynolds, Albert, 153–4
Ridley, Arnold, 96
Ghost Train, 70–1, 73–8, 84, 94–6
Riley, Sue, 205
Rix, Brian, 70
Rixon, Matthew, 6
Roach, Archie, 221–2
Roche, Johnny, 64, 66–71, 73, 84
Rolfe, Jill, 93
Rolling Stones, 41, 112, 166
Romeo + Juliet, 173–6, 216, 222, 243
Rostand, Edmond
Cyrano de Bergerac, 113
Roth, Tim, 133–4

Royal Shakespeare Company, 107–22, 125, 133, 157, 173, 176, 201, 224–5, 252
and improvisation, 204–5
Not the RSC Festival, 115–21, 219
understudy productions, 110
work schedule, 108–9
Royle Family, The, 231
Russell, Ronald, 95
Russell, Willy, 60, 90
Breezeblock Park, 99
Educating Rita, 106
Rylance, Mark, 108

St John, Louis, 221
St Mary's, Twickenham, 39–45, 50
St Thomas More, 48–9
Sartre, Jean-Paul, 134
No Exit, 43
Saunders, James
The Borage Pigeon Affair, 59
Saving Private Ryan, 200, 202
Scacchi, Greta, 191
Scales, Prunella, 60
Schindler's List, 155–6, 200
Scofield, Paul, 163
Scorsese, Martin, 216–17
Seaward, Tracey, 191–2, 225
Selick, Henry, 172
Serpent's Kiss, The, 191, 193
Shakespeare, William, 4, 108, 110–11, 115, 173–6, 205, 226
As You Like It, 264–5
Coriolanus, 64
Hamlet, 116, 140
Henry V, 116, 125
King Lear, 3, 6–21, 32, 44, 109, 202, 243, 249–50, 255
Love's Labour's Lost, 116
Macbeth, 109, 130, 200–6, 219

Measure for Measure, 175
A Midsummer Night's Dream, 173, 203
Much Ado About Nothing, 109, 113
Othello, 58
Richard II, 140
Richard III, 116, 125
Romeo and Juliet, 173–6
The Tempest, 109, 232–5, 239
Timon of Athens, 89
Titus Andronicus, 87
Troilus and Cressida, 89
Shallow Grave, 178
Sharpe, 164–5
Shaw, George Bernard
  Widowers' Houses, 65–9
Shea, John, 126–7
Sheehan, Robert, 255
Sheen, Michael, 233
Shelley, Rudi, 58
Sher, Antony, 3, 6, 61, 108, 117–18, 120–1, 157–8
Sheridan, Jim, 145–52, 154–5
Sheridan, Peter, 157
Shipping News, The, 215–16
Shropshire, 131–2, 190, 213, 225–6, 248
Shropshire Star, 239
Sicily, 159
Sillitoe, Alan
  The Loneliness of the Long Distance Runner, 35–6
  Saturday Night and Sunday Morning, 35–6
Sin Bin, 155, 161–3
Singer, Bryan, 165–71
Sins, The, 215
Sixmilebridge, 191–2
Slovakia, 172
Sluizer, Geroge, 173
Smith, Maggie, 123
Soans, Robin, 139

Soldier, 123
Spacey, Kevin, 166, 168, 171, 215–16
Spall, Timothy, 133–5, 224
Spencer, Charles, 16
Spielberg, Steven, 158, 172, 192–200, 202, 213, 241, 267
Stage, The, 92
Starr, Ringo, 5
Staunton, Imelda, 113
Steadman, Alison, 102–3, 123, 141
Steadman, Ralph, 65–7, 73
Stewart, Alan, 208
Stewart, Olivia, 137–8, 182
Stok, Witold, 207
Storey, David
  Cromwell, 86
Stott, Mike
  Funny Peculiar, 86, 90–1
  Thwum, 77
Strange Bedfellows, 222
Stravinsky, Igor, 117, 120
Strindberg, August
  The Dream Play, 116
Suchet, David, 133
Suite 16, 163
Sundance Film Festival, 197
Supertramp, 97
Swift, Graham, 140

Tales of Sherwood Forest, 139, 179
Taylor, Dennis, 114
Taylor, Shirin, 96
Tchaikowsky, Pyotr Ilyich, 104
Teale, David, 222
Teletubbies, 203–4
TFI Friday, 198
Thatcher, Margaret, 15, 17, 114, 178–9, 182–3
Theatre of Cruelty, 41
Theatre of the Absurd, 41–2

Thewlis, David, 171
Thompson, Emma, 151, 153–5
Thornton, James, 207
Thunderbirds, 212
Times, The, 16
To Kill a Priest, 133, 134
Todmorden, 90
Tomlinson, Ricky, 182
Tompkinson, Stephen, 178–81
Toronto, 223–4
Town, The, 245–7, 251
Towyn, 23
Trainspotting, 191
Troughton, David, 139
Tumbledown, 138
Tutu, Desmond, 228

U2, 252–3
Undertakers, 41
Uninvited Guest, The, 32
Upper Room, The, 28–30, 41–2
Usual Suspects, The, 165–71, 216

Van Load, 62, 105, 267–8
Vaughan, Peter, 128

Walters, Julie, 3, 63–4, 71–2, 75–6, 84, 86, 103
  relationship with PP, 105–6
Warrington, 1–2, 22–4, 36, 41, 45, 52, 61, 123, 179, 196, 246, 267
  and *In the Name of the Father*, 153, 156
  Padgate, 56, 124, 182, 230–1
  St Oswald's Club, 230–1
  and *TFI Friday* appearance, 128–9
Washington Times, 189
Waterland, 140

Weaver, Sigourney, 140
Webster, John
  The Duchess of Malfi, 99–100, 217, 245
Weisz, Rachel, 224
Wells, 162–3
West, Timothy, 59
West, Tony, 104
What's Eating Gilbert Grape, 156, 159
When Saturday Comes, 171
'White Cliffs of Dover', 66
Whitelaw, Billie, 138–9
Whitley Bay, 115
Wilde, Oscar
  The Importance of Being Earnest, 35
Wilkinson, Tom, 163
Williams, Michael, 106
Williams, Nigel
  Class Enemy, 90
Winston, Stan, 195–6
Wishaw, Ben, 237–9
Wolfe, Tom
  The Electric Kool-Aid Acid Test, 70
Wonder, Stevie, 81
Wood, Jane, 64
Wood, Victoria, 99
Woodeson, Nick, 67–8
Woodington, Albie, 93
Woodward, Peter, 230
Workhouse Donkey, The, 59
Wright, Nicholas
  The Desert Air, 116
Wringer, Leo, 93

Yates, David, 215

Zeffirelli, Franco, 140, 173
Zen in the Art of Archery, 55